BEHIND THE FLYING SAUCERS

BEHIND THE FLYING SAUCERS -- EXPANDED EDITION
By Frank Scully
With Bonus TRUTH ABOUT AZTEC UFO CRASH
Section by Sean Casteel
This edition Copyright 2008 by Global Communications/Conspiracy Journal

Revised Edition

ISBN 1606110209
       9781606110201

Published by   Global Communications/Conspiracy Journal
                Box 753 · New Brunswick, NJ 08903

Staff Members
Timothy G. Beckley, Publisher
Carol Ann Rodriguez, Assistant to the Publisher
Sean Casteel, General Associate Editor
Tim R. Swartz, Graphics and Editorial Consultant
William Kern, Editorial and Art Consultant

Sign Up On The Web For Our Free Weekly Newsletter
and Mail Order Version of Conspiracy Journal
and Bizarre Bazaar
www.Conspiracy Journal.com

Order Hot Line: 1-732-602-3407
PayPal: MrUFO8@hotmail.com

Disclaimer:

The publication of any and all content e.g., articles, reports, editorials, commentary, opinions, as well as graphics and or images in this book does not constitute sanction or acquiescence of said content; it is solely for informational purposes.

Fair Use Notice

This book may contain copyrighted material the use of which may not be specifically authorized by the copyright owner. We are making such material available in our efforts to advance understanding of environmental, political, human rights, economic, democratic, scientific, social justice, and religious issues, etc. We believe this constitutes a 'fair use' of any such copyrighted material as provided for in section 107 of the US Copyright Law. In accordance with Title 17 U.S.C. Section 107, the material in this book is distributed to those who have expressed a prior interest in receiving the included information for research and educational purposes.

Christianity has in no way excluded the possibility that God has created other groups of intelligent beings, who may or may not inhabit other planets. In fact the Bible tells us many times of a group of intelligent beings, called angels. It even records the visitations of a few of these beings to our earth. God has told us about the angels; there could be other beings He has created about which He has told us nothing. After all, there are some men who find it difficult to accept what He has told them.

BEHIND THE FLYING SAUCERS

Contents

BEHIND THE FLYING SAUCERS

Frank Scully and UFO engineer/
contactee Daniel Fry examine
something "alien."
Courtsey Center For UFO Studies

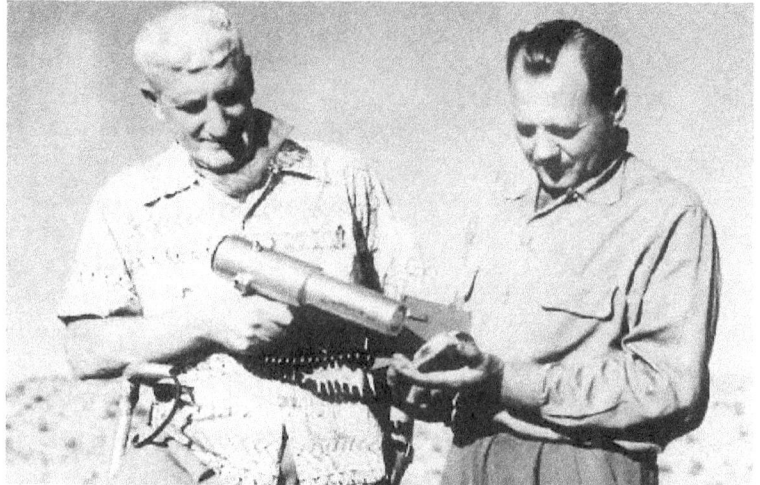

AZTEC-THE UFO THAT CRASHED THAT COULD STILL FLY

By Timothy Green Beckley
Publisher of The Conspiracy Journal

When Frank Scully wrote "Behind The Flying Saucers" and had it published by a major New York publishing house, it hit bestseller status shortly after its release.

It had all the elements of a bestseller-including a sexy Hollywood actress, Linda Darnell, who had passed the original tip onto Scully, then a writer for "Variety." Furthermore, it was the first book-length account of a spaceship said to have arrived on Earth, along with its humanoid crew, be they dead or alive. The story was written in an engaging, forthright manner and convinced many that the event had really happened, in spite of the fact that there were no direct witnesses. It hit at just the right time-a moment when everyone in the nation was looking up hoping to see a UFO for themselves, an era when thousands reported observations of unexplainable aerial phenomena all over the world.

Unfortunately for Scully, his work was refuted and disputed not long after it was published. The main "sources" were "exposed" as being conmen. The public has a short memory and the case was discarded for many years, until in the mid-1980s, when researcher/publisher Wendell Stevens printed 1,000 copies of a book by William Steinman called "UFO Crash At Aztec," in which Steinman rehashed the original crash at Aztec, adding material of his own-some of it credible, some of it undocumentable. Though the book had its "day in court," it was shortly out of print, having been read by only a handful of the public and Stevens' "inner circle" of fans.

The story once again died, until recently, when Scott Ramsey began to visit Aztec and search for long lost witnesses. Though the story has "aged," Ramsey and his wife Suzanne have earnestly tried to dig as deep as possible to uncover what really happened near this small New Mexico town over half a century ago. The clues may be cold and naturally the witnesses, when they could be found, are getting up there in years. But the Aztec crash is finally getting the attention it deserves. It may not be as well known as the Roswell crash, but serious researchers like Ramsey, nuclear physicist Stanton Freidman, Art Campbell and Nick Redfern have taken the case by the horns and are looking at it with wide open eyes.

Aztec has survived the test of time. It is the UFO crash that refuses to lie down and die. Hopefully this book will add to the weight of positive evidence that SOMETHING happened in a remote part of New Mexico these many, many years ago.

BEHIND THE FLYING SAUCERS

REDFERN ON AZTEC- FROM A TO Z

By Sean Casteel

* Did a pair of conmen named Silas Newton and Leo GeBauer serve ironically to reveal the dramatic truth about a UFO crash in Aztec, New Mexico?

* Declassified FBI files tell part of the story, but why were 200 pages of secret material kept classified for national security reasons? What did the conmen really know?

* Read about the fascinating twists and turns of behind-the-scenes maneuvering in a complex web of possible disinformation designed to keep the Aztec crash covered up.

* Do the UFO occupants themselves merely "stage" crashed saucer events to exert a kind of psychological control over us?

Nick Redfern is among a handful of researchers who have investigated the alleged UFO crash at Aztec, New Mexico, in 1948, in the kind of depth it deserves. This introduction to the long overdue reprinting of Frank Scully's book "Behind The Flying Saucers" will present not only Redfern's findings but that of well-known researchers Stanton Friedman, Scott Ramsey and Art Campbell, all of whom shed important new light on a subject that continues to be shrouded in the deepest of controversy. But first, let's start with the basic outline of our story.

THE BASIC FACTS

Frank Scully was a successful writer in the 1940s and 1950s who wrote for the Hollywood publication "Variety." In October and November of 1949, he published a pair of columns in "Variety" that claimed alien beings were recovered from a flying saucer crash. Scully said his source for the story was one of the scientists involved in the subsequent investigation of the craft's remains.

In 1950, Scully published "Behind The Flying Saucers," dealing further with the crash reports, which he now claimed had happened three times in New Mexico as well as once in Arizona. The book primarily focused on the aforementioned crash at Aztec of a ship 100 feet in diameter that was thought to have worked on magnetic principles.

Scully listed his sources as being a man named Silas Newton and a scientist named "Dr. Gee." "Behind The Flying Saucers" went on to sell 60,000 copies.

A couple of years later, San Francisco Chronicle reporter J.P. Cahn wrote an expose for True Magazine in which Cahn "revealed" that Newton and Dr. Gee, identified as Leo GeBauer, were a pair of oil conmen who had deceived a credulous Frank Scully. In his

BEHIND THE FLYING SAUCERS

follow-up book, "Armour Bright," published in 1963, Scully defended his earlier story on Aztec, and stated that he still believed what he was told by Newton and Dr. Gee. He further declared that Dr. Gee had been a composite of various scientist sources who he believed to have inside knowledge about flying saucers and the Aztec crash.

The remaining pages of this opening section will be devoted to fleshing out this story in more exacting detail.

NICK REDFERN'S RESEARCH BEGINS

Nick Redfern hails from the midlands of Great Britain and has researched UFOs, crytpo-zoology and related paranormal subjects beginning in childhood. He has written several books, including "On The Trail Of The Saucer Spies," "Strange Secrets" and "Body Snatchers In The Desert."

Redfern began his own investigation in 1986, after reading a book called "UFO Crash At Aztec" by Bill Steinman and Wendell Stevens.

"I read the book extensively," Redfern

Newton and GeBauer

said, "and made a lot of notes, noting names, places, dates, and the agencies involved. That really set me on the road from there, of chasing down the documents. Obviously, being in England at the time, there was no real way for me financially and geographically to get out to Aztec on a regular basis, if indeed at all, which is the main reason why I focused on documents. I felt that if I could add something to it, then chasing the paper trail would be the way to do it."

Surprisingly, it is legal to file Freedom Of Information Act requests even if you are not a U.S. citizen.

"Every other day," Redfern said, "the postman would be knocking at the front door with another parcel with a big FBI or CIA stamp on it. He'd kind of laugh and he thinks, 'What the hell has this guy got coming in the mail?'"

THE IMPORTANCE OF CRASHED FLYING SAUCERS

And what did Redfern conclude from all his hard-won paperwork?

"In my opinion," he said, "the Aztec story in general and Frank Scully's book 'Behind The Flying Saucers' in particular, are both very significant. The reason I say that is as follows: the Frank Scully book was actually the first published nonfiction book on the whole issue of crashed UFOs. Of course there are many aspects to the whole UFO mystery, to the UFO puzzle. And certainly crashed UFOs, today at least, are one of the standout areas of research. You have countless books out there on Roswell and things like back-engineering and Area 51, alien autopsies, that kind of thing.

"But in the early years of Ufology," Redferen continued, "if you look back at the subject, the crashed UFO subject, particularly in the late 40s through the 50s, even through

BEHIND THE FLYING SAUCERS

the 60s, was very much frowned upon by a lot of the established groups then. For example, people like Donald Keyhoe, one of the early researchers in the 50s and 60s, was actually very much against the idea of crashed UFOs, as were many other researchers. It was only in the late 1970s, with people like Leonard Stringfeld and then the publication of Bill Moore and Charles Berlitz's book 'The Roswell Incident' in 1980 that people began to look again at these crashed UFO stories, which had largely been forgotten after about the early 1950s. And this very early fluttering of interest that briefly surfaced in the 1950s was primarily if not exclusively due to 'Behind The Flying Saucers' by Frank Scully."

Redfern added that Roswell itself had indeed created a brief flurry of excitement when the announcement was first made that the military had its hands on a crashed flying saucer in the summer of 1947, but when the publicity died down and the Air Force delivered its weather balloon story, the issue of crashed UFOs pretty much died with it as well.

Origin Unknown

OUT OF THE BLUE

"And then of course," Redfern said, "out of the blue, you have the Scully book surfacing in 1950. Now what's interesting about the Aztec story and the book in general is that it has its detractors and its believers. Some people think that the Aztec story was a legitimate UFO crash. There are other people who take the view that it was nothing but a straightforward hoax by several conmen. And there are people who have offered the intriguing theory that yes, UFOs might have crashed, but is it possible that the Aztec story was a government disinformation scheme to divert people away from the real crashes and to make the whole subject seem ridiculous by setting up a couple of conmen into the story?

"So it has a lot of avenues and aspects to it," Redfern continued, "that regardless of what happened make it a great story. A lot of research has been done into the Aztec accounts, and it's one of these interesting stories that refuses to just roll over and die. It's kind of like a Ufological cockroach, if you like. No matter how many times you kick it and stamp on it, it gets back up on its feet and keeps going."

Redfern provided his own retelling of the basic story.

"The basic outline," he began, "is that in March of 1948, an alien spacecraft came to Earth and crash landed on this mesa in the town of Aztec, New Mexico. Reportedly, a number of small alien bodies were found in the wreckage by the military. I say 'the wreckage,' but the craft reportedly was very much intact apart from supposedly a fractured porthole-window type affair. The crew, apparently, were all dead and everything was whisked away to a secure military facility for analysis. Kind of the usual scenario.

"Well, when Scully's book came out," he went on, "it caused a sensation, not just amongst the small UFO community that existed back then, but also among the media. It actually went on to become a bestseller. It sold in the tens of thousands of copies, literally, which was just unheard of, not for just a UFO book, but bear in mind that this was one of the earliest UFO books as well. It really captured everyone's imagination."

BEHIND THE FLYING SAUCERS

FLIES IN THE OINTMENT

In the wake of the book's success, many people came forward with what they knew of the subject, and rumors and stories abounded. For the first year or so, things went relatively well for Scully. He had an interesting story and was getting the word out on crashed UFOs. But soon an investigation was undertaken by journalist J.P. Cahn into the book and Scully's sources.

"It was found," Redfern said, "that two of his prime sources-one was a guy named Leo GeBauer and the other one was Silas Newton. Newton was really the guy who was orchestrating getting all the information to Scully.

"Now, Newton himself was a shady character. He had a very controversial background. He'd been involved in various swindles and con operations. The FBI actually declassified their files to me on both GeBauer and Newton, neither of which put them in a particularly good light in terms of credibility or honesty. I guess the crux of the story was to what extent the legend, if you like, or the story, rested on the shoulders of Newton and GeBauer. Or were they simply go-between characters who were passing the information on to Scully from insider sources? That's a debate that has raged to this day, namely whether

THE VOICE OF THE ROCKY MOUNTAIN EMPIRE

DENVER POST HOME EDITION

DENVER, COLO.—Climate Capital of the World—TUESDAY, OCT. 14, 1952   52 PAGES

'Saucer Scientist' n $50,000 Fraud

Rocky Mountain Rodeo Ticket Offices Listed

Tickets for all performances of the Rocky Mountain Empire rodeo may be obtained at the following places: The coliseum, from 10 a. m. to 3 p. m. Sunday, and 9 a. m. to 5 p. m. on weekdays; The Denver Post and the downtown J. C. Penney company store; Engelwood Men's store, 3163 South Broadway; Reinert's Clothing stores in Boulder and the Cheyenne Travel Service in Cheyenne.

Military personnel can get tickets at special services offices at Lowry air force base and Fitzsimons Army hospital.

Telephone reservations may be made by calling AComa 4784. Tickets still may be ordered by mail through use of the coupon printed on page 2.

Ending War

Swindle Alleged In Oil Tests

By CHARLES ROOS.
Denver Post Staff Writer.

Silas M. Newton, the "Mr. X" lecturer of flying saucer fame, and a Phoenix, Ariz., radio parts merchant were charged Tuesday by District Attorney Bert M. Keating with operating a $50,000 confidence game swindle.

Keating accused Newton, an oil promoter, and Leo A. GeBauer of Phoenix of defrauding Herman A. Flader, Denver industrialist, out of $50,000 in a swindle involving oil well exploration tests with electronic "doodlebugs," one of them represented as costing $800,000.

Two similar machines have been examined and declared to be war surplus items worth about $3.50, the district attorney said.

BOTH MEN SOUGHT.

or not Aztec begins and ends with a couple of conmen or if they legitimately did stumble across something of a top secret nature."

The truth is that Newton and GeBauer did spend a great deal of time in northern New Mexico and also the Four Corners area as they conducted their various swindles, and it is entirely possible, Redfern feels, that given all the stories of crashed UFOs circulating at the time, that the pair may well have stumbled across rumors and stories similar to those UFO researchers typically encounter.

"So the irony is," Redfern explained, "that they may actually have picked up on real events, but being of a shady background, it may then cast aspersions on the credibility of the story-the fact that it ironically comes from a couple of guys you wouldn't trust as far as you could throw them basically."

Over the years, people have championed and denounced Scully in varying degrees. There were various "knockdowns" of the case, Redfern said, in the 50s and the 70s. Then researcher Leonard Stringfeld caused a revival of the subject in the late 1970s with his self-published crash reports. In 1986, the book that started it all for Redfern, "UFO Crash At Aztec," by William Steinman and Wendell Stevens was published.

"Which again thrust 'Behind The Flying Saucers' into the limelight from the perspective of yes, it really happened and okay there may have been some shady involvement with some of the early people but the essence of the story was true. That was the thrust of the book," Redfern said.

More debunker denunciations were heard in the 1990s, but by then Redfern had begun his own work in earnest.

THE PAPERWORK IS THERE

"What I did," Redfern said, "is to use the FOIA to try and pry out of the government and various agencies official files relating to Aztec. And unlike Roswell, where the amount of paperwork that exists is literally a couple of pages of teletypes-there's really nothing at all-the exact opposite is the case with Aztec, somewhat ironically and surprisingly."

Redfern found the FBI to be the most profitable source of material, and eventually received declassified files on Scully, Newton and GeBauer.

"Newton's file and Scully's file," he said, "were each about 70 pages in length, and both files made it very clear that the FBI were watching both men very, very closely around the time of publication of the book. They knew all the various things the two men were getting up to, who was speaking to who. And they actually had detailed files on the story surrounding the crash. I would stress that the FBI didn't have files or didn't release files concerning their insider knowledge of the crash. What they released were files making it clear that they were following very closely the stories that Newton was telling to Scully and they were aware of the tales at least."

When it came to the FBI file on Leo GeBauer, however, the story was a little different.

"The FBI released to me," Redfern said, "200 pages of a file that in itself is at least 400 pages in length, and at least half of which the FBI to this day will not declassify. And parts of that file are still classified in the name of national security 60 years later. Which is kind of surprising and often opens a lot of people's eyes. The idea that if this was a straightforward hoax, why doesn't the FBI release all the files? Then we won't be in a situation of wondering what's in the withheld files, which just kind of fans the flames of conspiracy

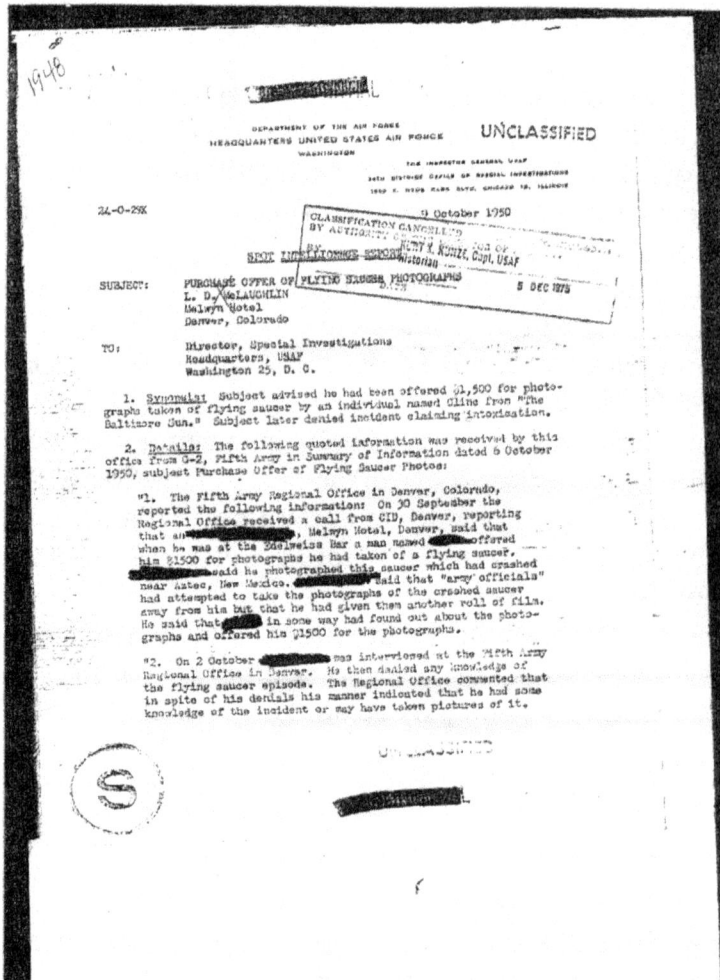

even more."

Redfern also received some pages from the army and the air force and slowly assembled a dossier that is now around 600 pages altogether on various key players and reports related to Aztec.

"Now unfortunately," he said, "like a lot of aspects of the UFO subject, we've got a lot of files on Aztec, but it doesn't really answer the question of what did or didn't happen. What it tells us is that Scully was pretty sure he was being told the truth. It tells us that yes, Newton and GeBauer were shady characters who were two of the prime sources for Scully. It also tells us that the military and the intelligence world were deeply interested in the fact that people were telling these crashed UFO stories from roughly 1948, 49, through to about 52. And they wanted to get a handle on who was speaking to who, who was publishing the stories and why.

"Of course," he continued, "what we don't have, unfortunately, is the reasoning behind this. Was the FBI concerned that Newton and GeBauer and Scully had stumbled upon real crashed UFO stories? Or were they just thinking, 'Hang on. Who are these guys? We just need to know what they're doing.'"

KARL PFLOCK IS HEARD FROM

The late Karl Pflock was in many ways a UFO believer. For instance, he felt the Betty and Barney Hill abduction case represented genuine alien contact and that there was in fact an alien presence on Earth from the 40s to the 70s, but that that presence had since gone away.

"You know, they came here, they surveyed us, they did whatever they were doing and then they left," Redfern said. "But although Karl was a UFO believer, he wasn't an Aztec believer. One of the intriguing things that Karl found out-during the course of his research he was exposed to and shown a copy of a journal that Silas Newton had written probably sometime around the late 60s or early 70s, kind of a diary, entry-type journal, which might have been the basis for a book that Newton was planning to write.

"One of the interesting things in the journal was that it made reference to how Newton, at the height of the Scully/Aztec controversy, was secretly contacted by a couple of guys who told Newton that they worked for a very high, influential U.S. intelligence department or agency. Now they didn't say it was the CIA or the NSA or who it was. But some people have said ironically it actually sounds almost like an MJ-12 type organization."

At that point, Newton was afraid that he was going to be in big trouble.

"As it turned out, though," Redfern said, "these guys from this intelligence agency told him, according to Newton in his journal, that they didn't care about the fact that the Aztec story was hoaxed and bogus. But they wanted him to keep on telling the story. They wanted him to keep promoting this controversial tale about crashed UFOs. Karl himself wondered if possibly this was a ruse to try and make the UFO crash subject look ridiculous by promoting a hoax. Then, if there had been a real crash, it would make people think, 'Well, theses stories are nonsense.'"

Karl Pflock also had another theory. Could the Aztec story be a concoction of the U.S. military, a kind of counterintelligence operation directed against the Russians, to try and scare the Russians-at the height of the Cold War-into thinking that the U.S. had gotten its hands on a crashed UFO and by definition highly advanced technology and weaponry?

"In other words," Redfern continued, "it was intended to possibly root out Soviet spies in New Mexico. Start spreading this story and then you see who follows the trail. It would allow the American intelligence community to see if any Russian spies started asking questions, and then, if they did, they could be arrested without any real secrets being compromised. And of course the other angle was just to screw with the minds of the Russians, to try to make them fearful that, 'Oh, my God, the Americans have got a crashed UFO.'"

WHAT ARE UFO CRASHES REALLY?

What are we to make, ultimately, about UFO crash reports? According to Redfern, we have to judge each case on its own merits.

"I think we're looking at several different things," he said, "that could lead to these crashed UFO legends, stories, events. Just because crash A might turn out to have been a prototype Stealth fighter, that doesn't mean that crash B was also a prototype aircraft. That could have been something weirder. One of the things that I suggest in some of my books is that some of the early crashes could well have been prototype devices captured from Nazi Germany and the Japanese and that we were flying ourselves. Some of these crashes were just due to us raiding the laboratories in Germany at the end of 1945. You know, bringing all these German Operation Paperclip scientists over, Nazi scientists, and working on things that really were highly controversial but were also prototypes that we didn't have a good handle on.

"Now I think that definitely accounts for some of these crash reports. But if you're talking about truly unknown ones, one of the interesting theories that's being put forward is the idea that some of these crashes, if they're genuine UFO crashes, that they actually are being staged by the aliens."

Redfern admits that theory is a little odd.

"Now that sounds strange," he said, "but the theory is that maybe, in the early years, rather than freak everybody out and land on the White House lawn, why not make themselves, their first appearance to us, as being kind of like vulnerable creatures, somewhat similar to us? Try not to overpower us with the idea that they're sort of massively advanced creatures that view us the same way we view an ant. You know, kind of appeal to a scenario that is more comfortable to us, the idea that they're not superhuman beings, they're as frail and fragile as we are. So stage an event. That's a possibility."

Still another possibility exists.

"Other people put forward the idea that maybe yes, they're more advanced than us, but perhaps they're not as advanced as we think they are. The idea that maybe they create this image that they're super-advanced, but perhaps they're the last sort of vestiges of an ancient civilization. Perhaps there aren't many of them left, and in simplistic terms they're driving around in the equivalent of a 1940s beat up truck or whatever. They're just down to their last few craft or whatever. The image that they're super-advanced and have this huge armada of craft could be an ingenious smokescreen to make them appear more powerful and less vulnerable than possibly they really are.

"These are all just hypothetical ideas of course. But when you're looking at how something could get from there to here and then at the very last moment crash, I'll be the first to admit that is an odd scenario."

REDFERN'S ASSESSMENT OF THE SITUATION

Origin Unknown

Having discussed the nature of UFO crashes in general, the question of just what Redfern himself believes about Aztec was addressed. Has he ever been tempted to play the hoax card?

"Oh, no," he said. "I sort of veer between the idea that something happened, or that Newton and GeBauer and Scully got wind of rumors of something having occurred in the New Mexico desert. I don't think they made the stories up out of thin air. A lot of people forget this, that Newton and GeBauer, because of all their oil scams and different things, they were spending a hell of a lot of time in New Mexico and the Four Corners area, and they were kind of like players. They were running around everywhere, making leads, hooking up with people, just to try to make a fast buck, so to speak. And traveling around in the late 40s, I'm pretty sure they did pick up on some of these rumors about crashed UFOs. Whether they were told the full story or whether they embroidered on it, I don't know.

"But in that respect, I don't think Aztec can be dismissed as a straightforward hoax, but equally we have to be very careful and recognize the fact that two of the very early players were conmen who were found guilty of crimes. There's no doubt about that. They were charged and found guilty of fraud in a case in the early 50s. And their FBI files don't paint them in a flattering light at all. There are lists of all sorts of things the FBI were watching them for.

"But that doesn't take away from the fact that a conman can pick up on something that's real. That's again the irony of the case. I'm kind of more intrigued by Karl Pflocks' discoveries that possibly Aztec was linked with disinformation games and operations to possibly either hide a real event behind a faked event that could be destroyed in terms of its credibility because of the people involved. Or maybe it was directed at the Russians to scare them into thinking America's got this advanced technology and weaponry from outer space. What the hell are we going to do now? As if the atomic bomb wasn't bad enough."

Another interesting aspect of the Aztec legend is the "little men" reported to have been found there.

"See, this is one of those things about Aztec," Redfern said, "and why I don't dismiss this story, is because when you talk to people today, who have spoken of their involvement with crashed UFOs, we hear these stories about little creatures and so forth. If you look back at a lot of the literature that existed around the UFO subject in general, in the late 40s and particularly the 50s, it was primarily UFO sightings or it was the classic contactee humanlike, long blonde-haired alien.

"There wasn't a great deal spoken about little men other than really, interestingly enough, in the early years by Newton, GeBauer and Scully. They were the ones who focused on the little men angle. Then in later years, we hear more stuff about the little men, the grays primarily. You didn't hear stories about them in the 40s and 50s. It was all 'Captain Zargon' or whatever, someone they'd been flying around Venus with. Those kinds of stories were the ones we heard.

"So I find it interesting that the Aztec story had an ingredient in it-namely the little men-that no one else was focusing on, and then, hey, 40 years later, everyone is talking about little men. Did they have an insider at the time who knew something no one else knew about until in the later years when it started to surface? As I said, everyone else was talking about, 'Oh, the aliens are very human-looking with long blonde hair' and the women looked like a cross between something straight out of 'Star Wars' mixed with Pamela Anderson or whatever. But Newton and GeBauer and Scully were saying something completely different and it makes you wonder why."

LIKE UNTO JACK THE RIPPER

So much remains unresolved and unknown.

"That's one thing that is unfortunate," Redfern said, "about a lot of these early cases like Aztec, is that they become a Ufological equivalent version of something like Jack the Ripper where there are a lot of theories, a lot of books out, a lot of ideas, but at the end of the day everybody's dead and the government is saying nothing. Or there's nobody to ask. And that is the danger now, that Aztec has fallen into that Jack the Ripper category of how do we resolve it? I truthfully don't know how to resolve it.

"I think it would either be via a smoking gun document that somebody leaks or that something is declassified by mistake. Something along those lines. I think it's going to come down to human error on the part of somebody on the inside or a Deep Throat-type source coming forward and saying, 'Hey, here's the files you're looking for.' Now whether that happens or not-we can't sort of foresee the future. But I think that's our only chance, and otherwise we're still going to be, 50 years from now, thinking, 'Well, I wonder if 'Behind The Flying Saucers' by Frank Scully was real or a hoax?' Which is what we've done for the last 60 years."

BEHIND THE FLYING SAUCERS

SEEING AZTEC THROUGH
A HAZE OF SECRECY

By Sean Casteel

* Is secrecy about UFOs sometimes enforced with intimidation and even threats of murder? Stanton Friedman says the government threatens witnesses with such extreme measures routinely!

* What is involved in analyzing recovered alien technology like the ship that crashed at Aztec? Will our scientists ever learn the truth?

* What was behind the mass flyover of UFOs at Farmington, New Mexico, in 1948? Was it a show of force by the aliens in the wake of the recent Aztec crash?

* Why was New Mexico such a hotspot for UFOs in the late 1940s? What was it about the region that drew such intense alien interest?

Nuclear physicist Stanton Friedman is one of the most publicly visible faces from among the UFO community. He has appeared numerous times on the Larry King Show and a slew of other television programs. He has authored landmark books on the Roswell Incident ("Crash At Corona: The Definitive Study of the Roswell Incident," coauthored with Donald Berliner) and the Betty and Barney Hill abduction case ("Captured! The Betty and Barney Hill UFO Experience," coauthored with Betty's niece Kathleen Marden), and has lectured at over 600 colleges and 100 professional groups throughout the world.

So with credentials like that, Friedman is more than qualified to discuss the still mysterious events that happened in Aztec, New Mexico, in 1948.

"I just think it's an outstanding story," Friedman said. "It happened after Roswell, so I still have pride of place, you know. Roswell's first. But I think the Aztec case is solid."

Freidman arrived at that opinion only after meeting longtime Aztec researcher Scott Ramsey, whose work will be featured in the next chapter. Friedman said that he had initially been most unimpressed by the research of others prior to Ramsey's appearance on the scene, but that speaking to Ramsey had quickly changed his mind about the believability of Aztec. Ramsey had spoken to many witnesses, including military personnel whose testimony sounded perfectly in order from Friedman's expert perspective.

"Scott's a terrier," Friedman said. "He gets after the facts and data. A man after my own heart."

THE WAY SECURITY WORKS

"Unfortunately," Friedman said, "a saucer crashed. The reason for what happened we may not know. If you hear an automobile accident out in front of your house, which

BEHIND THE FLYING SAUCERS

happened to me once, you don't know what happened. You're inside. You do know that there was an accident, though, even if you don't know where the people were coming from and going to, etc. I think what happened was the thing crashed, the military got involved, the fire department, the police got involved. They carted this thing off, they covered it up, they intimidated certain military people who were involved to not talk about it. And who knows what they learned from it? I don't know. I haven't seen any technical reports. It would be extraordinary if I or anyone else had."

Friedman, having been involved in classified government work for many years beginning in the 1950s, knows whereof he speaks.

"I know how security works," he said. "And after 14 years under it, you get a pretty good understanding of how things happen or what people do to intimidate others. So the military guys would all have had clearances and they would have talked to the police in no uncertain terms, and there would have been intimidation of the civilian witnesses.

"It all makes sense," Friedman continued. "When you've got a craft whose characteristics clearly indicate that it wasn't made here, it's going to be top secret material, no matter how you slice it. So I can't blame the government for wanting to cover it up, especially since we're talking about March 1948 when the world was in lousy shape. A good part of Europe was starving, the Cold War was certainly heating up by then. And what are you going to say? 'Well, a saucer crashed, there were aliens in it. We don't know what they want or where they're coming from or how they operate, but we thought you'd like to know.' They could hardly do that."

BLACK BUDGETS IN THE REAL WORLD

"I find that people have no idea," Friedman explained, "of the vastness of the resources that the black community, the intelligence community, can bring into the examination of things like this. They're accustomed to thinking of a few professors and a bunch of grad students. Well, that's peanuts by comparison. When I worked on the aircraft nuclear propulsion program, in 1958, at General Electric just outside of Cincinnati, there were 3,500 people there; 1100 of them were engineers and scientists. We spent a hundred million dollars that year. That was a lot of money in 1958. So if you want large scale, important technology development and review, all that sort of thing, you go to industry and you spend a lot of bucks."

All of which relates to what would have logically happened to the wreckage from Aztec.

"You've got the wreckage," Friedman said, "you figure out clever ways of moving it, and then you have an awful lot of people looking at various scientific aspects of the problem. What is this stuff made out of? What's the strength, what's the melting point, what's the composition? What's the function? These are difficult problems."

Coupled with the obvious difficulties involved with analyzing alien wreckage, one must recall that our analytical capabilities were much less refined in the late 1940s.

BEHIND THE FLYING SAUCERS

"Early on," he said, "you could measure percentages of things in tenths of a percent. Then it was hundreds of a percent. Then it's thousands and then it's parts per billion. So your understanding grows when your analytical capability grows. And anybody who thinks, 'Well, give me a saucer today and tomorrow I'll build you one'-that's ridiculous. The Stealth Fighter took ten years to develop and it only cost 10 billion dollars in development money. That's the scope we have to look at.

"So if we had wreckage from Aztec," he continued, "as I'm convinced we did, from an advanced alien vehicle-this is eight months after Roswell, where you had another one-there would have been a lot of work just comparing the stuff. Are these from the same place? People forget that during the war we used to grab pieces of downed German and Japanese fighters, if they were downed over friendly territory, and did our best to examine them, to find out what their capabilities were. These are not easy problems.

"And anyone who thinks that they're going to find a bunch of papers in a physical review, analysis and evaluation of an alien flying saucer from Aztec or Roswell in some journal is crazy. That's not where you publish that kind of stuff. So I get a little disturbed by the people who know nothing about security, nothing about the development of advanced technology or how our own government does things, and make their proclamations about Aztec or Roswell and several other cases like that."

Illustration copyright by Jim Nichols

KNOW YOUR ENEMY

There is a vast industry, according to Friedman, that is involved in the recovery of alien enemy/friend technology and analyzing it.

"One of the key factors here," he said, "is that anybody who's in-I'll call it an 'almost war' situation-the Cold War, a hot war, whatever, one of your first jobs is to find out the capability of your enemy. How fast can their vehicle travel? How rapidly can they turn? What kind of radiation are they emanating so that you can detect them from a distance? There are all kinds of questions like this. I'm convinced that there was a Majestic-12 and this certainly would have fallen under their purview.

"They had to be concerned about two different things. One is wreckage. How do you get it analyzed, who looks at it, who can determine what it's made of, what its features are, that kind of thing. The other is monitoring flight data to see how these things behave. Do they tilt when they turn? Does the color they give off at night change when they change their acceleration?"

Freidman said it was unfortunate that he had characterized the aliens as enemies, but then added, "We've treated them like enemies. We put out orders in 1952 to shoot them down if they don't land when instructed to do so. So just as we wanted to know the Russian flight capabilities and radar capabilities, we want to know alien capabilities and they want to know ours. How fast can we fly? How sharp a turn can we make? What kind

BEHIND THE FLYING SAUCERS

of offensive and defensive weapons do we have? These are all natural questions."

There were approximately 200 American fatal jet crashes between 1951 and 1955, some of which Friedman says may have been the alien response to our own aggression.

"We were trying to shoot them down," he said, "and they shot back."

Learning the capabilities of the enemy is an important part of preparing for war as well, which could just as easily apply to our efforts in the wake of Roswell and Aztec to learn what kind of firepower the aliens have at their disposal.

FRIEDMAN'S EXPERIENCE WITH THE FBI

"I read 'Behind The Flying Saucers' with great interest," Friedman said. "It's interesting that Scully did have, despite the fact that he's attacked so much, he did have a good reputation in Hollywood. I think he did make an effort to sort of make Dr. Gee out of a bunch of important people whose names he didn't want to use. He wasn't a science reporter, let's face it. And Silas Newton was a rich guy. A conman, sure, but there were lots of them around at the time."

Friedman talked about the FBI files on Scully, Newton and Leo GeBauer that Nick Redfern and Scott Ramsey had managed to unearth.

"It is interesting that they have such files," Friedman said. "So we know there was a strong government interest in these guys that was much more than would have been expected if they were just conmen. Who cares? So they're trying to take people for money? Well, a lot of people have been taken because they were trying to find oil, you know. 'I'm going to make a fortune for you, buddy, just invest with me.' You've heard that. So the government interest is an important part of the story."

Friedman's experience seeking to obtain his own file from the FBI has convinced him that the federal agency is less than honest in its dealings.

"I went after my files under Freedom of Information/Privacy Act with the CIA and the FBI," he said. "This was several years ago. The FBI wrote me back saying we don't have a file on you, even though I told them I'd had a security clearance. There aren't many people with my name and certainly not my name and birth date. Then I hear from the CIA and all they have is a negative name check request on me from the FBI with a file number. And they sent me that. So I wrote the FBI again and oh, yeah, we do have a file on you, but it's classified. How big was the file? What security level? That information is classified too. Sorry.

"So you know they will lie," he said. "They will cover up. It's a way of life for the government. It's a crazy world in which we live. The government gets by with as many lies as they can put into place. They're not aimed at me so much as at their enemies. Remember that the key part about security-I have to tell this to everybody-is you can't tell your friends without telling your enemy. They listen to the radio, they read newspapers, they watch television. So one of the reasons for government lies is not because they don't like Americans, but because they don't like the Russians or Chinese or whoever else is out there. Osama."

THE INTIMIDATION FACTOR

No one has yet been able to find a top secret report, something like "Technical Report of the Recovery of an Alien Spacecraft at Aztec," Friedman said, "but absence of

BEHIND THE FLYING SAUCERS

evidence is not evidence of absence.

"And many people say," Freidman continued, "that you can't keep secrets that long. That's baloney. You can keep secrets for a very long time. There's a whole chapter on the Cosmic Watergate in my new book, 'Flying Saucers and Science.' People who haven't had clearances think you can't keep secrets. People who have had clearances know you can. It's not that hard. There's the need-to-know aspect. That's really important.

"And there is intimidation here as well. I mean, the sheriff's granddaughter in Roswell told me that her grandmother told her that the government told her 'If you ever talk about what you saw we'll kill you and kill your family.' And the granddaughter's horrified and she asks, 'Did you believe them?' 'Barbara, I was there. Yes, I believed them.' So intimidation goes on all the time. And when people work for you, then you've got a real hold, because they have a security clearance. You're threatened with loss of benefits, loss of your life, little minor problems like that. That's the real world. I'm sorry. That's the way the world works."

THE FARMINGTON ARMADA
The over-flight of a sky-full of ships in 1948 in Farmington, New Mexico, near Aztec, also continues to be a controversial event more than 60 years later.

"I have talked to people," Friedman said, "when I was in Aztec, who saw that huge array of vehicles up there. There was a mass flyover. Now I'm not going to second guess and say I know why they were there or what they were doing, whether they were trying to intimidate someone or whether they were looking for their buddies who had crashed at Aztec. Who knows what motivates aliens? We have trouble understanding earthlings; we certainly don't know what motivates aliens.

"Are they worried about recovering bodies for their home burial? Are they worried about recovering technology? Or are they worried about trying to figure out how much we might have learned from what technology we recovered? Who knows? But there is no question that there was a massive group of craft there.

"There are other cases where there have been dozens of UFOs seen at once. One guy described how there were dozens that came out of this big mother ship. So if you release all your vehicles nearby and say, 'Hey, guys assignment one, check this region out. And after that, you guys go this way and you guys go that way.' So who knows how many of them were available for a quick look at Farmington?"

Friedman applied a similar logic to the type and number of bodies recovered at the Aztec crash, with some estimates as high as 16 bodies altogether, much more than were reported to have died at Roswell. Friedman answered by way of a human-centered analogy.

"Because of all the electronic gear onboard," he said, "one of our typical reconnaissance planes would have 15-member crews. But fighter planes, typically at most two members. Bombers, five to ten. So it depends on the function. How many guys were needed to do the job they needed to do? And I don't know what that job was. Reconnaissance? Recovery? Checking out the soil composition in New Mexico? Which incidentally is a big mining state. In the Betty and Barney Hill case there were really three different kinds of alien bodies, and that was an abduction mission. It sure doesn't sound like Aztec was that. We don't have anybody who was abducted there, as far as I know."

BEHIND THE FLYING SAUCERS

WHY UFO CRASHES? AND WHY NEW MEXICO?

"Well," Friedman began, "I think we have to separate the problem into two parts. How do you get here from another star system, through the vacuum of space, where there's not much in the way of gravity fields and they have no problem with air friction or anything like that. Until when you get here and you turn loose your Earth excursion modules and then you have all these problems. A very different environment, and subject to change. Lighting storms, for example, only happen on occasion. Sometimes they produce a tremendous number of hailstones. I've been in New Mexico and my car was dented by big hailstones. There are incredible lightning storms. I've been there for them, too. Boy, you want a display!

"Why is New Mexico special? Well, it had two of the three nuclear weapons labs in the country, Sandia and Los Alamos. It had Kirtland, which was the largest employer in the state back then. It had Roswell, the home of the only atomic bombing group in the entire world. It had White Sands Missile Range with the German rocket masters of the captured German V-2 rockets. If there was one place you would expect there to be spies, whether Russian or Chinese or alien, it would be New Mexico. No question about it.

"And you say, 'How would the aliens know?' Well, among other things, the Trinity site was where the first nuclear weapon was tested. It's still radioactive. You can do surveys from the air and plot these automatically and son of a gun, there's a hotspot here and there and a whole bunch more in New Mexico. So it would be rather astonishing if there wasn't major surveillance of New Mexico."

Extreme variations in the weather in what would have been for the aliens the new and untried atmosphere of the Earth, then, may account for the crashes, while our burgeoning mastery of the atom might have drawn them to New Mexico as one of their first ports of call. Meanwhile, our fear of the Russians was reaching a new extreme as well.

A 1951 national security memo that Friedman saw years later, after it had been declassified, said that the Russians had made more progress in the development of nuclear weapons and methods for delivering them in the past 18 months than had been expected for five years.

"That's a scary thought," Friedman said. "We expected that they were just dumb peasants, what do they know? What can they do? Well, they've got a little slave labor and a lot of Germans to help out. But the point is we were honestly expecting that Joe Stalin might want to attack us. There was a story a few years ago in which a Russian general was indicating that maybe Stalin was killed in 1953 because he wanted them to make war against the United States. You know, he trusted Hitler, why should he trust us? That sounds complicated, but what I'm saying is the Russians were actively working toward being able to attack, and we had to try to defend.

"So we had to find out as much as we could about them. Along the way we find out about flying saucers, and we had to worry about them, too. And they would worry about us. So things were going on, and New Mexico was a big part of it. So I'm not surprised that Roswell and Aztec happened. Who knows how many more there were?"

BEHIND THE FLYING SAUCERS

Scott and Suzanne Ramsey

LIES AND DECEPTIONS ABOUT AZTEC EXPOSED!

By Sean Casteel

* Learn how a chance remark by a New Mexico laborer sparked more than 20 years of research into the Aztec UFO crash mystery.

* Celebrated film actress Linda Darnell helped start a chain of events that is still impacting on Ufology today. What is the Hollywood connection to Aztec?

* Even after a smear campaign involving a jealous journalist and the FBI, among others, the Aztec story still has legs, says investigator Scott Ramsey.

* How does one answer the many arguments of the numerous debunkers of the Aztec story? Read Scott Ramsey's expert refutations of the negativists and their shoddy research.

Scott Ramsey is the foremost researcher of the 1948 UFO crash at Aztec. He is praised by many others in the field who defer to his expertise and dedication without hesitation.

For instance, in the interview conducted for this book, Stanton Friedman said that "Scott works exceedingly hard and has spent an enormous amount of money on his own, chasing after leads and finding some good ones. I've found him to be totally believable and honest. I'm very impressed with Scott."

But why did Ramsey take up the challenge of researching Aztec in the first place?

"I got interested in Aztec," Ramsey said, "on a business trip in the late 80s out in Farmington. I was calling on a company that employs a lot of Navajo Indians, and we were working late one night on a generator. That's what they do for a living, mainly, repair generators. What I do for a living is I supply mostly copper, but any alloy of magnet wire, which is wire that creates a magnetic field, such as motor windings, transformers, generators, that kind of thing."

As he and the others were working, one of the Navajos began to discuss his plans for the weekend.

"And one said that he was going to go hunt mule-deer, and he wanted to check out the old crash site," Ramsey recalled. "I didn't really know these guys well at all, I was my first trip there, and I said, 'What old crash site?' Just trying to make conversation really.

"They said that back in the late 1940s or 50s," he continued, "there was rumored to be a UFO that crashed out in Aztec, New Mexico, about 17 miles from where we were. That kind of piqued my curiosity a bit. I asked more questions, and they said, 'We really don't know much. It's just an old tale. We don't even know if there's any truth to it, but a lot of people believe it.'"

BEHIND THE FLYING SAUCERS

When Ramsey returned to his home in North Carolina, he began to dig further into the Aztec story, using newspaper articles and archived newsletters. He found very little information. He returned to Farmington on another sales call, and this time he visited an old museum in Aztec. After talking to the curator there, he again came up with almost nothing in the way of usable information.

"The town was pretty well split," he said, "on whether it was an event or a nonevent. But that's how my interest in Aztec came up."

What followed for Ramsey were many years of seeking declassified documents, primarily from the FBI, and many visits to the Aztec site and the area around it as well as interviews with witnesses, many of them now elderly. (Ramsey would also meet his future wife in the tiny New Mexico town, but more about that later.)

RAMSEY TELLS THE TALE

Ramsey's version of what happened to Frank Scully and the others at Aztec begins with Scully's decision to leave New York for work in Hollywood.

"Frank was a well-known writer," Ramsey said. "He wrote for 'Variety' and freelanced quite a bit. He moved from New York right before he wrote the book on Aztec and was living out in California, writing on the Hollywood scene. Actually, if Silas Newton and Leo GeBauer had approached him on their own, I don't think Frank would have taken their story seriously at all. It was the other people who were telling Frank, 'You really need to sit down and talk to Silas Newton.'

"Newton was well-known in the Hollywood area," Ramsey continued, "and he was a very, very wealthy man. Even the FBI files agree with that. I think it was the cred-

Film Star Linda Darnell

ibility of people like Linda Darnell and Peverly Marley [Marley was Darnell's husband and a cinematographer], who were big names in Hollywood that Frank had befriended. And they said, 'Hey, if you're looking for a story, you really need to talk to these guys.' Without that credibility from the Hollywood figures, I don't think Frank would have paid much attention to it."

Scully had known Newton years before through working on a previous book project that had nothing to do with UFOs, and Newton considered himself a fan of the popular writer and therefore wanted his help concerning the Aztec crash story. Scully met with Newton as Linda Darnell and others had advised and found his story interesting enough to warrant a book-length treatment. Scully wrote "Behind The Flying Saucers" in a mere 62 days and the rest, as they say, is history. But a very complicated history, to say the least.

One such complication involves the true identity of Dr. Gee. Was he a composite character, as Scully later claimed?

"I've read different things that Frank Scully wrote," Ramsey said, "and supposedly it was up to 8 or 9 different scientists, and those men of science were, in his opinion, after he saw their credentials, very important and had gotten his attention and respect as far

as who they were. The scientists told Scully that the Aztec story would break within a year, but they wanted it out sooner than later and they wanted Scully, as advised by Newton, to release the story to the public."

Meanwhile, along with the honorable men of science, Scully himself is worthy of a certain degree of respect as well.

"He really wasn't what the skeptics," Ramsey said, "make him out to be. It just seems like he's under the magnifying glass. I guess he's not here to defend himself. But they try to make him out as a sensationalist journalist, and he wasn't. Quite the opposite, actually. I don't think you can immediately get in with the Hollywood crowd if you're writing INcredible things about them and sensationalizing about them. He had their respect, and therefore they were willing to work with him."

THE CURTAIN COMES DOWN ON A SURPRISE BESTSELLER

"Well, Frank Scully's book came out," Ramsey said. "It was published by Holt and Company, out of New York. It sold somewhere around 62,000 copies in several different printings, which back then was phenomenal. It was on the 'New York Times' bestseller list. My mother's still alive, and she read it when she was a young lady. So it was a very popular book.

"It just seems like the curtain came crashing down," he continued, "when the FBI went after Silas Newton and Leo GeBauer. Then, all of a sudden, the credibility of the book got a black eye because of two people who had confided in Frank."

Even prior to the book's publication, the FBI was already keeping a file on Silas Newton. He was said to be a man of great wealth, a huge supporter of the Republican Party and "an all around great American," Ramsey said.

"Just about the time that the book came out," he continued, "the FBI has pegged Newton as being a source on the book and all of a sudden he's basically a dirty rotten scoundrel and a man of 'interest' to the FBI. Now how do you go from one extreme to the other when you've really done nothing but given Frank Scully information for a book?"

Newton was also accused by one of his investors, a man named Herman Flader, of outright fraud. It seems Newton had claimed to discover oil by means of a recovered piece of alien technology he called "the Doodle-Bug."

"You can write a lot of negative things about Silas Newton," Ramsey admitted, "because he did use some creative tactics to get individuals to put their money in with his investment. But the interesting thing is, he was also very, very successful, according to the FBI, in producing huge wealth for some of his investors. But the skeptics, the debunkers, and all the negative articles written about him would have you believing that, boy, he pulled this big con and sold Herman Flader and the other investors on alien technology and they're a bunch of con guys.

"Well, there are a lot of investors who would tell you differently. As the FBI noted, out of the around 32 investors in the specific oil well that Herman Flader complained about, only Flader wanted to complain. The other investors said they were quite happy with it. 'We don't care if he sold us on alien technology or what. We're starting to produce oil.'"

The FBI persisted in trying to bring charges of fraud against Newton, who had dealings in Arizona, Colorado, Utah and New Mexico, which necessitated going before four different federal judges, one in each state. None of the judges were impressed by the evidence enough to bring charges, since only Herman Flader was making the accusations. However, Silas Newton and Leo GeBauer were finally found guilty of "Confidence Charges," and ordered to pay back Herman Flader. The original judgment, made in a federal court in Denver, Colorado, was for $50,000 but was later reduced to $18,000 and court costs. It should also be noted that none of the other investors, who had no complaints in the case at all, were allowed to testify at the trial.

THE MYSTERIOUS GUEST LECTURER

Another thread in the confusing story concerns a mysterious guest lecturer who spoke before a crowd of students and faculty at the University of Colorado sometime around early March of 1950.

"He gave a lecture to the college students about UFOs," Ramsey said, "and said one had crashed within 500 miles of where they were sitting right now, and he gave the location as a mesa outside of Aztec, New Mexico. And that person turned out to be, to the best of everybody's research, Silas Newton.

"And then here comes Frank Scully, fresh into California, hanging around the big names of Hollywood who were going to be his sources for many articles. And he's told about a very influential, wealthy man by the name of Silas Newton, who has an interesting story. And that led to Frank Scully's meeting with the men of science. He refers to one of them as having 'more degrees than a thermometer.'"

Scully concluded, having met so many credible men, based on his encounter with Newton, that there must be something to it all. It was at that point that the FBI began its investigation into Scully's sources and put Silas Newton on their hit list.

The investigation was spurred on by a reporter named J.P. Cahn, who at one time worked for the "San Francisco Chronicle" and had heard through sources still unnamed to this day that Frank Scully was at work on a book about UFOs. Cahn himself was very interested in UFOs. His mother used to attend the frequent gatherings at Giant Rock, California, where contactees and other flying saucer believers would meet with one another and exchange UFO lore.

"A lot of times," Ramsey said, "you'll read that Cahn was employed by the 'San Francisco Chronicle.' But through his obituary we got the names of the people who attended the funeral, including pall bearers. They turned out to be former employees. And they all said, no, he had already left the newspaper. He was doing freelance work."

In any case, Cahn contacted Scully and offered to buy the UFO story outright.

"And Frank Scully said, 'Why would I sell it to you? I've already got the story.' According to J.P. Cahn, he offered Frank $25,000. Frank said it was actually far less than that and he never agreed to sell it. He said, 'I'm honored that you would want to buy my story, but I already have all the parts and people and places intact and I'm going to go ahead and write it on my own.'"

However, Cahn had already gone to his bosses at the "Chronicle" and guaranteed them he could deliver the story. When Scully again refused to turn over the story, Cahn was made to appear foolish to management and decided to take the story apart piece by piece. It was Cahn, according to his former fellow "Chronicle" employees, who went to the FBI and made the initial accusations against Newton after doing some background checking and finding some of Newton's shady past. It was also Cahn who put disgruntled

BEHIND THE FLYING SAUCERS

investor Herman Flader onto Newton's "creative" salesmanship.

"It seemed like a jealousy kick," Ramsey said. "'I thought I had the story and if you're not going to sell it to me then I'm going to just take you to the cleaners with it.' Cahn was trying to con the cons, basically."

WHAT ELSE COULD HAVE CRASHED AT AZTEC?

The preceding story also illustrates the exacting, detailed research conducted by Ramsey. Contacting Cahn's pall bearers is the kind of relentless search for meaningful data that he is so praised for within the UFO community.

Ramsey also spent a great deal of time researching alternative theories as to what might have crashed at Aztec, including military aircraft. He and researcher Andy Kissner journeyed to Maxwell Air Force Base in Montgomery, Alabama, to study crash reports.

"The military keeps impeccable crash reports," Ramsey said. "Especially back in that timeframe, in New Mexico, when there were so many secret military operations going around, there was so much restricted airspace, that the military kept a very good and very detailed record of civilian and military crashes."

The only crash officially reported in the Aztec area took place in the early 1970s, and appears to have involved a pilot who bailed out of his F-4 Phantom about 40 miles east of the town itself. Meanwhile, the hunt for records of the 1948 crash continued.

"We looked for all the obvious," Ramsey said. "Could it have been a flying wing? Could it have been a prototype jet? Could it have been a Soviet bomber? That would be a real good reason to keep it secret. We wouldn't want to admit that through our half-assed radar system back then that a Soviet bomber could have gotten through and, the fact was, one could have. But there is always a paper trail to an incident. The paper trail may lead you to 'That report is still classified,' and you can appeal it and they can deny it, but at least there's a paper trail that something took place. There is a paper trail to Aztec. The paper trail stops."

THE AZTEC LIBRARY FUNDRAISER

The story of the Aztec UFO crash is also a story of the people involved. Though many of the local residents were unwilling to talk about the event, perhaps due in part to the kind of government intimidation that Stanton Friedman talked about, the public library in the town of 6,400 decided to use the event for an annual fundraiser. In 1998, librarian Leanne Hathcock organized a symposium to be held around the date of the Aztec crash.

"She did it one year," Ramsey said, "just to see how it worked. The old Aztec library was a tiny building that had been outgrown for ten for fifteen years. And the symposium kind of took off. Leanne was lucky to get some very good speakers. I got involved in 1999. I called her long distance to say I wasn't an expert on Aztec but I could tell her that

BEHIND THE FLYING SAUCERS

she had some of her dates wrong. She had the crash happening in May. And she said, 'Well, I need all the help I can get if we're going to try to make this as accurate as possible.'"

The interest shown by the library led to the opening of new leads in the case as well as to some interesting confrontations with some of the lecturers attending the symposium. Debunkers and skeptics were also invited to speak at the event in the interest of fairness.

"It's one thing to have a bunch of UFO researchers at your library," Ramsey said, "but because you're a public library you also need to have the skeptical side."

The policy of inviting debunkers was discontinued after a few years, however, because the nay-sayers so often arrived ill-prepared. One such case was Albuquerque scientist Dave Thomas, who got up in front of an audience of 250 people and said, "I'm a scientist, and by doing very little scientific work I can prove to you that the Aztec crash never took place because Hart Canyon Road did not exist in 1948."

"Well, about half the room broke out laughing," Ramsey said. "Because there are people who have lived there all their life, and Hart Canyon Road used to be the best way to get to Durango, by stage coach. We had high hopes for Dave because he was a scientist that would give us a scientific view on why this could maybe not have happened or didn't happen. And he comes out with a remark like that. Later I said to him, 'Dave, that would have taken five minutes of research over at the county building to pull old maps.' He got his research from someone who said that Hart Canyon Road didn't exist. Well, I'm sorry, but that's not how you do scientific work, and I certainly hope he does better work as a scientist."

Another lecturer at the Aztec library was the late Karl Pflock, ex-military, ex-CIA, who lent credibility to some aspects of Ufology. Pflock denied that something extraterrestrial had crashed at Aztec, and offered the alternate explanation that it had been a P-38 Lightning that landed on Highway 550 because it had run out of fuel.

According to Pflock, the plane sat there for a number of days until flatbed trucks were sent to the scene. It was then disassembled and hauled away.

"Now if a P-38 Lightning lands on Highway 550," Ramsey contended, "you've got the Farmington airport, the Aztec airport, and the Durango airport all within 22 miles. Wouldn't you send a pickup truck with fuel, fill up the plane and take off? You wouldn't call Albuquerque, send up a flatbed truck with four or five mechanics, disassemble the plane and haul it out. But most importantly, since we already pulled all the incident reports, that would have shown up there."

Ramsey ran down a checklist of the typical paperwork that would have existed if the P-38 explanation were to hold water.

"If you run an aircraft out of fuel," he reasoned, "or do something else stupid, the report's going to be 50 to 60 pages long. Reprimands, corrective actions. How did this happen? What kind of weather was the pilot diverting? What kind of instruction did he lack that he ran out of fuel? Who were the civilians involved? Furthermore, just by asking anybody who lived up on Cedar Hill, to the people who still live there, do you remember a P-38 landing as kids? That would have been big news. They would have played on the thing. So again we have another skeptic with another empty statement of fact, that a P-38 landed and had to be disassembled."

BEHIND THE FLYING SAUCERS

To further make his point, Ramsey and friends measured Highway 550 and saw that it gave the pilot twelve times the Lockheed minimum of runway required for a plane to take off safely. That the highways in that period were often used in New Mexico as alternate landing strips is a well-documented fact, and the pilots are known to have no trouble taking off again, no disassembly required.

The next year, the debunkers returned with a slightly different story, this time saying that it was a trainer plane on a training mission.

"Again, five minutes of research at Maxwell, which is the archive of the United States Air Force," Ramsey said, "to look at an incident report saying, 'Hey, did you have a trainer land out here?' So basically, you look at what the skeptics have said over the years and nothing holds water. What happens is everybody likes to regurgitate old things. It takes a lot of time and money to do good research. A lot of people that want to bash any UFO incident-I don't care if it's Roswell, Aztec or Kecksburg, whatever-they don't want to take the time to research it."

SUZANNE RAMSEY COMMENTS

Suzanne Ramsey first met Scott when she was a local radio interviewer and they were working together promoting one of the Aztec Public Library events. The details are probably better left to the book the couple is working on as of this writing. Suzanne has since become Scott's primary research partner, and she has some very definite feelings about why the Aztec UFO crash story is so important.

"One of the things that drew me into it," she said, "was that it is an important part of history that has not been properly documented. It's had an effect on us technologically, and I think it says a lot about what was going on in the world and has impacted people's lives and still to this day impacts people's lives. The people that were threatened not to speak of it, or there could be harm to them or harm to their families, or financial problems could come from it because it was so important.

"And when I talk to folks," Suzanne continued, "some of the folks that have had these experiences, and how that has played out in their life, that's very important. It's amazing that over 60 years later that there is still information that we are able to locate and dig out. And as I'm sure you found out with my husband, he doesn't say anything unless he knows it to be a fact. If it's not, he'll tell you that. I don't think he leaves a lot of stones unturned. As he continues to find more stones to lift, there's more information. It's been a very powerful experience."

SCOTT RAMSEY'S SENSE OF THINGS

Scott Ramsey firmly and absolutely believes that the Aztec UFO crash was a real event.

As for the alien corpses rumored to have been scattered around the crashed spacecraft, "I spend so little time," Ramsey said, "on whether there was one alien onboard or three hundred. I don't consider myself a Ufologist. I don't have an overall general view of Ufology. I look at it that my wife and I are doing historical research on 'Did an object land or crash land on a mesa outside of Aztec, New Mexico, based on facts that we can compile?' When Suzanne and I go around the country and we talk and then do the questions and answers segment, 'Tell us about the bodies. What did they look like?' I don't think it's insignificant, but there's nothing we can do in our research to prove that there

BEHIND THE FLYING SAUCERS

were 14 or 16 dead aliens, whether they were childlike, midget-like, typical alien, gray, green, reptilian, it doesn't matter. The whole thing is, is there any fact and how much fact behind the original story that something took place on that mesa on March 25, 1948."

When comparing the Aztec crash to the more famous Roswell incident, Ramsey said, "I think Aztec got swept under the rug a lot quicker."

Ramsey also feels that Newton and GeBauer's questionable business practices were blown completely out of proportion.

"I think their biggest problem," Ramsey said, "was that there were a lot of different pyramid scams in the oil fields back in that timeframe. The big marketing thing was 'How do I get you to put your money in my oil well versus you put your money in some-one else's?' Of course, Newton and GeBauer went to market saying they were using alien technology. But if you take them completely out of the Aztec picture, with all the research we've done, the story still has legs. I think people tend to throw the baby out with the bathwater when it comes to those two characters."

So Scott and Suzanne Ramsey continue their diligent investigations. As this introductory chapter for the reprint of "Behind The Flying Saucers" is being written, in July of 2008, they are hard at work on the aforementioned and as yet untitled book based on their research, which Stanton Friedman for one says he is waiting for with bated breath.

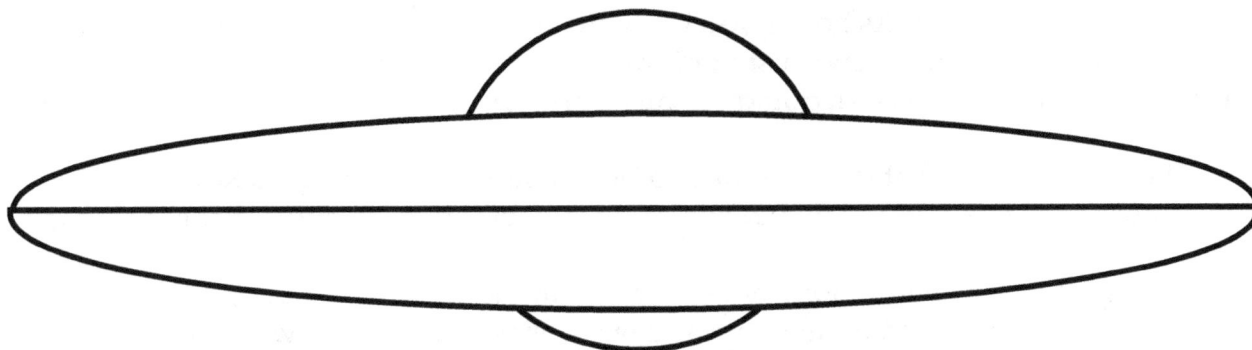

The Aztec saucer before it impacted courtsey Scott Ramsey collection.

BEHIND THE FLYING SAUCERS

Aztec crash investigator,
Scott Ramsey

The Witnesses:
KEN FARLEY

Our first witness was Ken Farley. When we interviewed Farley, he was dying of a respiratory disease. He was on bottled oxygen when we met, north of Phoenix, Arizona. As he later described to me during a three hour interview, he had been in Durango, Colorado on March 25, 1948, visiting his aunt on his way to San Diego, California.

He was supposed to meet a friend north of Aztec, New Mexico. and then continue his drive to San Diego. As he arrived early that morning at a planned pick-up spot near Cedar Hill (a small town just north of Aztec), his friend told him about a lot of trucks and a police car seen going out on a small dirt road just south of where they were standing.

The drivers of the vehicles seemed to be in a hurry, according to Ken. Thinking an emergency was underway, the two of them decided to go out and see what the problem was.

Farley and his friend (anonymous) arrived at the mesa, now busy with oilfield workers, what appeared to ranchers and two police officers who were at the scene talking to the locals.

As they moved toward the west side of mesa to get a better look at a large disc that sat silently on the mesa and had, as Farley described, "no noticeable damage". The craft was "perfectly smooth on the outside with no seams or marking except for around the middle".

Finally, one of the officers walked over to Ken and his friend and told them that the military had been notified and that they should leave the area at once. They refused to leave because nobody else seemed to be listening to the officer. Farley recalls that some of the oilfield workers were climbing "all over the damn thing, which was absolutely stupid. Some older folks started yelling at them to get the hell away from it".

Later that morning, Farley explained that the military arrived and discussed the incident individually with the people on the mesa. Everyone was "threatened with their lives" and sworn to secrecy.

Since Ken Farley was not originally from the area, he was unable to help to identify who the other people might have been.

BEHIND THE FLYING SAUCERS

DOUG NOLAND

Doug Noland and Bill Ferguson were employed by the El Paso Gas Company. Noland, 19 years of age, had just picked up his boss Bill Ferguson at 5 AM. Bill had told Doug that they needed to get out to Hart Canyon Road as soon as possible due to a bad brush fire that was spotted near a drip tank.

As the two arrived to the site, other oilfield workers greeted them explaining that the brush fire was under control, but that they needed to see something else. As they arrived on the mesa, Noland said that they could not believe what they were looking at. A very large metallic disk sat silently on the mesa. He explained that as they cautiously moved closer they realized the craft was smooth with no noticeable seams, rivets, bolts or weld marks. He said it looked as if it had been molded.

Noland and Ferguson climbed up on the craft and looked through a broken port-hole. He recalls seeing two bodies slumped over what he thought was a control panel.

Other oil field workers were climbing around the craft looking for a way to enter, when others started to arrive and advised the men to move away from the craft. A Mr. and Mrs. Knight (local ranchers running cattle out near the mesa) arrived in their pickup truck and began to walk slowly toward the craft. Nearing daybreak (as Noland would recall) a helicopter started to circle the mesa. Doug said this was un-believable as well, because he had never seen a helicopter before! (Keep in mind that helicopters had just recently been introduced to the military at that time).

During the interview with Farley he recalled that the first law enforcement officer to show up acted as though he had not known anyone. Doug approached the young officer and asked what they should do? The officer explained that he was from the town of Cuba, New Mexico and that he had followed the low flying disk in the early morning hours and then finally to the area of Hart Canyon Road.

The officer also explained that the town of Cuba had several sightings over the past few weeks. He remembered that when the second law enforcement officer showed up he was well known by most of the local people at the site.

This ties in with Ken Farley's story about two police officers at the crash site. Doug was able to name everyone at the crash site with the exception of the two young men who stood on the western side of the mesa. He had not seen either of them prior to or after the incident.

Second Hand Witness –
FRED REED

Fred Reed (who prior to 1948 had worked for the O.S.S., Office of Strategic Services) and his group were sent to Aztec, New Mexico to "clean up a crash site" early in April 1948. Shortly after they arrived it was apparent to them that something very large had been removed from the site. Their specialty was to make an area appear as if nothing had transpired there.

Fred revisited the crash site in 1999, and I was able to interview him one week later.

26

In 1948 they were ordered to collect any foreign items they found, bury them eighteen inches deep and to "soft landscape" any area where heavy equipment tracks were visible.

They were also to do an extensive survey on the entire mesa. He noted a newly cut road and an out-of-place, large concrete pad in the freshly altered and silty soil during the cleanup. Reed recalled thinking that they must have poured it to support a heavy structure, such as a crane used to move a large object.

At the time of the cleanup, his group was informed that it was simply a crash site. The entire clean up was done in the usual quiet manner that Reed had been accustomed to providing while in the O.S.S. Years later, one of Reed's former senior officers would explain to him that it was not an aircraft crash, but that of a large metallic "flying disk".

In my interview with Reed, he commented that the crash site today looks much the same as they had left it when they had finished. He recalled the tops of the trees were broken and was fascinated with how they had weathered with time.

The Police Officers –

The Four Corners area today is a busy and fast growing area. Farmington, New Mexico is currently the largest town in the area. The San Juan Sheriff's Department was formed in the late 1800's.The local Farmington Highway Patrol and many "Deputies" were at that time, the law enforcement throughout the area. The town of Cuba, New Mexico had two police officers from the research done so far. It appears that one of them was a full time officer and one a part time on the night shift.

Trying to locate and identify which police officers would have been at the site in early morning hours of March 25, 1948 has been a long and difficult task.

For this reason the names of these officers will be released when the documentation is firm.

BEHIND THE FLYING SAUCERS

Art Campbell

IKE AND THE ALIENS

By Sean Casteel

* Did President Dwight D. Eisenhower hold a 45-minute conference with the occupants of a flying saucer in 1955? Read a breathtaking account of a real-life extra-terrestrial summit meeting!

* Learn how Eisenhower cleverly eluded the prying eyes of the press by throwing a large party for them in a Georgia country club as he secretly flew back from his meeting with the aliens.

* Do the aliens have a vested interest in our ability to achieve peace on Earth? Why do they study our nuclear capabilities so closely?

* Was there a second UFO crash in New Mexico at the same time as the more famous Roswell Incident? What evidence was found less than 200 miles away in San Augustin?

He doesn't come away a believer very easily. He's the type of individual who has to test the waters, weigh things out.

Art Campbell is a longtime veteran of UFO causes going back to the founding days of the National Investigations Committee on Aerial Phenomena. It can be said that he did a little "legwork" for the man himself. When Major Donald Keyhoe, the acting head of NICAP, wanted to know if he should take seriously the imaginative tales of outer space travel being spun by George Adamski, he had Campbell check into the Polish-born contactee's claims. But that's another story, one that has no immediate connection with this tale of possible interplanetary wonderment.

The fact is Art is thought of in a positive light by most of his Ufological associates. You will seldom hear any snipping behind his back. His credentials are impressive, and his investigation into an alleged meeting between President Dwight D. Eisenhower and the occupants of a landed flying saucer has drawn a great deal of attention within the field. The exciting story Campbell is still in the process of uncovering is a distant cousin to the legends surrounding the crash at Aztec.

CAMPBELL'S SOURCE

Before launching into the story of Ike and the UFO, Campbell said he wanted to mention his sources.

"I got a letter from an airman," Campbell said, "who was stationed at the air base where this happened. He had tried to come out with a letter in the late 1990s, and he was kind of rebuffed by the UFO community. So he said the heck with it and just filed it away."

At some point after that, Campbell found out through a friend of the family that the airman was out there with a story to tell. So Campbell traced the airman down.

BEHIND THE FLYING SAUCERS

"Essentially," Campbell recounted, "he said that he was working at the base hospital at Holliman Air Force Base. He was a 'high altitude chamber' specialist, and there were just a few of those around the country in those days. He said that early on, about two weeks prior to late January, he was asked if he wanted to stand parade for President Eisenhower, who was coming to visit in a couple of weeks."

When the airman, to whom Campbell has given the pseudonym "Kirtland," asked to know what time Eisenhower would be landing, he was told 8:30 in the morning. Not wanting to miss any sleep over it, he declined and was assigned another duty for that day. Campbell said the airman had a little seniority and was therefore able to pick and choose his assignments to some degree.

MEANWHILE, BACK IN WASHINGTON

In Washington, Eisenhower announced that he would be taking a short vacation at the plantation of his Secretary of the Treasury, George M. Humphrey, in rural Georgia. The president planned to do some bird hunting. Ike had made the same trip before, and would do so several times while in office.

There was a great deal of international tension at the time. The Red Chinese were shelling the Island of Camoy Matsu, which was in artillery range, and it was assumed that it was preliminary to the invasion of Formosa, now called Taiwan.

"The international press was all over this," Campbell said. "People were starting to think the Red Chinese were going to take over Formosa. And Eisenhower, as a campaign promise, had promised to defend them if they were to be invaded."

In response to the Red Chinese aggression, Eisenhower said publicly that he would use tactical nuclear weapons, which was backed up by later comments by Secretary of State John Foster Dulles, who also said that nuclear weapons would be used if the Red Chinese chose to invade.

"Well, this is ten years after the A-bomb," Campbell said. "And the entire world was upset about the possibility of nuclear war, and they were upset at Eisenhower and Dulles. So the entire press corps was clamoring to get news from Eisenhower in February of 1955. So Eisenhower announced he was going bird hunting in Georgia, which was being well-publicized."

THE TRIP TO GEORGIA

Eisenhower took two planeloads with him to Georgia, one consisting of his hunting party, six people, to be accompanied by 13 secret service agents, which was very unusual for a domestic trip. The group left on February 10, flying down to Spence Air Base, which was located 25-30 miles north of Thomasville, the eventual destination.

"It was a very convenient place for him to fly into," Campbell said. "It was secure."

The press chartered their own plane to be on the scene when the president arrived, a group of at least 30 reporters, many of them from large news agencies like "TIME" and the wire services as well as several big European papers. There were several media cameramen sent as an advance wave to film the landing and the motorcade. The group made its way through tiny rural towns on its way to Humphrey's plantation. Eisenhower wanted to go hunting as soon as they arrived, and he quickly changed into his hunting togs and waited for the others to join him.

BEHIND THE FLYING SAUCERS

Eisenhower had brought with him his wife Mamie, her mother, a Mrs. Dowd, Humphrey and one or two others. They went out shortly before dark and the hunting dogs quickly flushed out some pheasant or quail, and the hunters bagged a couple of birds each. The press was kept out of the plantation, where Ike and his party were staying in a guest cottage.

"So essentially it was well-known," Campbell said, "that Ike was going hunting, which seemed kind of an interesting thing to do in the middle of such international tension. I've seen presidents sneak off for a game of golf or two, or shoot at a couple of birds. It just seemed a little strange to some people at the time. That night, the temperature gets down to 20 degrees above, and the reporters think the bird hunting is pretty well shot, so to speak. Ike does go out that morning, according to his press secretary, and of course bird dogs can't pick up the scent of birds on frozen grass.

"So the story was that Eisenhower had come down with the sniffles," Campbell continued, "and he and his valet were nursing it. He's going to sit by the fire for a couple of days and Mamie and her mother were playing scrabble and drinking hot toddies, this kind of thing. So here was the press stuck down at a place called the Scott Hotel, with nothing to do on their hands."

THE SECRET MEETING

"So while the press secretary is making the pronouncement," Campbell said, "that Ike's going to be tied up for two or three days, nursing the sniffles, 1,300 miles west and five hours later, Eisenhower was landing at Holliman Air Base in southern New Mexico. It's a super-secret, secure base. Lots of work was done there, lots of pre-space work. The astronauts, for instance, those sled runs they ran to see how fast a man could go, those people were there."

Eisenhower landed around 8:30 am local time. According to Campbell's airman

BEHIND THE FLYING SAUCERS

source, soon after Eisenhower's plane touched down, they shut off the base's radar capabilities.

"Then shortly after that," Campbell said, "two saucers came in. One hovered over the base and one landed in front of Air Force One. Air Force One had landed on the far runway, turned around and taxied back about 50 yards, apparently by prearrangement, and the UFO was said to have landed there.

"Now this information is secondhand. Our airman did not see it but did hear some officers talking about it, his boss and another officer talking about it later that evening."

The story continues. The president's plane did not come around to where the VIPs normally were, but instead went back up the runway a short distance, after which the runway was closed. No planes could take off while the president was there.

The airman, who Campbell identifies with the pseudonym "Kirtland," had an enlisted supervisor named Dorcy, who walked up to him that morning and asked, "Did you see what was out over the runway?"

When Kirtland replied that he had not, Dorcy said, "Well, it's a disc."

This was before the acronym "UFO" had entered the familiar lexicon, and Campbell believes that most of the enlisted personnel knew as little as the general public did about UFOs at the time. Kirtland asked how big the disc was, and was told it was about 25-30 feet across. Dorcy urged him to go out and look at it, but when Kirtland asked permission to leave his desk to see the disc, his request was denied by the doctor he worked under. The doctor apparently was unaware of the saucers and felt that the president's arrival was "business as usual" and did not warrant relieving Kirtland of his duty.

Holloman A F B 1957

"Now, the saucer was not hiding," Campbell said. "It was hovering over the flight line as kind of cover for the one that was on the ground in front of Air Force One about a half mile away."

Another officer on duty at the time said that he had been in the flight tower and though he didn't have binoculars, he was able to see a man, presumed to be Eisenhower, but in any case a "figure" get out of the plane.

"Apparently, they had some kind of prearranged exit stairs there," Campbell said, "so he could come down easily. And the man presumed to be Ike walked from Air Force One to the UFO. He was inside for 40 to 45 minutes, and then walked back to Air Force One."

WHAT WAS SAID ONBOARD THE UFO?

"That is speculation," Campbell replied. "In 45 minutes-you're not meeting somebody for the first time, obviously. You're confirming something. We believe that it was probably connected with the international crisis. Also, that July, there was to be the first

31

BEHIND THE FLYING SAUCERS

peace conference in Geneva, and it very well could have been that he was encouraged to attend and to get other people to attend. A lot of the international powers were there: France, Germany, Russia. I think there were two Chinese delegations there. It was nicknamed 'Geneva One.' My guess is he was being encouraged to seek peaceful solutions to the international crisis.

"And being the kind of guy he was," Campbell said, "I think Ike wanted to see who he was talking to, who he was negotiating with. We know nothing else about what he may have said or done, but the chances are it had to do with the international tensions and the threat of a nuclear war."

Campbell did allow as how he had heard that Ike's first meeting with the aliens may have taken place a year earlier at Edwards Air Force Base (called Murdoc at the time of Ike's meeting) and located near Palm Springs, California.

"I have no information on it," Campbell said, "but I do know people who swear by it. There are a lot of kooky people who assume we were signing galactic treaties and so on. I think that some of the aliens we had found, dead or alive, might have been at Edwards in those days."

The cover story for the Edwards meeting explained Ike's absence at the time as being for a trip to the dentist to repair a broken tooth. A check of the dentist's office records by his wife did not list any such visit with Eisenhower.

THE STORY CONTINUES

Campbell said that "Kirtland," while he had missed the president's arrival and the coming of the two saucers, was able to see Air Force One depart. After spending four or five more hours at the base, the president's party departed at around 4:45 pm. Campbell estimates they would have arrived in Georgia around 12:30 am Eastern Time.

"And here's what is interesting, and also funny," Campbell said. "In the 'Thomasville Enterprise,' the local paper, there was a story saying that Secretary of the Treasury Humphrey had thrown a big party for all the press at the local country club with an open bar and so on. So I think Ike was waiting for that party to get started and get people moving along on their alcohol intake. But they were soon well under the weather.

"This is a slightly amusing thing, but it is quite feasible that if you have a planeload of press you want to kind of dodge or not have around, you would throw a party. They had all the press in that one room there at the country club so there wasn't anybody in the media who could see Ike's plane coming in. There are five or six back roads from Spence down to the plantation in Thomasville, so it was easy to get in and out of there."

THE UFO CRASH AT SAN AUGUSTIN

Along with his expertise on the Eisenhower/UFO/Holliman incident, Campbell is also an expert on the UFO crash at San Augustin, 165 miles due west of Roswell, which took place on the morning of July 2, 1947. Campbell said that a civil engineer named Barney Barnett made the initial discovery, and he was quickly joined by a group of archeolo-

32

gists said to have been working at a place called Bat Cave about ten miles away. The archeologists had made camp the previous night and would have had no trouble seeing anything, particularly something with prominent lights, coming down in the darkness over the desert.

The leader of the archeological party, Herbert W. Dick, was in a sensitive position career-wise. He was not only in competition with another archeologist to exploit the site at Bat Cave, but he was also nearing completion of his Ph.D, and so he wisely, according to Campbell, denied any knowledge of the crashed UFO.

In 1994, Campbell visited a rancher in the area who said he thought something had happened out on his property.

"Some others had been there," Campbell said. "I wasn't the first. But we went down there and looked around and took some photographs. Then I went back a year later and started finding stuff."

An object Campbell calls "the artifact" was discovered there.

"We haven't finished our work on it yet," he said. "All we can do is speculate about what it is, but it might be some artificial body part. But that's as far as I'll go with it. I found it underneath the sage brush, and then I had some cattle inspectors look at it at a local restaurant that evening and asked if it was part of a cow or something. They said, 'That ain't no part of no cow.'"

Campbell has written a book about his work there, called "UFO Crash At San Augustin," which includes a chapter on the mysterious "artifact."

He worked the area for twelve years and made other discoveries, such as strange forms of metal foil and the bizarre sole of pair of shoes.

What had drawn the archeologists to the area in the first place was the peculiar weather patterns found there. The frequent wind and rain served to uncover Native-American artifacts and leave them lying near the surface where they could be easily found.

"They'd be buried two or three feet down and over the years," Campbell explained, "the wind would scour out the surface and you'd have what are called 'blow sides' and you'd actually find artifacts there. Well, I think this is what happened, after 50 years. Where the crash was, it was thoroughly cleaned up by the government, I'm sure, and maybe on a second occasion too.

"We ran into a family who lives in Arkansas, and one of them had been hired by the guy who owned the property at the time the crash happened, and he'd helped the army clean up some of it. I don't think he saw the craft, but there were a lot of things laying around that he got in on the cleanup of. I think they hustled the craft out within eight or ten hours."

A SECOND MAJOR CRASH

Barney Barnett, the civil engineer who made the initial discovery, said that when he saw the craft, it was 25-30 feet in diameter, stainless steel colored, with three or four bodies nearby. The early investigators of Roswell had tried to place all the witnesses at just the one crash, but it has gradually become apparent that there were in fact two separate crashes in the same general timeframe.

"After the stuff that I found," Campbell said, "it was impossible to me that it could be anything else but a second crash. I started finding a lot of things and had everything analyzed by laboratories. I never told the labs what they were working on. I said, 'Please analyze this for me,' and then they take your money, it costs you an arm and a leg, and then they send you back the results. I would then add the results to my stack of research."

The pieces of foil, for instance, were found to be of no known foil formulation on Earth. While the metals in the alloy were not in themselves exotic, the way they were combined into the aluminum was checked against the standards maintained by the Aluminum Association, who have kept a storehouse of over 600 possible combinations, none of which were a match for what Campbell had collected.

The shoe sole that Campbell found fits no known Earth size.

"It is too long and narrow," he said, "to belong to a child whose foot is seven or eight inches long. Do you have children? Well, you know they have wide feet. When your child was say two and a half, and the foot was four to eight inches long, it was also three inches wide. This particular shoe is only an inch and a half wide. I showed it around to shoe manufacturers. I got all kinds of information back, that they belonged to some native tribe from Brazil or might belong to pygmies, but none of the podiatrists or anybody we talked to had ever seen a foot this size to fit that shoe."

DO WE REALLY NEED DISCLOSURE?

"I started speaking on UFOs in 1958," Campbell said. "And one or two percent of the audience would believe in people living on other planets then. Now we're looking at 65 or 70 percent. A good part of those people, and this is a non-UFO audience, would probably agree that UFOs are here and are interplanetary. So we've come a long way in 50 years.

"I'm not sure we'll ever have disclosure," he continued. "I don't think it will be necessary. In another generation, everyone is going to believe it, though disclosure might come back with some missing details. If, during the Reagan administration, the disclosure had been made that we were in contact with or had been visited by extraterrestrials, a lot of his political base would have been eroded, because he was working primarily with conservative religious people. And they're probably the ones who would be in great denial about life on other planets and thus our being visited by extraterrestrials. So there are lots of political reasons why these things are not announced, and I'm sure we had quite a few in Eisenhower's day too."

The aliens' interest in our various nuclear facilities in New Mexico in the late 1940s may imply a certain amount of self-interest on their part.

"Whether it's concern for us or concern for themselves, I have no way of knowing, but that would certainly be in keeping with them not wanting us to perish in a nuclear war. We had hundreds of nuclear test, and this seemed to be high on the extraterrestrials' agenda.

"I think it was in our best interests," Campbell said, "that we not learn early on of the nature of the UFOs. As I look back at the all the people I've known and all the places I've been, it would have caused quite a bit of confusion, especially if we were trying to keep it from the Russians. I think it was the right thing to do to keep it in the dark. I don't particularly enjoy being lied to and told this has no meaning whatsoever, that UFOs are not here, but that isn't government people doing that. That's some of the people they put on these talk shows who are paid, by the way, to say that UFOs don't exist."

BEHIND THE FLYING SAUCERS

CAMPBELL ON SCULLY

Campbell said he bought a copy of Frank Scully's "Behind The Flying Saucers" for a quarter at a garage sale in Kansas in 1952. It was the first book on the subject he had ever read.

"So I read Scully in '52," Campbell said, "and I just remember being mildly interested in the subject. I had no idea I'd be an investigator later on. Just like anybody who'd taken a book off the rack, I didn't really have much information on Scully other than what anyone had at the time.

"Scully had been discredited in 'True Magazine' by an article probably planted or encouraged by some of our government officials. I think he got out of the starting block too quick on the UFO thing and people had to find a way to get him discredited so they could go on with it."

[Art Campbell has a website located at www.ufocrashbook.com and is available as a speaker.]

So now, having read the latest in updated research and educated opinions from Nick Redfern, Stanton Friedman, Scott and Suzanne Ramsey, and Art Campbell, it is time to move on to the original and unabridged text of Frank Scully's pioneering work "Behind The Flying Saucers" in all its ragged glory. Having suffered trials for fraud, media ridicule and defamation, and various forms of libel and slander, it remains alone at the top of a heap of groundbreaking investigations into a truth we still have not mastered, though our need to penetrate the veil grows ever more urgent.

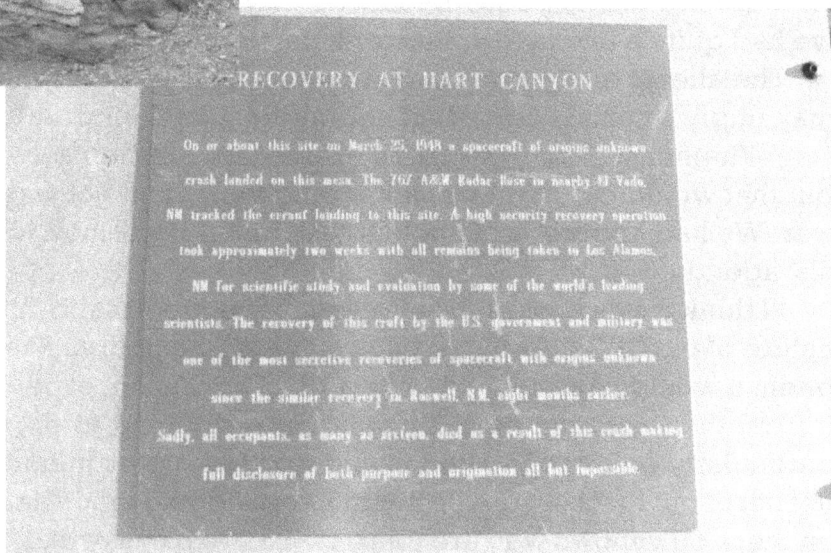

BEHIND THE FLYING SAUCERS

By Frank Scully

BEHIND THE FLYING SAUCERS

BEHIND THE FLYING SAUCERS
Frank Scully
Dedicated to The Scully Circus, our trained fleas from heaven—Skip, Syl, Pat, Non, and Mike—and may they some day fly in one.

PUBLISHER'S NOTE

We are publishing Behind The Flying Saucers because we believe it to be an exciting, timely, and straightforward interpretation of one of the strangest phenomenon in modern times. It is obvious, of course, that any discussion of flying saucers from whatever point of view is bound to be controversial. This book is no exception, for Frank Scully's conclusions as to the nature of these craft differ sharply from those held officially by the Department of Defense.

However, we are as convinced as any thoughtful publisher can be that Mr. Scully has approached his subject with probity and has interpreted the facts and figures given him with care and caution. In writing this book he has had extensive interviews and assistance from scientists and other experts in such fields as magnetic energy, astronomy, and aerodynamics men who are reputedly high in their profession but some of whose names, as will be apparent in reading this book, must be kept anonymous.

We, like most people, including Mr. Scully, have never seen a flying saucer. But from the mass of evidence as reported in the press and magazines by reputable persons, there is much reason to believe that they actually do exist. What they are, where they come from, or how they fly, we do not presume to know. Mr. Scully attempts to answer some of these questions and we're sure that you'll find his answers both fascinating and provocative. We did.

BEHIND THE FLYING SAUCERS

AUTHOR'S PREFACE

BETWEEN THE PEOPLE and government today lies a double standard of morality. Anything remotely scientific has become by government definition a matter of military security first; hence of secrecy, something which does not breed security but fear. If we see anything unusual, even in the skies, we the people must either freeze our lips, like a Russian peasant at the sight of a commissar, or give our names, addresses, business connections, and testimony to be screened and filtered by anonymous intelligence officers.

Feared and respected by many people, these anonymous creatures can deny what we say, ridicule what we say, and sometimes (and in an increasing number of countries) jail us for what we say especially if our timing does not match to the second their intended official pronouncements on the subject.

Just as the communists have made a god of their Uncle Joe, we have begun to deify our faceless spokesman. Both should be fought by free men as word oppressors.

Without going into it at too great a length, this all ties up with the loss of faith in formal religion, which forces people to cling to the New Sublimation.

The only way for a free people to fight such encroachments on free inquiry is to say in advance, "What I am telling you will be denied," or "This is true but those who say so now will be branded as dreamers, and if they persist, as liars."

It completely destroys American sportsmanship standards when we, the people, stick to the rules while an opposing team of censors who have usurped our rights are permitted, by their own handpicked referee, to pull rabbit-punches on defensive play, hamstring us from the rear if we seem to be running well in an open field, and even machinegun the ball in midair if we are kicking an almost certain field goal.

There is only one thing to do under such a setup. Expose their tactics. Show that more offenses are committed under the word "defense" than this world dreams of. Insist that what we say is the whole truth, and what they say is not the whole truth.

BEHIND THE FLYING SAUCERS

That may seem a dreadful way to treat our own flesh and blood, our commissioned sons who have been trained for combat but have been assigned in peacetime to espionage and counter espionage. But since our sons in uniform do not report to us, the people, but to Central Intelligence (which as far as we can make out reports to nobody and is answerable to nobody), how otherwise can we get our current findings to our own friends?

Scientists believe they have suffered more than any other group from the postwar loyalty hysteria but writers cannot be far behind them. The "thread of intolerance" which runs through our history has now become as thick as a noose to hang us. Under the circumstances, to write a book, knowing not only that you will be ridiculed, but also knowing who will do the ridiculing, and not have a counteroffensive ready, is to be starry eyed and unrealistic.

Rather than be rated dreamers by such obvious interior proof that we are dreamers, it is a good deal smarter to swing first and say that all bureaucrats, whether in tweeds or bogged down with salad dressing, are incompetent time servers, hanging on the public payroll till pensioned or rewarded with a stuffed shirt job in private enterprise (privately endowed universities, naturally, included) and are truth trimmers to boot.

In order to regain this lost freedom we will have to say "a pox on both your houses" and cease to be brushed off by the perpetual hocus-pocus involved in such phrases of these spokes men as "top secret," "secret and confidential," "restricted," and, "withheld for reasons of security."

Such brush-offs are almost invariably followed by a statement from another department of the defense arm, that what we are hiding isn't really worth concealing, that we are defended by old and obsolete equipment, and that, finally, unless we grant them an additional billion dollars for new equipment overnight, we are dead ducks, saucers or no saucers!

Propaganda has made true—and—false practically obsolete in our language. In fact, if a spokesman has served time in intelligence, it may fairly be said, the truth is no longer in him. Spies cannot even buy or sell lies with skill. If so, why are they being arrested all over the world and almost invariably getting a sentence of fifteen years? Has that become the fair trade practices act on the international level?

Perhaps it would be clearer to readers if I illustrated with a few samples of this dismal wallpaper pattern. On June 24, 1947, businessman Kenneth Arnold of Boise, Idaho, flying his own plane, first reported he had seen several flying saucers in the area of Mt. Rainier, Washington. Reports of other saucers from other areas followed.

Then on August 9, Lieutenant Colonel Donald Springer, assistant to the chief of staff of the Fourth Air Force, decided to stop the nonsense. Despite the fact that his command had an unsolved mystery on its hands concerning molten material

BEHIND THE FLYING SAUCERS

claimed to have fallen on Maury Island, and the death of two army pilots who were transporting the material for further examination, Colonel Springer said, as far as he was concerned, there was no basis for belief in flying disks in the Tacoma area "or any other."

Newspapers took this as some sort of hint and piped down on the subject. With what result? That by January, 1948, six months after Colonel Springer's dismissal of the subject, the Pentagon set up Project Saucer to investigate the hundreds of reports that had been coming in. Fate devoted almost half of its first issue to flying saucers and led off with an article by Kenneth Arnold entitled "I Did See The Flying Disks."

Project Saucer proceeded in a quiet unhysterical way for eighteen months before issuing even a preliminary report. The Saturday Evening Post apparently got the idea that the report was going to be negative, so it had Sidney Shalett prepare two articles on the subject for almost simultaneous release with the Air Force report. The articles turned out to be rather long winded recapitulations of various flying saucer case histories previously explored, and the general impression left after reading them was that believers in the actuality of flying saucers appeared as not quite bright.

Shalett's first article appeared in the Post issue dated April 30; the second, May 7. The April 30 issue was on the newsstands several days before April 30, of course. In fact, it was on sale when the Air Force issued its April 27 preliminary report. The Air Force report crossed up the Post. This was in line with the pattern I have previously outlined of making fools of collaborators.

Far from confirming Colonel Springer or the Post, the official report held that there was something to the flying saucer stories after all. It even entertained the idea that the saucers might be from another planet. It left many of its case histories with no solution, as far as this earth or Air Force Intelligence was concerned, but promised more light on these later.

Having thus proceeded to lure the Post into "fronting" for a negative approach, the Air Force proceeded to accentuate the positive. This naturally opened the door to those rival editors who thought they saw a new trend. True magazine figured it could cash in on the Post's loss of face. Its publisher, editor, and a contributor reassembled much of the Fate and Post material and told the tale again, except that instead of casting doubt on all believers in aerial disks, True followed an older party line established by Fate in the spring of 1948 and declared in December, 1949, "Flying Saucers Are Real."

Hardly had True's copies reached the newsstands when Air Force Intelligence denied True's position from beginning to end. Its spokesman announced on December 27, 1949, that Project Saucer had been closed. It classified believers in flying saucers practically as psychopaths or hoaxers. It left no other way open as an escape hatch for True or anybody else.

40

BEHIND THE FLYING SAUCERS

This Machiavellian pattern of inflating and deflating those who agreed or disagreed with the military on flying saucers continued and was not likely to be altered even if, and when, the whole truth came out. The formula seemed to be: "Play ball with us and we'll let you have it between the eyes."

Though I have not the slightest interest in what the military may or may not say about this book, I want my readers to under stand my position. I have never seen a flying saucer. I have never had a hallucination that I have seen a flying saucer. I have never joined in any mass hysteria on the subject, and to the best of my knowledge and belief I have never participated in the perpetration of a hoax on flying saucers.

I have talked to men of science who have told me they have not only seen them but have worked on several. I have tried to the best of my ability to find flaws in their stories. But to date I have not succeeded in placing them in any of the three categories laid down by the Air Force.

Scientists do not want to go to war with the Army over the issue. They have to get essential materials for research, and certain branches of the Department of Defense might find it difficult to find such essential materials for scientists who will not cooperate. Do they make themselves clear?

Is it any wonder therefore that I advise readers to treat any official comment as no more to be considered than old news papers blowing in the wind? In fact, if such faceless men should say that the objects are (a) newspapers or (b) not newspapers but fragments of flying saucers, they are not to be believed either way. Not until we, the people, we who, have names, addresses, and the courage of our convictions, not until we say there are such things as flying saucers, is it authentic. And we have been saying it for sometime.

Now read Behind The Flying Saucers and throw in the fire unread all the Pentagonic denials from this day forward.

Decoration Day 1950
Frank Scully

BEHIND THE FLYING SAUCERS

"There are more things in heaven and earth, Horatio,
than are dreamt of in your philosophy."

BEHIND THE FLYING SAUCERS
Chapter 1
The Mystery of The University of Denver

AS THE SECOND HALF of the twentieth century began, three things experienced strange news emphasis. Two practically did not exist for The New York Times. The third, which did not actually exist at the time for anybody, was featured for months in this great newspaper as well as all others.

The two that had practically no news value to The New York Times were numerous reports of the presence of flying saucers over our mainland, and the birth of Ingrid Bergman's baby in Italy.

The third item had not been verified as anything more than a terrifying nightmare, and many of the scientists who were expected to turn it into a reality were not sure that it would work if, and when, made. That was the hydrogen bomb. But to the newspapers, without exception, the unmade bomb was un fait accompli.

It is hard to believe that to all people living in the spring of 1950 this thermonuclear monster was already a reality, while to the majority flying saucers, either from here or elsewhere, remained the stuff of which dreams are made.

A bomb which might destroy fifty times as many persons as did the atomic bomb released over Hiroshima, in the process of construction, was of course news. But it certainly had less reality in 1950 than the stockpile of stories about flying saucers in our atmosphere and possibly on our soil.

Such a story, if true, might well be among the greatest stories told since the creation of the world. It would seem that, if a choice had to be made, almost any government surviving on deficit-spending or lend-lease, or even on the sweat of its people, would decide to budget millions for studying interplanetary space ships, rather than to spend the same amount making bombs which could contribute nothing new to man's knowledge and understanding of this world or any other.

Yet given such a choice, at least one government chose to close down a Project

BEHIND THE FLYING SAUCERS

Saucer after two years of researching on a modest budget and report that its Air Force had traced most reports of unidentified flying objects to:

1. Misinterpretation of various conventional objects,
2. A mild form of mass hysteria,
3. Or hoaxes.

Its unidentified spokesman briefly explained that the project had been established two years previously at Wright-Patterson Air Force Base, Dayton, Ohio, headquarters of Air Materiel Command.

"Since that time" [January, 1948] "some 375 incidents have been reported and investigated," the report concluded. "Assisting special investigators were scientific consultants from universities and other governmental agencies."

No names of investigators, consultants, or colleges were mentioned. Indeed between that brief dismissal and a fairly long report of six months previously which, despite its length, left 34 of 375 incidents still unsolved (even to the Air Force's satisfaction) the 34 unsolved mysteries were closed out without any explanations whatever. If they were ever solved at all they remained top secret to all but the military.

Yet hardly had Project Saucer's final press release been printed when a series of reports on flying saucers began bombarding newspapers from every corner of the Western World. As the government's project was closed, the bearers of these tidings had nowhere to go except to their local newspapers.

There had been an entente cordiale between the press and the Department of Defense to ignore these stories during the two years of the Air Force's official inquiry. But when the Air Force pulled out, the floodgates opened. Some newspapers continued to throw flying saucers into their wastebaskets. Others broke down under the persistent barrage of reader reports and reader interest. By Easter time every radio commentator of any standing, every comedian, every legislator, every televisable personality, even The New York Times, had had his or her say. Walter Winchell was sure he had had it first and that the missiles were from Russia. Henry J. Taylor had tried his hand twice. His version was that the saucers were American, not Russian. He assured his listeners his elaborate radio accounts of the authenticity of flying saucers contained only half the story, and when the rest was released by the armed forces it would be good news tonight. In fact, he sounded more like Gabriel Heatter than Henry J. Taylor. David Lawrence threw all the prestige of his U. S. News and World Report behind the believers in the reality of flying saucers and said they were "a revolutionary type, a combination of helicopter and a fast jet plane." Even the President had to be dragged out of his Key West retreat to blow that one down. Eleanor Roosevelt had interviewed Captain Jack Adams and First Officer G. W. Anderson, two veteran pilots of the Chicago and Southern Airlines. They reported the flying saucer they had seen over Arkansas, which they insisted was not a visitor from another planet but a secret

BEHIND THE FLYING SAUCERS

experimental type aircraft and not jet-propelled either. Walter Kieran said he wished Drew Pearson would confirm the story and get it over with. "I'm willing to believe it," he added. But a week before Kieran's broadcast Drew Pearson had confirmed it. Fulton Lewis, Jr. had aired his version. Bob Hope, Red Skelton, Fibber McGee and Molly, Edgar Bergen and Charlie McCarthy, Amos 'n' Andy, and, of course, Jack Benny had also kicked the saucer around. Everybody, including Jimmy Durante, had got into the act.

But the real inside story had been missed by all of them. It happened on March 8, 1950, in Denver, Colorado. On that day at 12:30 P.M. 350 students of the University of Denver skipped lunch to hear a confidential scientific discourse delivered by what the press described later as "an unidentified middle-aged lecturer."

He delivered what was probably the most sensational lecture about this earth or any other planet since Galileo said, "It moves!" He gave the whole inside story of a flying saucer which he said had landed within 500 miles of where he was now talking, and he described the space ship and its personnel in such detail that the undergraduates and faculty members left the lecture room with their heads spinning.

Such is the nature of man's distorted sense of curiosity, however, that who the lecturer was soon began to overshadow what he had said. He, not the flying saucer, became the mystery that had to be solved by the students first.

It was recalled some hours later that the lecturer had been escorted by one George T. Koehler of 315 Franklin, Denver 3, Colorado, a staff member of an independent Rocky Mountain radio station, with the call letters of KMYR. It was commented upon by those faculty members who attended the lecture that Koehler never introduced the lecturer by name to anybody. (But the lecturer later explained to me that the professor whose job it was to guard the speaker's anonymity in his introduction certainly knew who he was.)

Before beginning the main body of his talk, the lecturer explained that he would purposely have to leave out certain names, dates, and places, and must not be asked about them, as some of the scientists were working on security projects, and therefore were not free to talk even about such flying saucers as they were reported to have examined personally. With that even the professors got out their notebooks.

He talked like a faculty member who knew how to time his well-considered words so that the scribbling students would not fall off at the first turn. He spaced his revelations, which at the end of the lecture were described as "startling," "sensational," "spellbinding," and "electrifying," by the majority; and "absurd," "ridiculous," and "unbelievable," by the minority.

In actual figures his lecture, which took 50 minutes, left about 40 per cent of his audience still with their mystery. The lecture was arranged for students of a basic science class, on the condition that it was not to be publicized. But from a group of

BEHIND THE FLYING SAUCERS

90 students, the gathering had grown, by grapevine, to a capacity audience. Professors of astronomy and engineering, as well as their students, piled in. There wasn't even standing room only.

The negotiations between the faculty and the spokesman for the lecturer took months to arrange, as the speaker wasn't keen about being "evaluated," but when the science students voted 100 per cent to hear the lecturer, he acquiesced. Of these, 80 per cent said, after the lecture, that they were "impressed." By a show of hands 60 per cent indicated they believed the man knew what he was talking about, that he obviously was a member of the group of scientists he described as having examined space ships which had landed on this earth from, in all likelihood, another planet. More, they believed the mystery man of science had the best answer to the secret of propulsion behind these flying saucers and that it was neither combustion nor jet.

Another poll taken later reduced the college-bred believers in this staggering story from 60 per cent to 50 per cent.

This was considerably higher than the over-all credence in flying saucers. According to a nation-wide survey by the United Press, one out of every four believed the objects were real ships. Actually 26 per cent believed they were and 8 per cent weren't sure. The rest agreed with the Air Force spokesman who said they were hallucinations, mass hysteria, or hoaxes. These would include those members of the University of Denver faculty who thought their speaker's performance was at best a very good act. It would also include those who suspected it was a hoax played on the fair name of a proud university. But all agreed that the mysterious stranger talked as plausibly, as conservatively, and as scientifically as Einstein, Oppenheimer, or Busch might have talked if placed in the position of presenting equally sensational revelations to an equally skeptical audience.

After the mysterious scientist had been plied for fifteen minutes with questions, George Koehler cried: "Great Scott, we have to get out of here! You have only twenty minutes to catch your plane!"

With that, the pair hurried out of the building, climbed into a high-powered car and drove off.

The conversation piece on interplanetary travel had set up such a chain reaction that within the hour members of the faculty, students, newspaper editors, and radio commentators were trampling all over each other in their mad haste to violate a confidence. Within two hours they in turn were being questioned by Air Force Intelligence officers.

The first thing the investigators wanted to know was what was the man's name. Nobody quite knew. One freshman remembered he had been referred to as "Great Scott" just before he and Koehler took off. A faculty member recalled introducing him to another as "Mr. Sears," and being corrected; but he couldn't remember what the man said his name was.

BEHIND THE FLYING SAUCERS

"I think he said it was 'Newton' or maybe that he was a friend of Newton."

"You mean the Mayor of Denver?"

No, they were sure he wasn't the Mayor of Denver.

"You mean a man can lecture at the University of Denver and not be identified at all?" the military demanded.

The faculty didn't quite mean that, certainly not in the face of all loyalty oaths, witch-hunting, and security taboos which were bogging down what was left of their academic freedom, but the man had been vouched for by Koehler and, after all, he only had talked harmlessly on a fascinating subject about which man had speculated for hundreds of years.

"Harmlessly?" the military repeated. "How do you know the subject is harmless? Did anybody get the number of his car? Or overhear what hotel he was stopping at?"

Well, one auditor remembered that Koehler did say that the man had to catch a plane in twenty minutes.

"Did he say to where?"

"No," the informer remarked, "but Koehler would know."

"Oh, Koehler!" the investigator cried in disgust.

Why that? Well, for months it seems Air Force Intelligence as well as editors-from Publisher Ken Purdy of True who was out on a limb because he had proclaimed in giant type *"FLYING SAUCERS ARE REAL,"* down to an unby-lined reporter on The Kansas City Times-had been badgering Koehler about details concerning flying saucers. Actually Koehler had none firsthand. He told them so. Purdy rushed Donald Kehoe out to Denver from Washington to get the story. Money was no object. But Koehler said he had no firsthand information. So, incensed, they threw the book at him. One Kansas City reporter who hadn't met Koehler, called him "Coulter" and said it was all a hoax. An A.P. feature writer who hadn't met Koehler either, repeated the fallacy. Kehoe picked it up on the bounce and repeated it, too. Koehler called them the sort of names which would be out of place here, since this is not a modern novel.

No one would believe him, least of all Air Force Intelligence, whose members acted as if they were quite sure Koehler had a pipeline into the very cabin of a flying saucer which was reported by some to have landed somewhere in the Great American Desert, and was further reported by others to have been dismantled by the very souvenir-hunting military of which Air Force Intelligence was an integral part. Were the military Dick Tracys seeking information or were they trying to bottle up all who had the same information they had? Were they fearful that their own experiments in space ships would leak out, or did they believe the flying saucers were being hurled like boomerangs from behind the Kremlin wall?

Months before this tempest in a university teapot the Air Force had announced that Project Saucer, which it had set up at Wright Field, Dayton, Ohio, in January,

BEHIND THE FLYING SAUCERS

1948, had been ordered closed by the end of 1949. The preliminary report issued in April, 1949, had discarded 341, remember, of 375 reports which had been investigated since a businessman in Boise, Idaho, had reported that in the summer of 1947 while flying his private plane he had sighted nine saucer-like objects which shot through space at a speed too fast for him to compute.

Of the remaining 34 case histories concerned with flying saucers the Air Force officers could find no satisfactory answers. Seemingly they could not ascribe these to hoaxes, hallucinations, and sure-fire devices of nobodies hungry to see their names in newspaper headlines. Nevertheless, despite these unsolved mysteries, the Air Force announced late in December, 1949, that the whole project had been shelved and as far as its investigators concerned flying saucers were a myth and the belief in a form of mass hysteria in which it was taking no further part.

Despite this shunting of strange disk-like objects sweeping the sky at tremendous speeds to the file-and-forget file by the Force, persons who reported objects whirling through our themselves playing host soon espionage echelon of the military on local levels. Newspapermen and others in the know laughed at the idea that Project Saucer had been closed. Some even openly printed their derision. The Pentagon didn't bother to deny that their saucerian inquiry had gone underground and was now operating under another name.

Koehler had been one of many private citizens who had had a brush with a counterespionage body. But having been an old professional football player on the Chicago Bears before he got into the selling end of radio, he was not one to take a roust without delivering a counterpunch. When an army investigator turned up at Station KMYR on the hunt for flying saucer data, Koehler decided to record their conversations.

On a subsequent visit from another officer representing Operation Hush-Hush (which presumably had supplanted Project Saucer) Koehler was surprised when at the end of the interview he was ordered to surrender the reel. "We know you have been recording these interviews," the officer told him. "Now hand them over."

Caught off guard, Koehler said he'd have to consult the station's owner before handing over company property to anybody. "If it's for reasons of security" [the magic word], "by all means," the proprietor agreed.

Koehler left the conference, explaining he'd have to have the engineer rewind the recordings, which happened to be on tape. Having also learned how to handle government bureaucrats from their own double-talk, Koehler went to the engineer's booth and with his back to the military winked at the technician and then ordered, "Fix up the recordings for the gentleman."

He sure fixed them. In rewinding the spools the engineer demagnetized the wire, completely wiping out all recorded conversations as if a wet sponge had been rubbed over a chalk mark on a blackboard. Thus when played back later by

BEHIND THE FLYING SAUCERS

the exultant espionage officers the result was exactly nothing. So when in the pursuit of the mystery man of science who had lectured at the University of Denver the Air Force Intelligence boys cried, "Oh, Koehler!" they were practically adding under their breaths, "We could wring that bird's neck!"

What they did instead was to summon all passenger lists of commercial planes out of Denver on March 8, from 1:30 P.M. On. They combed these to see if any scientists whose names had ever come up in relation to the late Project Saucer had defied an unofficial directive for all scientists remotely connected with defense (and that about included everybody with a B.S. degree) to button up about flying saucers. The manhunt got nowhere.

The mystery man of science hadn't left town on any plane from Denver that day.

Scarcely had Air Force Intelligence swallowed the bitter pill of a lost suspect when flying disks began flying around like an August festival of moths around an arc light.

Within the week Mexico City; Los Angeles; Durango, Colorado; Mazatlan; Dayton; Gering, Nebraska; Orangeburg, South Carolina; Lima, Peru; and even the Chilean Navy were reporting saucer-shaped objects in their skies. Most of the stories were one-day wonders: streamer headlines one evening, watered down or reduced to hearsay the next. But here and there a story showed surprising staying power.

Surprising, too, was the double standard of identity maintained in these matters. Every citizen who thought he saw a flying saucer had to turn in a report that left no doubt about who he was, where he was, and the alcoholic content of his blood for one week before and one week after he had observed "a silver-like saucer whizzing through space." But in two years of sitting in the reviewing stand, the Air Force rarely identified so much as one officer or civilian technical adviser it had used to blow down these ever-increasing reports.

Even in the case of the University of Denver lecturer, it would not permit him to enjoy the same anonymity which it claimed for itself. The faculty and students were pledged not to publicize what they had heard but to evaluate it for what it was worth to them as science students. The speaker told them to disregard all but what he said. For this reason he was not introduced by name or by his degrees.

One of the things the lecturer said was that the first flying saucer found on this earth was discovered by his colleagues within 500 miles of where he was talking right there in Denver. This didn't send the science students scurrying into the field in all directions, as it should have if they had any feeling for research. It sent some to newspaper offices and the rest spent the afternoon lying on the lawn and gazing at the sky. By the next day the horizontal scanners had increased to nearer one thousand students.

That behind all this smoke was no fire whatever continued to be the unyielding premise of the Air Force High Command, officially, though its officers continued

BEHIND THE FLYING SAUCERS

to hop around like chameleons on a scotch plaid, unofficially. Outwardly the Air Force took a detached position in the Christmas season of 1949 and maintained it unperturbed right through the Easter sunrise services of 1950, even though warned by men of high standing in the electromagnetic branch of science that these alien objects in our skies were known for years to pile up in heaviest numbers in January, February, and March. Judging from the piling up of newspaper reports, the scientists were certainly right in their calculations and the weary Air Force spokesmen were wrong.

The second phase of the University of Denver story was either to find the name of the lecturer who might, for all the faculty knew, be an agent from Moscow, Idaho, or to find a "patsy" to blame for the affair. While this was going on, a report came in from Santiago, Chile, quoting Commander Augusto Vars Orrego, head of the Chilean Antarctic Base, as saying that several explorers under his command had photographed flying saucers. The commander denied the possibility of optical illusions because the pictures, he insisted, corroborated what was observed. Whether these would be published depended on his superiors in the Chilean Navy, he told the United Press. So far they haven't been.

This report had scarcely found its place in the line of march before another report out of Santiago from the country's meteorological observatory added that "a spheroid celestial body" (astronomical slang for flying saucer) had been sighted at an estimated height of 18,000 feet. It supposedly crossed the sky in an east to west direction. It remained, according to the naval astronomers, in the sky from 10 A.M. to 1 P.M., and then disappeared. It was observed by thousands.

As Chile is outside the boundaries of the U. S. Air Force Intelligence, this one elicited no comment from the Pentagon.

As for things at the Denver level their investigators were too busy tailing that mystery man of science to bother with scuttlebutt from the Chilean Navy.

The same day, unfortunately, for those on the negative side of the debate, the director of the Tonantzintla Astronomical Observatory in Mexico reported photographing a flying saucer. The photograph didn't turn out any too well, but the newspaper Excelsior printed it nevertheless. Luis Enrique Erro, director of the observatory, said it was photographed on March 2 when the strange circular object crossed the Mexican sky.

Then on March 9, Roy L. Dimmick, Los Angeles sales manager for the Apache Powder Company, the sort of man who would be welcome on almost any jury, started a veritable stampede of disk jitters when he reported the wreckage of a flying saucer picked up near Mexico City. It had a dead pilot on board. The space ship measured 46 feet across, he said, and the pilot measured 23 inches.

"American military men have viewed the strange object," Dimmick testified, "but for military security reasons the entire matter has been kept very hush-hush."

The next day Dimmick dropped back to what the military call "a previously prepared position" and said he hadn't actually seen the space ship personally but had talked to two important men-one from Mexico and the other from Ecuador-who had. One had given him a strip of metal from the saucer. It looked like aluminum, but wasn't of a metal known to this earth, he added. This had a familiar ring. I've handled some of that stuff, too.

"I think the government ought to make its position clear," Dimmick complained. "If it doesn't want to discuss these things for reasons of security, why not say so?"

But the Air Force was not saying anything of the sort. The saucers were "a mild form of mass hysteria." (Except in cases like Dimmick's. He would fall, I suppose, according to their rigid classifications, into either the group suffering from hallucinations or the perpetrators of hoaxes.)

Brigadier General Rodriguez Cardenes, chief of the Mexican Air Corps, added his disclaimer, indicating that the good neighbor policy was not dead when it came to reciprocal agreements on press releases of this sort. It was getting so that pilots, navigators, and others trained to observe objects in the sky were not keen about reporting their observations any longer to Air Force Intelligence. There were too many kickbacks. To observe was to be suspect; to know was to be guilty. It was a crazy situation for America to find herself in, but there it was.

Most persons in responsible posts learned to take the official position as if it had all the force of a directive. Almost to a man you could bank on such persons accenting the positive, if the Pentagon was going that way, or adding their ridicule if the trend was downhill.

In the midst of positive reports from here, there, and everywhere, Dr. Gerard P. Kuiper, professor of astronomy at the University of Chicago, laughed at the idea that the pilot of the saucer reported in Mexico was a small man, but suggested that pilots of space ships could be smart bugs or small plants because that's all, in his opinion, the planet Mars could produce at present.

This sort of smart-alec rebuttal couldn't possibly receive an official rebuff at the time because it was in the "right" direction. Moreover, it sort of set the party line for other astronomers.

Off the record you could find dissenting opinions from astronomers whose standing was just as high as Kuiper's. Many kept an open mind on the issue. Some believed the objects were flying saucers but were still at a loss as to their origin. A few favored one planet or another as a possibility. But from Kuiper's whimsy you'd think that everybody had agreed the space ships were from Mars. Who said they were from Mars? Orson Welles? The ghost of the long dead R. A. Locke? Or was this a device of the military, a negative approach, to condition us to further revelations later involving Mars?

Though no Air Force officer has been known to have written on the subject, True magazine managed to get two Navy men to break loose from the corral during this era. Donald E. Keyhoe, a former Marine pilot, and Robert E. McLaughlin, a commander still on active service, wrote about flying saucers they had seen or had heard about. The articles were long on sound and fury, and while it might be harsh to say they signified nothing, that was more because of poor writing rather than poor material. True was not the first in the field by any means. I was at least ten weeks ahead of True with articles in Variety, and Fate was ahead of me by a year. But mine was not a rewrite. I used material never previously printed by anybody anywhere Fate, the Post, and True included.

Much of this was subsequently reprinted from Variety in papers as widely scattered as Boston, Buffalo, Kansas City, and Los Angeles, and a good deal of it has been released over one radio station or another.

During most of these exposes, Air Force Intelligence maintained a weary silence in the face of aerial observations which had turned the peoples of all countries from discussions of the cold war to hot speculations about flying saucers.

As for Denver, and its mysterious lecturer of March 8, 1950, the music went 'round and 'round. Someone remembered that a tape recording had been made of the scientist's talk and that it probably was stashed away at Station KMYR where Koehler worked. Koehler's employer permitted a group of Denver businessmen to listen to the recording so that they could better understand the ridiculousness of all the espionage and counterespionage on the Denver campus.

By then the Chancellor, who had been out of town when the lecture was delivered, was sounding off. He issued a directive to his faculty. They would have to screen speakers more carefully in the future. An anonymous writer on The Denver Post liked this approach to the problem. So he tried his editorial hand at rebuffing anonymity among visiting lecturers. His rebuff had all the moral force of pots calling kettles black.

In the audience of leading citizens at the radio transcription was a reporter of the same Denver Post. He broke the story anew in a Sunday edition. This brought the Army Air Force Intelligence into the picture again. Finally Koehler said he could take the third-degree stuff no longer.

"The name of the mystery scientist is Edgar B. Davis!" he cried.

It was agreed by all who heard it that this was a nice honest sounding name.

But who was Edgar B. Davis? The hunt started out anew.

At the very hour, however, when Denver was listening to a recording of the lecture, several persons in Hollywood were listening to a tape recording of the same lecture. It was taken from the original tape recording. In Hollywood it was heard in the private home of a doctor and his wife who had been a graduate nurse and a former airline hostess. The recording was in the custody of a geophysicist, a man known to me for years.

All were unquestionably astounded by the revelations and even more so by the fact that the voice on the tape and the one of the geophysicist were almost beyond a shadow of a doubt one and the same voice. Of course, since the flying time between Denver and Los Angeles is only a matter of six hours his presence in both places in the same day could not be advanced as conflicting testimony.

But on March 17, Denver's faculty, student body, press, and Air Force intelligence officers were pretty well convinced they had identified the lecturer who had had the temerity to write the bad words "Flying Saucers For Beginners" on their cloistered walls.

Four students, as well as Barron Beshoar, Denver's bureau manager of Time-Life Incorporated (a gate-crasher to the lecture incidentally), were sure from Denver Post photographers that the man was Silas Mason Newton, president of the Newton Oil Company, amateur golf champion of Colorado in 1942, graduate of Baylor University and Yale, who did postgraduate work at the University of Berlin, a man who had never made more than $25,000,000 nor lost more than $20,000,000, the rediscoverer of the Rangely oil field, patron of the arts, and man of the world generally. In brief, a man of substance as well as science and as American as apple pie.

One student later admitted he remembered the lecturer and knew who he was all along because he had caddied for him at the Lakewood golf course many times. But he hadn't spoken up before because he understood there was to be no publicity. Hadn't the subject matter been announced as confidential, he wanted to know?

This tempest in a university teapot, cooked up to make modesty appear as scandalous and tattletelling as a virtue, was all but obliterated from even The Denver Post by a wire story out of Farmington, New Mexico, on the afternoon of March 17. The sky, it appeared, had been cluttered with flying saucers for three days. But on St. Patrick's day in the morning half the town reported saucers in the sky. Some saw hundreds, none saw less than nine.

Farmington is an oil town of 5,000 persons. Its citizens are given more to looking down than looking up. Their living is way down there in the bowels of the earth in the San Juan Basin of northern New Mexico, close to the Colorado line; within, significantly, that 500 miles of Denver the lecturer referred to.

The town has one newspaper, the Farmington Daily Times. On one ear of its front-page masthead it proclaims, "Our Mission-Truth; Our Faith-New Mexico." It was established in 1884, a long time before Air Force Intelligence, and its reputation for veracity in the community is good.

So when on the morning of March 18 it ran an eight-column banner headline proclaiming "Hugh Saucer Armada Jolts Farmington," it was reporting the news as the entire staff and most of the town's population saw it. Clayton J. Boddy, the paper's business manager, and Orville Ricketts, the associate editor, had a hand in it, but the story was actually written by Walter Rogal, the managing editor.

The main story told that fully half the town's population was still certain the morning after that it had seen space ships or some strange aircrafts-hundreds of them-zooming through the skies on the previous day. The estimates ran from several to more than five hundred. "Whatever they were," the writer reported, "they caused a major sensation in this community which lies only a 110 air miles northwest of the huge Los Alamos Atomic installation."

The objects appeared to play tag high in the sky. At times they streaked away at almost unbelievable speeds. One triangulation estimated the speed at 1,000 miles an hour, and guessed the saucers were about twice the size of a B-29.

The newspaper office was deluged with calls from persons who saw the objects and wanted some explanation of their origin. Most observers described the space ships as silvery discs, and a number agreed one was red in color.

Clayton J. Boddy, a former captain of the engineers of the American Army in Italy, was just one of the number who testified as to what he saw. He was one in fact among those who thought there appeared to be about five hundred of them. His account was confirmed by Joseph C. Callioff and Frances C. Callioff, grocers from Antonito, Colorado, and Robert Foutz, and John Burrell of Farmington. The Callioffs were in Farmington inspecting sites for a proposed new store in their chain, and they contributed the opinion that the saucers seemed to be flying in formation.

Harold F. Thatcher, director of the Farmington unit of the U. S. Soil Conservation Service, was the one who made the triangulation. Not an engineer, he had engineers working under him and knew how to make a rough triangulation of an object. He laughed off the idea that the sky might have been full of pieces of cotton fuzz floating around. "I was not sighting on any cotton," he said. The cotton theory was a contribution of a state patrolman named Andy Andrews.

The first reports of flying saucers were noted at 10:15 A.M. and for an hour thereafter reports kept streaming in.

The second large-scale sighting appeared at 3 o'clock in the afternoon.

The first report that one of the saucers appeared red came from John Eaton, a real estate salesman, and Edward Brooks, a garage employee. Brooks had been a B-29 tail-gunner, and was the first to discount the objects as that of modern aircraft. They were "too maneuverable" he said.

John Bloomfield, another garage employee, said that they traveled about ten times faster than jet planes and frequently made right-angled turns. "They appeared to be coming at each other head on," he added. At the last second one would veer at right angles upward and the other at right angles downward."

"From the ground they appeared about the size of a dinner plate," said Marlow Webb, another employee. "They flew sideways, on edge and at every conceivable angle. This is what made it easy to determine that they were saucer-shaped."

No one reported seeing any vapor trails, or hearing any engine noises.

In general the town accepted the phenomenon calmly enough. Except for a few isolated reports there was no indication of Air Force's tired old trinity-hallucinations, mass hysteria, and hoaxes.

As to whether the objects were from another planet or some new craft of American design, the town's opinion was divided.

At 11:15 A.M. the clearest view and reports of the largest number of saucers came into the Farmington Times. By 11:30 all had disappeared.

Nearby Las Vegas reported that at 11:35 observers caught a glimpse of the saucers. Twelve postal employees witnessed one that sailed till noon. One employee was Robert Hilgers, a lieutenant in the naval reserve. He said the object was very high in the sky, "probably twenty miles."

The Las Vegas Daily Optic gave the Farmington story an eight-column streamer too. "SPACE SHIPS CAUSE SENSATION" it proclaimed.

All previous official explanations in the Air Force stockpile, that these things could be kites, balloons, reflections, debris from atomic bomb tests at nearby Alamagordo, wind-blown merry-grounds, suggestibility, hallucinations, mirages, and postwar psychoses didn't seem to cover the Farmington revelations. A whole town couldn't be seeing things.

Without knowing it, that Farmington fish story had come awfully close to landing a whale, because it was in that general direction where it all started in the spring of 1948 when a colleague of the lecturer of the University of Denver tempest got a hurry call to fly to New Mexico. This colleague (I shall call him "Dr. Gee") had been in government service on top secret defense projects for seven years and had played a part in 35,000 experiments on land, sea, and air, involving 1,700 scientists. He was still on call and getting pretty tired of these consultations, which at government salaries represents a loss to a man much in demand by industry.

But this time he was too thrilled to be tired. It took him only three hours to fly from Denver to his destination. There on the ground, having gently pancaked to earth, seemingly without having suffered a scratch, he saw the first flying saucer ever known to have landed on this planet.

Not long afterward I heard about it, first from that University of Denver lecturer and later from the lips of Dr. Gee himself.

"I don't believe a word of it," I remember saying at the time, "but tell me more about it. What did it look like? Where was it found?"

The scientist told me but he also told me so many other things that I had forgotten the name of the town. He explained about magnetic fault zones particularly in Oregon and on the Mojave Desert and how the pilots of these ships seemed to be as curious about them as bees about honey. He said he was checking to see if this curiosity was a likely source or had any connection with the propulsion behind their ships. He told me he suspected they had mastered secrets of flying, which we were only now seeing most dimly.

I kept my own counsel for months. But when others less well informed began sounding off in all directions about flying saucers, I thought it was about time that I told the world if nothing more than proof that I knew more than I had read in the papers.

In fact the night the Denver Post was exposing Scientist X and the Farmington citizens were exposing Operation HushHush, I was dining in Hollywood with the man all Denver was hunting for. He had just talked to George Koehler in Denver by long distance. Koehler had worked for him and had married his nurse. The Farmington report had set Denver uproar, Koehler told him.

"Do you remember my telling you," Scientist X said hung up, "that the first flying saucer was found on a ranch twelve miles from Aztec?"

I remembered when he reminded me "Yes," I said, "I remember now."

"Well," he said, "Farmington is only twenty-eight miles from that ranch. In fact they flew over the exact place where one of their number had fallen a year ago."

"I wonder why they keep scouting that area?" I asked. "Is it a tribute to the saucer that failed to come home or to show that they have mastered the particular fault zone that grounded an earlier patrol?"

"I covered that in my Denver lecture," he said. "Weren't you paying attention?"

BEHIND THE FLYING SAUCERS

Chapter 2
What the Scientist Said

THOUGH PERHAPS not too much thought has gone into the saying "nearer to church the further from God" (else how explain the piety of monks and nuns?), it-nevertheless happens that a hermit on a faraway hilltop sees more clearly into your windows now and then than your next door neighbor. Such an explanation of the vagaries of reflected light might explain also why it was not the Denver newspapers that gave the best report of what Scientist X had said to students of the University of Denver. The reflected prize for the best reporting would go to the Summerside Journal, a modest sized publication quartered on Prince Edward Island, Canada; between Newfoundland and New Brunswick at the mouth of the St. Lawrence River.

This newspaper obviously got its story from a Denver correspondent, but it recapitulated what the speaker said so well that it's better than a transcript in helping readers arrive at an understanding of what went on that March afternoon.

A transcript of a speech doesn't necessarily leave the reader with a well-rounded picture of what happened. The reason for this is that when a man talks he is primarily appealing to the ears of his readers; when he writes he is appealing to their eyes. Therefore, a complete transcription such as The New York Times frequently employs would not necessarily be the truest picture of what a man said. It would certainly lack his emphasis, his gestures, and (in this case) his chalk sketches on the blackboard.

Basically, the questions brought to the surface by this mysterious talker at the University of Denver were: (1) had science really found flying saucers to be real, (2) what did they consist of, and (3) where were they found?

A listener would like to know if the speaker thought the flying saucers had their origin on this earth. If they were, on the other hand, from another planet, what planet? Were they operated by pilots aboard them? And if by pilots, what were the appearance, size, coloring, age, clothes, and some of the other census-taking facts?

Did their knowledge of aerodynamics go deeper than ours would be another natural question.

BEHIND THE FLYING SAUCERS

In a fifty-minute address, it would be too much to expect any scientist to cover this whole field completely. At best he could subdivide the already divided camps between those who believed in flying saucers and those who disbelieved in them. He might reveal certain information along the way :fortifying the general suspicion that he was a man of education and standing in the community, that he was not only a man of science but of substance.

Well, he was saying, to begin with, that there is such a thing as a flying saucer. He was saying, moreover, that the Air Force, despite its announcement to the contrary, had not abandoned its Project Saucer, but was operating on another level and under possibly another name. He was saying that t four of these flying saucers had actually landed on this earth.

Three of the four, he added, had been captured and had been inspected by men with whom he was currently identified in geophysical research. Thirty-four men, measuring between thirty-six inches to forty inches in height had been found dead in three of the saucers discovered.

The first saucer to land on this earth, he said, landed less than two years previous to his talk, "on a site within 500 miles of Denver."

The saucer not only didn't appear to come from any part of this earth, but the question of where it came from still remained unsolved. The best speculation, he added, was Venus, but he continued to stress the point that it was still a wide-open question.

Under research, he said, the materials used in the saucer had disclosed two metals unknown to us. This convinced him and his co-scientists that the saucers were not likely made by us or rival powers.

Found in the first space ship were instruments which seemingly measured lines of magnetic force. These instruments were a key to something which his group was still working on and believed when they solved it, they would have solved the whole problem of the propulsion of these saucers. He said such ships capable of traveling with the speed of light could leave such a planet as Venus, say, which is 161,000,000 miles from us when our orbits lie in extreme positions, and return to Venus in less than one hour.

According to the correspondent of the lecturer never identified himself speech was calculated, well thought enough for the slowest student to absorb and record.

There was no particular accent or diction which the correspondent could detect. The speaker used scientific terms and spoke with a familiarity of a man who knew many sciences. He repeatedly used the word "we" when referring to experiments being done on the strange crafts. He didn't associate himself with any particular experiment. He also indicated that a full disclosure of the government's interest in flying saucers, though officially denied at present, would be forthcoming in the not too distant future. He said the first disk that landed was 99.9 feet in diameter and had a cabin measuring 72 inches in height. The second measured

BEHIND THE FLYING SAUCERS

72 feet in diameter, the third, 36 feet. All measurements on the ships seemingly were divisible by nine, which may have been a clew that they used our system of measurement.

The disks, he explained had revolving rings of metal, in the center of which were the cabins. The cabins were geared to the disks, which revolved around the stabilized cabins. The gears, which had no lubrication, were of a gear ratio unfamiliar to our engineers. He thought they might have traveled by using the magnetic lines of force known to encircle planets of our solar system.

From its appearances the researchers assumed that the first saucer was capable of maneuvering in any given direction. Like helicopters, which these ships were not, they could be maneuvered to land anywhere. The smallest had a landing gear built like a tricycle of three metal balls, which could revolve in any direction.

Accepting the theory, which he did, that the craft could operate by harnessing magnetic lines of force, he said it was entirely logical to assume these saucers could travel up to virtually unlimited speed-at least up to 186,000 miles per second the speed of light-in this atmosphere, and where there was no gravitational or wind resistance it would be impossible to compute how fast they could travel.

Sixteen men, ranging in ages, he would guess, from thirty-five to forty years old, if we use our calendar of time, were taken dead from the first craft. Their bodies had been charred to a dark brown color.

Sixteen dead men were also found in the second craft. These, however, had not suffered from burns apparently, and were all of fair complexion. Otherwise they were like the first space travelers-of small stature. No different from us, except for height, and lack of beards. Some had a fine growth resembling peach fuzz.

The third ship was also manned and the men in it were also dead. This one, a small saucer, 36 feet in diameter, had a crew of only two. These men had lived to land, because they had died while attempting to climb out of their cabin.

Those connected with the research, the speaker said, believed that all three craft landed under the guidance of their own instruments and did not crash, despite the fact that their crews were dead. They may have landed on instruments or they may have been guided the whole distance. But they did not crash and in only one ship was there any mark of imperfection.

In construction, they were quite dissimilar to anything we have designed. There was not a rivet, nor a bolt, nor a screw in any of the ships. Their control boards were a series of push buttons. Their outer construction was of a light metal much resembling aluminum but so hard no application of heat could break it down.

There was no reference to the means of propulsion beyond that the craft presumably operated on lines of magnetic force and the designers had conquered the problem of how to switch from Venus (which is positive) to this earth (which is positive), and therefore repel each other.

The ships carried no weapons, and the speaker assumed that they had solved the problem of disintegrating an object which might pursue or threaten them.

He gave details of the water and food found on the board the saucers. He also told of sleeping accommodations on one craft that had wall-enclosed bunks which could not be seen when closed and ingeniously disappeared in the curtains when open.

As he neared the end of his lecture he told of the discovery of a fourth saucer which members of his group stumbled on near a government proving ground. It was unoccupied at the moment.

The scientists returned to their car for cameras and equipment and as they neared the ship they saw several little men hop into the saucer, and the ship just disappeared like one of those hallucinations we hear so much about.

At no time did the speaker indicate where the ships disappeared to after being broken up for research. Nor did he give any clew as to what happened to the bodies of the 34 men found dead in the first three saucers. "He said simply," concluded the reporter for the Summerside Journal, 'There is a flying saucer.' "

He might have added for the benefit of any eavesdroppers scouting for the Air Force that the ships were as real as the planes over Pearl Harbor, which the Air Force never saw either. He might have, but he refrained.

Comparing this news summary with an actual transcript of the lecture, the reporter for the Summerside Journal comes out with flying colors. That he skipped such technical matters as the speaker's reference to William Gilbert-(1544-1603)-as the father of magnetism, and other milestones, such as July 16, 1945, at 5:30 A.M. when the atomic age was born at Alamagordo, New Mexico, and Max Planck's theories advanced in 1903 when he was professor at the University of Berlin is not important. Tying all these things to the age of the flying saucers was part of the speaker's general introduction.

He drew four designs on the blackboard. One showed the "System of Nines," believed to have been used in constructing the saucers. Two others showed two views of the saucer, which was 99.99 feet in diameter, 18 feet across the cabin and a clearance of 45 inches above the rim for pilots to see what might be around them. The design looked very much like the photographs taken by Paul Trent of McMinnville, Oregon, and published in the June 26, 1950 issue of Life. The fourth design showed how magnetic lines of force travel from the sun to the various planets, particularly to the earth and to Venus.

After his lecture had caused such a stir, the chalked designs were preserved by lacquer, and unless the lacquer has been removed are there to this day.

The reporter missed too that the space ships apparently had no doors, no exits. They did, however, have portholes. One was broken and it had a hole about the thickness of a pencil. Through this had rushed either gases or air with such speed that it burned the 16 passengers inside to a brown crisp.

The speaker made it quite clear both in the transcript and subsequent fireside chats at my home that the passengers, although approximately 40 inches tall were not midgets. They had no bad teeth, no fillings. They all wore a sort of uniform but there were no insignia on collars or caps.

There were two or three instruments which the scientists judged to be time-pieces. It took 29 days for the instrument to make a complete circumference. This was their first clew that there might be something between the ship's means of propulsion and magnetism, because a magnetic day is 23 hours and 58 minutes, which works out at 29 days for a magnetic month.

Another thing the reporter missed, one that was really significant, was the speaker's solution as to what happened to Captain Thomas F. Mantell. This case had been hashed and rehashed many times, but never once had anybody come near a remotely plausible solution as to what happened to Mantell and his plane.

All reports agreed that on January 7, 1948, an unidentified object was sighted over Godman Air Force base, Fort Knox, Kentucky, by both military and civilian observers. Four national guardsmen in F 51's, flying in the vicinity, were requested by the Godman control tower operator to investigate the foreign object. Three of the planes closed in and reported that it was metallic and of tremendous size. One pilot described it as "round like a teardrop and fluid."

Captain Mantell contacted Godman tower and reported the object was travel-ing at half his speed at 12 o'clock high. "I'm closing in now to take a good look," he said. "It's directly ahead of me and still moving at about half my speed. The thing looks metallic and of tremendous size...It's going up now and forward as fast as I am. That's 360 m.p.h...I'm going up to 20,000 feet and if I'm no closer, I'll abandon chase."

The time was 3:15 P.M. January 7, 1948. That was the last radio contact by Mantell with the Godman Tower.

Five minutes after Mantell's disappearance from the formation the two remain-ing planes returned to Godman Field. One of them refueled and equipped him-self with oxygen. He covered the territory for 100 miles and climbed as high as 30,000 feet, but found nothing.

Later that day Mantell's body was found in the wreckage of his plane near Fort Knox.

This at least is the official opinion of the Air Materiel Command. According to them, subsequent investigation revealed that Mantell had probably blacked out at 20,000 feet from lack of oxygen and that the mysterious object which he chased to his death was the planet Venus.

"However," the report continued, "further probing showed the elevation and azimuth reading of Venus and the objects specified time intervals did not coin-cide."

The object, in fact, is still considered "unidentified," and as far as is known has never been identified or cleared up by the Air Force to this day.

BEHIND THE FLYING SAUCERS

But the speaker in Denver cleared it up to the satisfaction of many. He first prepared his hearers by explaining that members of his group had been engaged in government research since 1942. At least 1,700 scientists were involved in top secret projects. They had worked together for five years and had found out more about magnetism in those five years than the whole world had been able to do in centuries previous.

They had come to the conclusion that everything existing owed its shape and being to magnetic lines of force. He explained there are 1,257 magnetic lines of force to the square centimeter. That is to say, to about a half inch.

Around certain areas of this earth are places known to have magnetic fault zones. Here blow-outs occur, similar to the perpetual eddying of the waters around Cape Hatteras. On this continent areas around the states of Oregon and New Mexico are known to have these sort of faultings.

If the saucers fly on these magnetic waves and have an intelligence operating them (like ours or even superior to ours) it follows that they would show a curiosity about areas that were troublesome. Also atomic explosions might disturb magnetic lines of force and certainly be not unknown to their instruments.

This could explain their frequent appearances over areas like the White Sands Proving Ground. Since the air is so much clearer in Wyoming, Colorado, Arizona, New Mexico, and Texas it obviously is easier for land-based observers to spot them.

Much of the magic, the scientist explained, which has baffled both trained and untrained observers, is not magic at all. A good deal of what is claimed to have happened to ships in the air, such as disintegration, suspension for a period of time, immobilization of their instrument boards, and such can be duplicated in the laboratory. Mantell's plane and every portion of his plane from the motor to the tips of the wings hung together by reason of magnetic frequency. This was true of even Mantell himself. Therefore all that a flying saucer had to do to disintegrate Mantell's plane, the lecturer revealed, was to demagnetize it.

No two lines have ever been known to cross each other naturally. If forced to do so, or if crossed by "accident" you get disintegration and fire.

Anybody who could create such a magnetic disturbance could wipe out every living thing on this earth in a second.

This, then was the magnetic research scientist's explanation as to what happened to Captain Mantell and his ship. The captain was proving a source of annoyance in his pursuit of a magnetically controlled flying saucer. A button was pushed and Mantel] and his plane were no more.

Another thing the speaker pointed out that should have been of more durable interest was that the water on the flying saucer was almost twice as heavy as our drinking water. It was carried in two small containers and was very similar in fact to the heavy water the Nazis wanted so badly from Norway in their haste to be the

BEHIND THE FLYING SAUCERS

first to make an atomic bomb.

The food was in concentrates, non-toxic when tested and of a sort familiar to our vitamin-concious civilization. The little wafers, apparently the food supply, were so condensed that when one was put in a gallon of water it swelled up and overflowed. It was fed to guinea pigs and they thrived on it.

From the outside the whole cabin of the first flying saucer examined seemed hermetically sealed and if it had not been for that break in one of the portholes the researchers might have spent months getting into the ship. But from the inside there was a visible knob in the wall and on the knob was another smaller knob. When the smallest knob was pushed the door flew open, but once it was shut again it was impossible to see the door from the outside.

It had not yet been determined what the two materials found on the ship were. Heat had not been able to melt one down, not even up to 10,000 degrees. It was strong it was light. A dozen men could stand on it and not dent it; two men could raise up one end of the ship, it was that light.

More than 150 experiments had been tried to break down the gear structure of the ship, with no success. It was hard and of a ratio different from the Swedish system which we employ. Instead of being three to five it was three to six, giving no allowance for lubrication or play or wear expansion under heat. The speaker said that one ship had defied all effort to get inside of it, despite the use of $35,000 worth of diamond drills.

Though the 72-foot ship had sleeping quarters and even a toilet, the third ship had neither of these features. The latter was piloted by two little men, who sat on bucket seats in front of a control board which was entirely manipulated by push buttons. One, when found, was halfway out of is cabin. The other was sitting with his head on his chest; both dead.

It was the little ship that had the three-point landing gear. The locomotion was not on wheels but steel-looking balls. If all the balls were spinning in the same direction, any number of men could not tilt the ship. However, if the were no movement to the steel balls, a child could tilt the disk ship. This helped to convince the researchers that magnetic laws were involved. The speaker guessed that the two-seater must have been a later model, based and built on the knowledge that the trip from wherever they came and back did not require sleeping accommodations nor toilets, any more than automobiles require them on this earth.

Certainly any flying saucer which could travel from the planet Venus, say, to this earth and back in an hour would have no need for overnight bags.

The speaker also said that the thread used to sew the buttons on the jackets of these men had been tested, and it took 450 pounds of weight to break the thread.

This was the lecturer's story. Later we will get to Dr. Gee's own story, but I have a story to tell, too. And after me the Air Force has its story, for in this court all will get a hearing.

Chapter 3
Some Personal History

LONG BEFORE this point, many readers must have asked themselves, "How did Scully get into all this?"

Frankly, I wrote my way into it. Years ago I wrote the inside story of how I happened to be the author of Frank Harris's life of Bernard Shaw. I later incorporated the articles into a book called Rogues Gallery-a title which I subsequently gave to Ellery Queen for a book of detective stories, only to find it used without permission in movies, radio, and everywhere else as time went by.

Among the readers of Rogues Gallery was one who wrote in substance: "You keep picking around the edges of Harris. Why don't you write a book about him?" It was signed "Silas M. Newton."

The name rang a bell in my memory. When Harris and his wife made a trip from Nice to New York in the winter of 1929/1930, Silas Newton paid for it. He housed them in his Park Avenue residence and arranged for their invitation to talk to Washington officialdom on Shakespeare.

Months later, after he had returned to the French Riviera, Harris told me that on the steamer to America he got a call in his cabin from port authorities. He was seventy-two at the time and in no mood for detention at Ellis Island for having written his *Life and Loves*. In his pocket was a vial of potassium cyanide.

"My God, Nellie," he cried. "They've got me!"

But it turned out the official had come to his cabin to inform him he had been extended the freedom of the port.

He was overwhelmed by Newton's beneficence. Newton offered him a $10,000 grant to make a world tour and compare what he saw with what he had observed as a young man. But Harris was not up to such an assignment. His memory simply wasn't there from day to day, let alone to be trusted with a fifty-year perspective.

For years after that I had thought of Newton as a fine old Southern gentleman— tall, slender, with possibly a white goatee, born in Kentucky, raised in Texas, mellowed in New York.

BEHIND THE FLYING SAUCERS

What I met instead was a short stocky man in his middle years, with not a gray hair in his head, a great athlete in his college years at Baylor and at Yale and a golf champion on some level almost forever after. His interest in literature had remained at a high level all his life. He was one of the great geophysicists of the oil industry, with a record of successful exploratory operations that was surpassed by none. He had made and spent millions and how he had rid himself of at least one million is an interesting sidelight to his character.

He was married to Nan O'Reilly at the time. She was New York's top feminine sports writer. After ten years of happily married life, he learned from her doctors that she was doomed to die in a year.

He put $1,000,000 in the bank in her name and said, "Nan, you simply do not know how to spend money. This has to be learned like anything else. I want you to practice with this million. Do what your best impulses tell you to do. Back plays, throw Park Avenue parties for people who never got out of Greenwich Village, publish their poetry—*anything*—but get rid of that million in a year."

In a year it was gone and she was too.

So he left New York and for the next ten years sublimated his loss in exploratory operations, chiefly from the Rocky Mountains to the Pacific Ocean. He traveled hundreds of thousands of miles, checking on likely sources of oil. He set up and independent company in Denver. It's still there and he's still president.

He took me on long rides through Wyoming, Colorado, California, trying to talk me into doing that book on Harris. His own tales of early wildcatters were far more interesting to me than twice-told tales of Harris.

He hunted for oil with instruments which had cost a fortune and were a closely guarded secret. With them he had rediscovered the Rangely oil field, years after the major oil companies had written it off as a failure.

Once an oil field was in operation he practically lost interest. Soon you'd find him out on the hunt to trap a new prey. His latest hunch was that there was more oil under the Mojave Desert than all of the Saudi Arabias, which at that time were sanding the smooth quality of our international relations.

Sometimes he'd come in with a collateral piece of research which couldn't possibly interest him except as a means of checking his highly complicated instruments in another field. Once it was a gold deposit which he was certain was within thirty miles of a huge nugget he had picked up. The nugget assayed $82,000 to the ton! About $750 to the ton is commercial gold.

While it's nice to know gold is within thirty miles of where you're standing, the problem is, in what direction? With 360 degrees to pick from, the radius doesn't help much. Newton put his instruments into operation and said, "There!"

He pointed northeast, set his compass and told us that over hill and crater we would go in a straight line from where the nugget was found and 27 miles away we would find the ore body that fathered it.

64

BEHIND THE FLYING SAUCERS

"Obviously it's an outcropping," he said. "No prospector would know how to get it otherwise."

He organized an expedition. He ordered equipment, men, and a jeep dispatched from Denver. They were to meet us at a motel near the California-Nevada line. We were routed out at 3:45 in the morning. We traveled to a jumping-off place in a new Oldsmobile and the jeep.

Four of them transferred to the jeep taking instruments, water, and food with them. I was left to guard the pass. From what? The nearest sign of life were some dinosaur's hoof prints-and they were 30,000,000 years old.

"If we don't come back by noon, don't worry," said Newton. "If things go bad we might be held up till 4:30."

"And if you don't come back by sundown?"

"We're lost," he said.

Then he drove off with the keys to the rescue car. That meant if they were lost, I was too.

They left just as the sun was coming over the mountains. I was parked on a volcanic lava bed-barren of the slightest vegetation. Not even a buzzard flew over the area all day.

By noon the heat became stifling. I stripped nude except for army boots and crawled under the car. Never had I seen such a God-forsaken spot.

I began to think of myself in terms of Captain Scott, that my end would be simply a matter of "these few notes and my dead body will tell the tale." In fact I even feared that the notes would burn up and never be found. I could see fifty miles in any direction and I could see nothing. I could get a radio station from Salt Lake City but they didn't help because they couldn't get me.

A sandwich and a canteen of water were gone by noon. I began to dry out, to salivate. I could have tried the radiator water, but it was full of rust and I felt that all that was left of me was ferrous oxide, the sodium chloride having long since evaporated.

Even if rescued I wouldn't know where to hunt for the others. There are 360 degrees in even a secret circle, leaving a 359-to-1 shot that a searching party would find them.

They didn't return at noon. They didn't return by 4:30. So by Newton's own definition they were lost. It was too late to try hobbling back to civilization, so I decided to spend the night in the car, without food or water.

But after the sun had set I saw the lights of a jeep weaving in and out of the cactus, sage, lava beds, and sand. After three attempts to get to me they finally found a way in.

They returned gasping for water, pooped, glass-eyed. They drank some of the radiator water, threw a sack of ore, some tools, and their gold-crazed bodies in the car. Newton took the wheel and tore across the open valley to the crib where we had spent the night.

Once refreshed by a couple of coyote sandwiches and some diluted marijuana the natives used for coffee, Newton gave out with the big news. They had found the outcropping all right.

"Only it's on a reactivated military reservation," he said, "and we'll get our butts shot off if we go in there again. So I guess we'll have to shelve the project till the cold war is over."

The others agreed.

"Well, it vindicated my hunch that we could find other things besides oil by instrumentation," he added. "Let's get some sleep. We've got to get back to business."

The sack of ore he lured from a government military reservation weighed fifty pounds. It assayed $1,250.

It was a year almost to the day, after this adventure in the broadcasting of microwaves from a gold outcropping to Newton's instruments, that Newton introduced me to his newest secret. I had introduced him to a girl, Sharon Chillison (he has since married her), and he invited her, Mrs. Scully, and me to dinner at the Sportsmen's Lodge in the San Fernando Valley. He had just come from Arizona, where he had been referred for some improvements in his geological research equipment. At the time of the dinner he had made thousands of surveys in the Mojave Desert and had just about decided to drill some test wells. All the big oil companies were convinced there was nothing in the area, but by instrumentation he was sure there was.

"Petroleum in place," he contends, "radiates magnetic energy and this is measurable."

The trouble was, how much? How deep did the wells go? Petroleum deposits hidden deep in the earth were constantly broadcasting through magnetic microwaves, he believed, what had been trapped in the various fault zones. The only handicap his instruments showed was that they could come within inches of telling him where oil could be found but could not tell him how much volume to expect. Thus he might come out with so little oil that for all practical purposes, he had drilled a dry hole.

In 1945 Newton told Walter Russell that the broadcasting of microwaves by his instrumentation never exceeded 32 miles. He didn't understand why. Russell explained why.

"Under one of my laws covering circular motion," he said, "the radius is limited to 32 miles because that is the limit of the earth's crust. Beyond that depth is a solid substance. Without knowing it you have discovered the thickness of the skin of the earth."

Newton was delighted to hear this and the delight was not lessened when 17 months later the telephone company announced that they were setting up a line between New York and Boston with relay stations every 30 miles because that seemed to be as far as microwaves would reflect. They did the same thing when setting up television relay stations between Los Angeles and San Francisco in 1950.

Meanwhile Newton was applying the knowledge of microwaves to "petroleum in place." Since trapped oil was what he was looking for, that's all he was concerned about. That of course and an estimate of how much would be there before he started digging.

In the summer of 1949 he met Dr. Gee, a magnetic engineer who had been released in July after seven years of government servitude on all sorts of top-drawer projects. He had become a master of magnetic energy but $7,200 a year was all he could make for all his mastery. So he begged off government projects to get back to a more profitable_ business. He and Newton exchanged views and he told Newton that he thought Newton was operating, not merely on microwaves but on magnetic waves. He thought a magnetron, such as was developed during the war, might be able to detect the volume of oil. This, he explained, was possible because magnetic waves will not go through oil. They move over and under the petroleum. Thus it would be easy to subtract the difference and tell you how much volume there was in a given oil trap.

This was the answer Newton was looking for and he signed Dr. Gee and his equipment to check on the Mojave Desert field before starting any wildcat operations.

While driving with Dr. Gee from Denver to Phoenix one day early in the summer of 1949 Newton tuned in on a news commentator who happened to be reporting a flying saucer story.

"Do you think there's anything to these things, Doctor?" Newton asked the magnetic research scientist.

The doctor nodded his head. "Too bad we weren't associated before," he said. "I could have worked you into the project of the first one we were called in to examine."

He pointed south of where they were driving.

"It landed down near Aztec, New Mexico. I got a call and flew down from Denver in three hours."

It was his group that had worked out the means by which Japanese submarines were detected by magnetic devices. So successful were the instruments, that we were able to knock out as many as 17 Jap submarines in one day. They had conducted 35,000 experiments for the government on land, sea, and air. They had moved magnetic research ahead hundreds of years and had spent a billion dollars doing it.

Newton was explaining all this to us at dinner and then, as if he could keep a secret no longer from old friends, he started to tell the details of two saucers the research magnetic scientist had *personally seen, examined, checked on, and re-*

searched.

His story was so fantastic, that if he weren't a solid man of industrial service, you might have suspected that he had gone crazy in a quiet, plausible way.

He said that Dr. Gee of their group was coming to the coast very shortly to check on some government defense work which for the present was top secret. He was then going to check on Newton's own geophysical findings in the Mojave Desert and maybe he would tell us what he had told Newton.

Dr. Gee might show us some of the things that had been taken off one flying saucer-some small disks of a metal unknown to this earth, a tiny radio which operated under principles quite unknown to our engineers, a strange cloth, some gears and other small things which he could carry with him, and which he had taken off one of the ships for research, after he found members of the Air Force picking off pieces just for souvenirs.

Frankly, I never expected to hear any more of this but a few weeks later, I received a call from Newton asking me if I'd like to drive up to the town of Mojave, which is about ninety miles from Los Angeles, to see how his exploratory operation was getting along. The geophysicist who was the top man in magnetic research would be with us. This was on September 8, 1949. He said that Peverly Marley, cameraman at Warner's and the husband of Linda Darnell, would be coming along too.

We failed to make connections with Marley and went on without him, but at the cutoff at Newhall we heard a honking behind us and there was Marley who had pursued us and caught up with us. He parked his car at a gas station and we all repaired to Mojave in Newton's Cadillac.

Marley and the magnetic research scientist sat in the back; Newton and I in the front.

As on most long trips, people talk about all sorts of things. So we got started on flying saucers. There was no secrecy, official or otherwise, at the time and the scientist answered any and all queries. His explanations were as phlegmatic as those of a combustion engineer explaining how gas explodes in the cylinder of an automobile. On the oil field proper, the magnetic scientist got out his magnatron and Newton got out his own instruments.

Though their instruments looked in nowise alike, these men kept checking each other and invariably coming out within a foot of each other's estimates. Newton would ask the magnetic scientist what depth he thought oil was at a particular point at which they agreed there was oil and within seconds the scientist would say something like 2,750. Newton would check in his book and say, "I got 2,749 when I checked here last May."

There would be a calm exchange of how this discrepancy of one foot could have arisen, but the difference was so small that it constantly amazed a layman like me that they could split hairs about digging one foot more or less into what

BEHIND THE FLYING SAUCERS

must have been millions of dollars either way.

Instead of staying overnight on the desert, we decided to drive back to town, a matter of only two hours and the eminent geophysicist stopped off at our house for a short visit to meet Mrs. Scully and our family.

Showing no feeling whatever that he was airing confidences which might be violated, he answered all sorts of questions concerning the possible origin of the flying saucers and how they might have got to this earth from another planet, and, more important to his mind, how they could have got back to where they came from. The smallest detail, which a woman might bring up, about the interior of the cabin of the flying saucer, matters of water, food, clothing, were quietly explained just as one might describe the furniture of his own home.

His knowledge of magnetic energy was as far ahead of us as, say, the knowledge of atomic-energy scientists must have been to the average person in relation to nuclear fission ten years ago. Indeed, he said some things at that time which since have been heralded far and wide by Albert Einstein in relation to his modified theory of the universe, wherein he discounted Newton's law of gravity in favor of one involving electro-magnetic forces. This didn't mean much to me at the time but it means a lot more to me now.

It means more because the geophysicist said he had checked over two of the saucers and believed they were driven, not by fuel, jet, turbojet, or even athodyds, but by magnetic power and that due to certain metals not found on this earth but found on the saucers, he suspected the space ships were from another planet. In fact he ridiculed the idea of anything getting even as far as the moon on jet propulsion or anything like it. As at this time he was doing research for men whose living came out of oil, and was in fact a partner in their properties, he could hardly be suspected of feathering his own nest by discounting gas or petroleum as a means of propulsion from one planet to another.

Another thing I remembered from that first meeting was his interest in my infirmity. I have only one leg and have not had much luck with artificial legs, chiefly because they are too heavy and my stump too short.

He suggested a suction socket, eliminating all shoulder and waist harness. He said he could make one of a material as strong as steel and as light as plastic. I told him it would still have to be manipulated. He suggested he could install a small motor that could be operated by push button.

"The whole thing shouldn't weigh three pounds," he added.

"Fine," I said, "but suppose I stopped to shake hands and chat with a friend, and the leg should keep on walking. Wouldn't I look silly?"

"I'd control that with a push button too," he said.

It gave me a clew to the practicality and sweep of his mind. Before he left he promised us he would show us small parts of one of the saucers on his next trip from Phoenix. A radio had him particularly baffled. It had no tubes, no aerials, no wires. He guessed the cabin must have been its antenna. He was trying to rig up a substitute antenna. He could hear a high singsong note 15 minutes past the hour. But the dial was so micrometrically keyed it was difficult to stay on the wave. He was thinking of setting up something like a block-and-fall which permits a clumsy hand to lift a heavy object. Anyway he'd take it along. Wasn't much bigger than a king-sized cigarette package.

He said he regretted the ship was dismantled this way but the Army seems to breed souvenir hunting as it does rank. When he saw what was happening he grabbed a few things himself, not to put in his trophy cabinet but to use for research.

The Air Force took some film, he explained. But it fades in two hours, for reasons of security. A special chemical, got only on license, restores the image for another two hours. Naturally this film was not available to him. He said he shot some film of his own, but it wasn't very good. He'd bring that along, though.

In time we saw all those things-all except the jacket. We examined the radio, the gears, the film.

Then began the reign of error. Air Force closed Project Saucer and went underground. All were told to forget what they knew. "Hallucinations" became a routine answer. "Psycho" became a veiled threat. Everybody shut up but the people. The official dams were closed but the public spilled its observations into the lake of a free press.

But the conflict between free inquiry and official censorship grew. Men who talked freely in the summer of 1949 wouldn't tell their story for $20,000,000 by the summer of 1950. But I remembered. Better than elephants, I remembered. In fact, elephants come to me when they forget.

Chapter 4
Theories in Collision

BEFORE GROUNDING believers in flying saucers perhaps it might be fruitful to hear what dissenters (by no means accepted by other dissenters) have to say on interplanetary travel.

Naturally if you follow any rival theorist too long, you'll either be sucked in by his prop wash or be blown over a cliff by his exhaust gases. It also naturally follows that men who are wedded to rockets as the only plausible means of getting from one planet to another (and that in 1950 included the Air Force) are not going to junk their rockets and embrace flying saucers merely because others may say saucers are already here, while the best military information puts rockets to the moon twenty-five years into the future, and a four-day trip even then.

Men stay with what they believe, or fight for buggy whips in an era of automobiles for the simple reason that their livelihoods are all tied up with buggy whips.

That rocketeers should pooh-pooh the reality of flying saucers while giving painstaking details of trips to the moon in their imaginary rockets reveals how theories as well as worlds can suffer collision.

Yet who can read Willy Ley and not be convinced that the man is writing about a trip to the moon that he actually took? And for those who may still doubt, they will be gathered in like daisies if they look at Chesley Bonestell's "documentary" paintings which support Ley's text. No camera could add anything to such an interplanetary understanding.

Viking, which gave The Conquest of Space (1949) the glamour treatment, published a more thorough if less glamorous book on rockets by Ley in 1944. Ley must have forgotten some of his own researches, because in the earlier book he lists a volume published in 1931 written by David Lasser. It bears the fetching title The Conquest of Space.

Both books commendably play down the lethal prospects of rockets and stress their possibilities for interplanetary travel. Ley is particularly persuasive, whether appealing to astronomers, engineers, or those who like a good story. He has been enamored of rockets for twenty-five years and has been publishing pamphlets on them since at least 1926. The Russians, however, were at them as early as 1893, and the French go back to 1814 when William Congreve published his first book on rockets. His theories spread to England, Ireland, and Germany and were the military vogue of the next fifteen years.

After the First World War there was another upsurge of interest-especially among those obsessed with the belief that one new weapon can win a war. The V2 of the Second World War convinced many enemies of the Nazis that perhaps the fanatics were right. Were it not for the fact that the Americans invented the atom bomb, war rockets would be completely in the saddle today. As it is, rockets hold a secondary position and their proponents, both among the military and civilian, must console themselves with such sublimations as trips to the moon instead of to Moscow.

Though Ley has a tendency to belittle what he calls second-rate novelists dealing with matter in the science-fiction field, he is really in the same field himself. He starts from a basic and believable premise, such as a rocket being shot off at the White Sands Proving Ground, New Mexico (north of El Paso, Texas), and overwhelms you with such a detail of engineering data, in connection with such a release, that you go with him into areas where, if you thought about it, you would realize he had moved from fact into a strictly fictional field with more laughable brass than any Jules Verne of flying saucers.

He calls the signal for firing "X minus 20," and he works you with a palpitant pace all the way down to X minus 1. After that there are only fifty seconds to go. . .forty. . .thirty. . .twenty . . .ten. A hand in a steel glove pushes an ignition button. A pinwheel burns, valves jump open, liquid oxygen and alcohol rush from tanks into the motor. Contact! Ignition!. . . A noise which can be heard one-half a :mile away like the roar of a waterfall, or of distant thunder. Peroxide and permanganate come together, the turbine wheel spins, the pumps move, the fuel is forced. There is a deafening roar. Zero! Rocket away!

How can anybody deny that such excitement is real?

There is a thrust of twenty-seven tons on a rocket weighing less than fifteen tons. Fifteen miles up the velocity climbs from forty feet per second to one mile per second. After sixty-eight seconds, there is a mechanism which shuts off the fuel flow. Ley insists on calling it Brennschluss because the Germans called it that. After that the rocket keeps moving on kinetic energy. It reaches a height of 110 miles, before gravity begins to reassert itself.

In five minutes it is back to the earth. And though it went straight up it has landed thirty miles away. Like all planets or other objects in space, it has followed Kepler's law of elliptical conformity. It might have been set to follow a different ellipse as war rockets do. In that case it might have landed 200 miles from where it was fired instead of thirty.

BEHIND THE FLYING SAUCERS

Of course if the rocket could have got outside our gravitational pull, it might have kept right on do the moon. But high performance depends on high velocity. With a high mass ratio, and a high exhaust velocity, a rocket slanted to land where the moon would be four days from now, would hit it right on the nose. There is an experimental rocket airplane called XS-1. Ley believes the winged, long-ranged rocket of the future will resemble this type of airplane. But he gives no thought to the idea that the rocket principle which he hugs so close to his breast may also be involved in the propulsion of flying saucers. If a rocket, simplified, is fireworks, a flying saucer, equally simplified, can be a pinwheel in the same pyrotechnical display.

The atmosphere of the earth extends 250 miles, but at forty miles the density is nearer a vacuum than anything else. Apparently Ley cannot conceive of any propulsion beyond our combustion engines, turbines, turbojets and, in his dreams, athodyds. Though believers in flying saucers have frequently been classified as beautiful dreamers, Ley talks about a rocket with flawless down-to-earth logic-until you find that his rockets do not have enough power to get to the moon. In that case they can become orbital rockets! That is to say, sort of artificial moons, there to revolve in our atmosphere and be used for navigation purposes or stations in space, for later rocket ships to refuel on their way to the moon.

What Willy Ley is cooking up, a group calling themselves the Borderland Scientists believe is here already. They call these space ships and the people moving around on such a plane between this planet to another, "Ethereans."

Once he has got an unmanned rocket to overcome all barriers and actually reach the moon (possibly with a load of gypsum so that its crash-landing will show up white against the moon's habitual greyness) Ley would be ready for a moonship manned by a crew conditioned to all sorts of atmospheric pressures and vacuums. Because man on this earth functions at 1 g. (gravity), the rocket could not exceed an acceleration of 4 g. without tearing him apart. Thus it would take 500 seconds of acceleration at 4 g. before the ship hit a velocity of 7 miles per second- a speed it would have to maintain to get out of the earth's gravitational pull. In its fall toward the moon, there would have to be enough fuel reserved to resist the pull of the moon's gravitational pull. And in fact enough fuel left over, to get out of it again. There would be no way to relay a message, as there is no air around the moon where the temperature varies from 250 degrees below zero to 200 above. Unless the crew hit a happy medium, their chances of coming back on Ley's slow boat would be academic.

Coming back to this earth, Ley hoped the engineers could work out a series of breaking ellipses, so that the rocket could eventually get home like a glider. He also suggested a two-step rocket, one inside the other, and the smaller one to take on the final job of getting to the moon.

Funny thing that Lucian of Samosata, who wrote the first story of a trip to the moon, in the third century, had a ship caught in an Atlantic storm and had the ship carried to the moon. It took eight days. That's not bad calculating, considering that the best figures today, according to those unfamiliar with magnetic energy (Ley apparently among them), would be four days.

Johannes Kepler who discovered the laws of planetary orbits also made an imaginary trip to the moon. But his wasn't as believable as Ley's. Ley's own imaginary trip takes place on a mountaintop near the equator. It will be out of sight within a minute. Its path will be vertical, and then tipped eastward so it can gain some of the earth's rotational momentum, and then pointed to a spot where the moon will be four days hence. It will leave the earth's atmosphere three minutes after taking off, and the rocket's motors will work for eight minutes.

Once the terrible acceleration has stopped, and the Brennschluss set, the pilot will no doubt have a hard time getting his breath back as the gravity goes down from 4 g. to 1 g. to zero. At that point the pilot will find everything around him devoid of weight. He may have to drink water that has become bubbles and is floating all around him. Of course he could eat, because bodily functions do not depend on gravity. Men can drink when standing on their heads. But everything would have to be strapped down, including the crew until it was time for the rocket to back down and decelerate to the moon four days later.

On the moon the pilot would not find those craters as such, at least they would not be extinct volcanoes, but peltings that had hit the moon from an outside atmosphere, and left huge circular indentations, some as wide as 150 miles.

Simon Newcomb described the moon as a world without weather on which nothing happens. Apparently that's why there is such a frenzy to get there. It might be the sanitarium of the solar system.

But four days is a long time for such a short trip. Fritz Lang produced a picture years ago in Germany called Frau im Mond and the rocket got to the moon and back in two hours of playing time. George Pal produced Destination Moon in Hollywood in 1950 and cut the round trip down to 90 minutes. Almost any planetarium can give a really comfortable trip to the moon and back and by removing all the fictional sex appeal considered essential in motion pictures, complete the voyage in 45 minutes. In fact Dr. Dinsmore Alter, director of the Griffith Park Observatory, Los Angeles, has taken more than 100,000 persons on such trips since 1935. But magnetic energy engineers believe that anybody who has mastered magnetic propulsion can go from the moon to the earth in two seconds on a flying saucer. That puts the rocket ship realists practically back among the buggy whips.

Illustrations of Immanuel Velikovsky's Worlds In Collision (Doubleday) portraying balls of fire striking wide-mouthed primitive men whose only weapon was a spear were by no means as convincing as Bonestell's astronomically certified illustrations in Ley's The Conquest of Space, but the net result in both instances seemed to move the whole subject back to the days when Camille Flammarion's features were the life of Hearst's American Weekly. That was in the good old days when agnostics read the magazine sections instead of either going to church or reading the comic sections.

Waldemar Kaempffert, science editor of The New York Times and the author of Science Today and Tomorrow and a history of astronomy, took the view that were it not for the years it took Velikovsky to compile his hundreds of citations and footnotes "a critical reader might well wonder if this quasi-erudite outpouring is not an elaborate hoax designed to fool scientists and historians."

Oddly, neither Kaempffert nor any other first-rate critic seemed to observe the deadly parallels between Worlds in Collision and H. S. Bellamy's Moons, Myths and Men, which was published by Harpers in 1938, a year before Velikovsky landed in America after a strange Odyssey that took him from Russia, to Montpellier, Edinburgh, Berlin (where he studied medicine), Palestine (where he practiced it), Zurich, and Vienna before almost burying himself alive in the Low Library of Columbia University only to emerge after ten years with not only *Worlds In Collision* but *Ages in Chaos* and *The Orbit*-a stupendous tribute to the art of learning even if much of it wasn't so in the first place.

But why has the astrohistorical continuity from Bellamy to Velikovsky been ignored by practically the whole critical fraternity? Both set down biblical catastrophes and miracles side by side with cosmic disturbances, except that Bellamy is more enthralled by what the moon did and Velikovsky by Venus.

Bellamy's main concern was not planetary conflicts but the popularizing of Hans Hoerbiger's *The Cosmic Ice Theory*. He even went into the fall of cosmic material, fragments of which could easily be confused with flying saucers. Hoerbiger's book, incidentally, was snowed under by the First World War, having been first published on the eve of combat. It failed to work itself free of that blizzard until 1925 when the battle for and against his glacial theory started anew.

Indeed, in warming up to Hoerbiger's subject, Bellamy carried the torch as well for Charles Fort without quite realizing it.

The Cosmic Ice Theory, which considers the moon as a body composed of ore minerals covered with ice, contends that it was captured out of space not so many thousands of years ago.

Bellamy has a very snug theory of the birth of our solar system, which comes out of capture itself followed by a subsequent generative explosion. He shows hydrogen, oxygen, water, steam and ice going through aerial gymnastics through millions of years and reduces one operation to a particularly impressive design. He takes a group of orbital cones. Mercury is deepest inside. Venus is outside of Mercury. The Earth has the next outside position, then the Moon, and then Mars. Bellamy moves the cones from their widest diameters to their points. You see the Earth's capture of Luna, which is the present state of things. Next, coming up, you see the end of Mercury, then the capture of Mars, then the end of Venus, then the end of the Earth. If Mars slips by uncaptured it will finally plunge into the sun and will do that before the Earth does. It will be Bellamy's trick of the light-year, if it comes off.

In the capture of the planet Luna by Terra, Bellamy gave a blow-by-blow description that almost seemed as if he had a ringside seat. Instead of being 220,000 miles away in space and 10,000 to 15,000 years away in time, he wrote as if he were right there when it happened. The moon, it seems, had dodged an open trap many times before its capture. This was due to the fact that it lagged behind the earth in those days. Then it began moving somewhat faster than our earth, and on the next elliptical swoop around it could not resist the earth's superior gravitational pull. It thereby became completely entangled, as if caught in the earth's tendrils, and henceforth was no longer an independent planet. It became a satellite of the earth.

Before its capture it was brighter than Venus and seemingly growing in mass (as viewed of course by earth-bound observers) until it appeared sixteen times its normal size. A sudden shock, according to Bellamy, sent trembling crowds to their knees, a series of throes and tremors sent them groveling in the dust. From above and below came a thundering, rumbling, roaring, raging voice. The houses heard it and crashed. The trees shivered into splinters. The hills reeled, and the earth opened up its womb and fire flashed forth. Dust storms swept over the survivors. Then from the north and the south, waves mountain-high swept over the land, drowning all but a very few in a cold, cold sea.

Thus Bellamy describes the capture of the moon. (Velikovsky applies most of the same stage directions to the tail of Venus swishing close to the earth, but the general idea is the same.) A little thing, the moon, compared to the size of the earth, but it was big enough to pull the earth out of shape, making it bulge more at the equator, flatten more at the poles, and leaving there barren and ice-bound, where once they had supposedly enjoyed a temperate climate.

Curious, where one writer will prove that the poles had mild temperatures before being squeezed of their human juices by citing examples of prehistoric monsters found buried with grass still in their teeth, others will use these skeletons to prove that the upheavals threw these monsters from their equatorial homelands to the arctic areas.

Velikovsky himself, unaided by melodramatic illustrations, had worked long of course to prove that such things as the opening of the Red Sea, the flood that enveloped all except Noah and his Ark, Joshua and his transfixed sun, and such recordings of the Old Testament, were matched by similar occurrences on many other places of the earth as well. The Exodus became the sufferings of man caused by the gaseous tail of Venus, at that time a comet-a brush which pulled the earth out of shape, and consequently submerged land in some places and raised mountains in others, while pelting the earth with meteorites, flaming rocks and steam-

BEHIND THE FLYING SAUCERS

ing air. (Does it differ essentially from Bellamy's mad moon?)

Velikovsky, like many others attempting to fit phenomena into a plausible mosaic, constantly strove for a figure that would show some order in all this chaos. He settled on fifty-two. By stretching forty years of wandering in the desert and adding twelve years between the crossing of the Jordan and the battle of Beth-horan, he managed to come out with fifty-two years between the crossing of the Red Sea and Joshua's command to the sun to stand still. He found two catastrophes in old Mexico which also had a fifty-two-year span.

When the planet Venus moved closer to the earth and passed on without catastrophe, that was listed as a near miss. When Moses told his people to hallow the fiftieth year, this too was worked out to be really fifty-two years. Lucifer became, through Velikovsky's painstaking research not a fallen angel but a fallen star. He pointed out that the Arab name for the planet Venus was Al-Uzza, giving rise to the suspicion that Venus was a comet before it became a planet-a belief supported by early Greek philosophers, because "comet" is derived from the word "hair" and the tail of the comet looked like the hair of a goddess being blown backward by the wind.

The pressure of such a comet's tail could distort the shape of the earth in passing and make it appear as if the sun had stood still. A rain of meteorites would in all probability follow such a comet's sweep past this earth, and fortify the theory of magnetic research scientists who point out that meteors are composed of metals which make them actually giant magnets.

Velikovsky even advanced the suggestion that the battles Homer described in the Iliad really referred to Venus and Mars. Since that conflict, Mars and the earth approach each other amicably every fifteen years. The earth rotates in twenty-three hours, fifty-six minutes, and four seconds. Mars rotates in twenty-four hours, thirty-seven minutes, and twenty-seven seconds. For all practical purposes this leaves these two planets on friendly, almost synchronized, terms. This alone could account for the suspicion that the space ships, people insist they see, might be guided by nosy neighbors who are just as interested in our planet as we are in theirs.

Velikovsky's first book knocked out Darwin's theory of evolution, which was dying a slow death anyway as a theory, and modified Newton's laws of gravitation, which researchers in the field of electromagnetic energy had modified before either Velikovsky or Einstein got around to it.

Velikovsky and Bellamy suffer a parting of the ways at this point, because Velikovsky saw shifts in planets but no liquidations in the foreseeable future, whereas Bellamy moved all planets in this solar system to an explosive end, the way he believed they began. Otherwise, the two have a lot in common. And both of them fortify those scientists who believe that the planets in our solar system are really giant magnets. Indeed the magnetic research men describe the earth as a

BEHIND THE FLYING SAUCERS

big dynamo wrapped in magnetic lines of force. From this they argue that anybody who can master propulsion on these lines of force could fly around the planet with the speed of light, and if he could overcome the repelling lines of say Venus and Terra he could move from one planet to any other planet as easily as we step from a moving stairway to a lingerie department of a department store.

To say Velikovsky may have something in his theory that everything from the sun to the moon is an electromagnetic dynamo, is to ask for the back of the hand from such as Waldemar Kaempffert. Nevertheless, he has.

BEHIND THE FLYING SAUCERS

Chapter 5
The Lunar Fringe

IN ASTRONOMY, it may be a long voyage from the lunar to the lunatic, but they frequently cross each other's orbits when the subject of flying saucers comes up. In fact, one of the hardest things serious men in the field have to deal with is the partisans they attract to themselves.

It should of course be no reflection on a magnet that some of the steel filings it picks up spent their youth in a Nazi hand grenade, or were rust on the bars of a madhouse. But juries do have a weakness for such irrelevancies, however much a judge may warn them to ignore such things.

Some of the supporters of flying saucers have rocked even me, a man with the balance of Gibraltar. It might be a mark of discretion to hide them in a closet, but unbelievers would find them and seek to blow up the whole case with such concealed evidence.

One pro-Saucerian, a most fantastic witness, even submitted photographs of God with his brief. His case was that flying saucers were connected with the throne of God "a spiritual nebulous, standing 49 trillion miles in height." His photograph was taken through a one-hundred-inch telescope on an exposure of 4 hours 47 minutes.

Like Immanuel Velikovsky he was able to drag in Ezekiel, Ephah, Zechariah, and other Old Testament prophets, to back up his contentions. The angels referred to by the prophets were really flying saucers and could travel far faster than light—372,400 miles per second, according to this photographer's cosmographlex. He had been spotting flying saucers since 1922 seven in all by 1950—and had exchanged information with everybody from the late Robert Ripley to Dr. Walter S. Adams of Mt. Wilson Observatory. Seemingly, they all agreed he had photographed God, and even the Century of Progress at Chicago in 1934 had found a place for his camera's revelations.

The flying saucers, he stoutly maintained, were not people from other planets snooping around this earth. They were chariots of fire that angels employed for space travel when sent by the Almighty on certain missions. The first report on them could be found in Zechariah, chapter 5, verses 1 and 2. That was in 519 B.C. Their size was given: "20 cubits in length and 10 cubits in breadth."

Lest this confuse those who think of a saucer as round or oval and having diameter rather than length and breadth, the celestial photographer added, "You don't have to be an Einstine (sic) to figure that out."

I suppose he was referring to the scientist who usually spelled his name Einstein.

By referring to Ezekial, chapter 1, verses 8 to 26, this Wyoming research scholar was able to describe flying saucers in detail. They were a wheel in the middle of wheels. Their wings were so high they were dreadful. He interpreted this to mean that they must have been more powerful than radar. They reached from the earth to the Throne of the Almighty. When the living creatures were lifted up the wheels (saucers) were lifted up, "for the spirit of life was in the wheels."

The Wyoming scholar explained that meant that "the spirit of God was in the flying saucers" and he warned all, particularly Air Force pilots, "don't never try to shoot down a flying saucer," or you will be "instantly crisped up" as were those who pursued flying saucers in army planes over Fort Knox.

It would be easy not to take such a scholar and his cosmographic findings too seriously, but how about believers in St. Joseph Cupertino who had the gift of levitation? He reportedly had it so marked that he was ordered to desist by his superiors. Once he saw a man falling from a roof and by employing his heavenly powers stopped the man in mid-air. Then remembering his vow of obedience he sought the permission of a superior before allowing the laws of gravity to complete their earthly mission. Even so, he intervened enough to let the man down gently.

Then there are the Lost Planet boys. Ever since Ceres was discovered, and that goes back to 1801, there have been hunters of the heavens trying to piece a planet together, which they are certain blew up between us and the Sun. More than 1,200 such asteroids have been listed; 50,000 believed to exist. Hermes, the smallest, measures, one mile in diameter; Vesta, 240 miles.

On the assumption that the asteroids are exploded bits of a planet not unlike the Earth, they would be neither balls of fire nor balls of ice. They would, in fact, be just the right temperature to be used as stepping stones by space ships. In fact, the smaller ones might be hauled into our orbit and given the job of space stations along the asteroid way.

The example of the Arizona asteroid, which if it had landed in midtown Manhattan instead of Arizona could have wrecked the whole city, does not seem to sober the Lost Planet boys. It was composed like any meteorite of magnetically attractive metals. But in hitting this earth at seven miles per second it got burned so badly by the resistance of our atmosphere that it was set on fire. This is what hap-

BEHIND THE FLYING SAUCERS

pens when a meteor gets out of line. Imagine what would happen if some space-ship wrecking crews tried to move one around in the heavens!

Not quite so far out in space nor so far back in time as the Wyoming biblical scholar nor St. Joseph Cupertino, nor the Lost Planet boys, were the Borderland Sciences Research Associates. Between 1945 and 1950 they appeared with bulletins almost as often as a flying saucer was reported, and that, for a while, was almost daily.

Set up in San Diego and Los Angeles and dually directed by N. Meade Layne and Max Freedom Long, BSRA were interested in happenings which orthodox or official science could not or would not investigate-"such as the officially 'damned' facts which Charles Fort and his associates studied at great length."

Among these were "the problems of underground races" and "the origin and nature of the ether ships and other unknown aircraft now visiting our planet."

Before treating their researches to a fraction of the length their own round-robin bulletins, pamphlets, and mimeographed books have done, perhaps it would be a brisk and possibly revolting therapy to give an example of what they mean by a borderland science.

This underground race problem they refer to was advanced by Paxson C. Hayes, "a discoverer," according to Who's Who, "of mummified remains of an ancient Mongoloid civilization and lost city in Sonora, Mexico." He one time managed the political destinies of Brigadier General Herbert C. Holdridge, U.S.A. retired, and myself when we ran for governor and lieutenant governor of California, and that one never got off the ground either.

A man of assured convictions Hayes believed the mummies he unearthed lived in huge caves 9,000 feet deep as long ago as 23,000 B.C. Unlike Saucerians of today they were reported to be big men, at least seven feet tall. Hayes found their remains far below the levels of civilizations which have come and gone since.

How many civilizations are buried between the presently accepted six feet of sod and the center of the earth 4,000 miles below, Hayes didn't know, but he claimed at least five have been lost.

He believed this earth was a ball of fire thrown off by the sun (the first hydrogen bomb), millions of years ago, took its place in the orbit of the planets and tried to keep up a long-range battle of bombarding the sun with its own radioactive rays and getting pelted back until a leaded vapor was formed between them. This currently circles Hayes's concept of the earth, as the rings encircle Saturn, to a height of 800 miles.

The earth began to cool off. Not all at once of course. In fact it blew hot and cold for a long time. The center of the earth remained a ball of fire. The contractions and expansions indicated something had to give and so, according to Hayes, the ends blew out. Nice warm caves were the result. People moved there.

It is a Hayesean guess that the atomic explosions have stirred these underground people into a curiosity and they have flown out of their caves at the terminal ends of the earth (polar vents), and are cruising around on magnetically-directed saucers trying to determine what manner of neighbors have taken to living upstairs.

This would explain, according to Hayes, the Chilean Navy's Saucerian reports in the spring of 1950.

He didn't share the view of other borderland scientists that the space ships had come from outside our atmosphere. Asteroids would knock them around like ping-pong balls. He believed they came from down under. Away down under.

Thus softened by a subterranean attack on his credulity, the reader may prove an easier victim for other borderland scientists, many of whom, though otherwise quite sane, take even more fantastic liberties with academic and industrial scientists than does Paxson Hayes.

To the ribaldry attending testimony that the crews of flying saucers were dwarfs or little people, a doubt which even Associate Hayes shares, the Borderland Sciences Research Associates advanced a solution. In fact, they advanced two. One was that the Etherians suffer shrinkage when they and their craft penetrate into this atmosphere too rapidly. The other was they chose to materialize in small forms "simply for convenience of operation and flight."

And why are they here in the first place? Because it may be their intention to prevent destruction of the omniverse by makers of hydrogen bombs, an eventuality that could prove as deteriorating to them as to us. "Unfortunately," added one BSRA, "not everyone will find the explanation easily understandable."

What explanation? Well, Mead Layne's for one. His mimeographed booklet published by BSRA in 1950 was entitled: *Flying Discs: The Ether Ship Mystery and Its Solution.*

Though Meade Layne was its author, other borderland associates, notably Millen Cooke, John A. Hilliard, and Edward S. Schultz, contributed. Together they hadn't the slightest doubt about the presence of flying saucers in our atmosphere, nor the likelihood that some have landed, crewed by little men.

They called them ether ships, and claim they were manned by Etherians. Since BSRA opened its doors to metaphysicians, theosophists, mediums, trances, and students of the occult, it is a little difficult to reduce their far-flung beliefs to the confines of a book as small as this. They have been exchanging information among themselves and their associates for years and have quite a library of papers dealing with everything from the Problem of Disk Propulsion by Hilliard to the Mystery of Ether Ships, as edited by Layne.

"The basic statements," one bulletin reported, "concerning etheric origin of ether craft come to us from the 'other side.' They were first made in the fall of 1946 by the trance controls of the medium, Mark Probert, during a sitting held in the city of San Diego."

They do not agree with the Air Force which announced officially after Christmas, 1949 that no genuine and factual basis for the belief in flying saucers exists. They insist they do exist and feel it necessary to inform at least their public to mitigate the danger of panic if and when the facts become officially recognized.

They do not believe the saucers come from a foreign and unfriendly government or even another planet. Neither Russia, Venus, nor Mars figure in their explanations of the source of these space ships. They not only do not believe they are not constructed by a foreign power, but they also do not believe they are put together by our own authorities.

They believe they come from a place they call Etheria, which to them is one of the seven planes between this earth and the next planet. They touch a possibility that the ether ships travel along magnetic meridians, north and south. They have explanations too as to why these planes seem to appear and disappear, and give off various colors which are confused with vapor trails.

A widely circulated story that these saucers originated from a mother ship at least ten miles long and more than five hundred miles above our earth, a giant airship thought to be revolving around the earth at enormous speed, but slowing down even so, seemed to derive from Oahspe, according to borderland scientists. This is a book which described Etherians as ancestors of both the Chinese and Aryan races-originators of the Sanskrit language, but long removed as taxpayers on this earth.

According to the borderland scientists, four-fifths of our world lies outside our normal range of vision.

Flying saucers are observed when they slow down-much as the blades of a plane's propeller are countable when the speed of their revolutions approaches zero. They give credence to the belief that several of these ether ships have fallen and the contents examined in utmost secrecy.

"There is no motor," one borderland report said, "no propeller nor any mechanism inside the falling disks, so far as we have been able to learn. The outer skin of the falling disks is harder than steel and is an unidentified substance."

They hold to the belief that from nothing, no thing was ever born. They illustrate if you hold a magnet over a nail, a miracle occurs. The nail jumps as if prodded by demons. It was first believed nothing existed between the magnet and the nail so scientists postulated the presence of ether.

This assumption becomes an eight-lane boulevard of travel among borderland scientists, whose "postulates" seemingly have the value among their associates of infallibility.

The borderland scientists informed newcomers in the field, who may feel at a loss to count all the states in the union, and who therefore look bewildered at the word "Etheria," that the place has been known to occultists, adepts, and initiates "for thousands of years." They quote Cory's translation of *Ancient Fragments* and Blavatsky's *Isis Unveiled*.

BEHIND THE FLYING SAUCERS

In *The Ethership Mystery and Its Solution* Layne says: "In spite of a policy and an unofficial censorship, it is widely believed by this time that a number of ether ships of the disk type have landed in the United States, through accident of some kind. We have no reports that any of the 'dwarf' occupants survived the landing, and we are told that the propulsion and control of these craft is very much of a puzzle to scientists who have inspected them. They are said to be without motors, propellers, or anything recognizable as a drive mechanism. This suggests, of course, some kind of magnetic propulsion. And the performance of these crafts, their extraordinary speed, power and maneuverability far outclasses anything our own engineers have been able to achieve."

Obviously some of these men have either contacted magnetic engineers who researched flying saucers reported in the Denver lecture, or had access to sources of material of scientists who had researched some of the ships.

John A. Hilliard, of the borderland associates, gives an entertaining theory as to the propulsion of these ships. He takes the analogy of a piece of steel heated to a thousand degrees above normal, and points out it will stretch .00743 of an inch. If this could be done three million times a second and the steel directed to move along in one direction like an inchworm, the bar would move along at 1,254.59 miles per hour.

From here he goes into even greater speculation-and then tosses the baton to Edward Schultz, a fellow believer in the theory that this is a septenary universe and that everything goes by sevens. (We now have 52's, 9's and 7's as secrets of the universe.)

Leaning on the "abundant and irrefutable observations of thousands of persons who claimed they have seen flying disks," Schultz concedes that the originators of these space ships are centuries ahead of us in their science, that they make the transition from one plane to another independent of air for support, and that they can travel at terrific speed. He adds that there is reason to suppose that they travel to other planets and if sufficiently provoked on this one they can retaliate in a manner to set the world "into a frenzy of misinterpretation and fear." He postulates further than the force of gravity at their place of origin may be twice what ours is, thereby giving the pilot a greater freedom of movement here.

The theory that these ships may travel on alternate currents of intense heat which would expand and contract their skins, was a postulation derived from a Science News Letter of 1949 in which Dr. J. D. Cobine, General Electric engineer, reported that he had generated enough heat to melt tungsten. (Tungsten at that time had the highest melting point known—3,370 degrees centigrade.) The heart of the electronic torch was a tube known as a magnetron, which produced radio waves of one billion cycles per second. The jet flame was nine inches long, and though the heat it generated was strong enough to melt down tungsten, the jet itself, it is claimed, wasn't particularly hot.

BEHIND THE FLYING SAUCERS

It is a short step from here to applying the discovery to the propulsion of space ships. Assuming their outer skins could move like an earthworm's and that the intense outside heat would not burn up the passengers inside the ship, the concept is not too fantastic for even intermediaries in the field of science.

Unfortunately, these borderlanders rarely take the middle way. They go from science to fantasy. They suspect that in an earlier civilization the survivors of a previous collapse immigrated to another chemical island in space. Etherians, it appears, populate planes around several planets and the ones observed in flying disks here, the borderland researchers believe, might be coming from an area surrounding Venus, Mars, and even Saturn.

They believe that the Etherian observers are hundreds of years ahead of us in their knowledge of sound and speed. No doubt they have caught disturbances on this earth; such as our explosions from our atomic proving grounds in New Mexico and our atom bombs in Japan and at Bikini. They are curious to know what is causing these disturbances. If disturbed themselves by attacks of persistent pursuit, these Etherians, we are assured, have the power to disintegrate every earth-made production from a hydrogen bomb to the jet plane that might have dropped it.

Because of the diffusion of their pseudo-scientific interests in an age of specialization, the borderland scientists, up to now, have had a difficult time getting themselves taken seriously. They, in turn, have found it hard to absorb some of the dogmatic writings of those on the outer edges of their scope of inquiry.

Grant them that it is possible to change $H2O$ from a solid to a liquid, to a gas (that is, from ice to water to steam), and they will move forward with Saucerian dispatch and insist that it is equally possible for little men in the ether beyond our atmosphere to materialize space ships from thoughts of space ships; easier, in fact, than it is for a carpenter to materialize a table from a thought of a table by building what is in his mind from material that is within reach of his body.

Such a space ship would be visible, they contend, once it came within the three remaining planes which are within our perception-at least within the perception of those who are occultists, mediums, adepts, clairvoyants, vortexans, serious students of Oahspe, or specialists in astral-etheric-mental deep trances.

As the borderland scientists warn writers and publishers that they have a high duty not to treat these phenomena with ridicule, because even at the eleventh hour things can and do happen for the first time, it would be flying in the face of storm warnings perhaps for me to do so.

The Hindus illustrated the fallacy of a barrel supposedly full of apples, by putting a bushel of rice between the apples and a sack of flour between the grains of rice. The idea was to show that there is no such thing as *nothing* and no such thing as *full*. The borderland boys use this to fill in the empty space between here and their Etheria and once you admit that by concentrating on it you can see particles in the air, they will proceed to fill it with everything from rice to little men in space ships carrying apples, ships which can be seen and then not seen, depending on how fast the power is being put on and off, which is the key to their propulsion-materialization and dematerialization.

In advancing this theory of materialization and dematerialization the borderland scientists believe they have a secret (which they call MAT and DEMAT) of the propulsion behind space ships.

You might get a better idea of what they mean by this MAT and DEMAT by observing the workings of an electric newspaper or flash-cast in Times Square, New York. These intelligences materialize through a series of small dots and dashes. Lights go on and off according to a design. The total effect is a flow in a certain direction. A space ship might conceivably scoot through the atmosphere on such an on-and-off current.

Anatomically if a caterpillar could be speeded up to thousands of miles a second, he too would serve as a good example of what these men believe is the type of propulsion behind ether craft.

They have another bait line to believability and that is the spectrum of color. They believe there are colors far beyond what has been so far accepted by the physicists, and since the color spectrum was widened a good deal by the Bunsen and Kirchoff discoveries, they do not believe it is the mark of a true research scholar to close off both ends of the spectrum and say, "This far and no further." They insist there are colors we can not see, sounds we cannot hear, and solid bodies which we can not discover by touch.

Oddly, seeing things which may not be there is not considered by psychiatrists but hearing things puts you within recognizable distance of the 20,000,000 crackpots currently adjudged insane in America.

Since every physicist knows now that colors have their wave lengths-from red with 0.0007594 cms. to violet with 0.0003968 cms.-how can we dismiss without a hearing the testimony of others exploring beyond present-day frontiers who claim they have additional wave lengths and can even see flying saucers before the rest of us can? They will point out to you that there are animals that cannot see the colors that we see. On the other hand, there are animals that hear sounds inaudible to us. Beyond the supersonic is the ultrasonic, and beyond ultrasonic, they ask, who knows?

"Seriously," they sum up, "what we face in the ether ship situation is far from amusing. On the face of it we have what seems an equal chance of utter disaster, or of making in a few years the leap from our present bedeviled condition into a comparatively golden age of knowledge, reason, and morality."

They point out that men of scientific reputation have remained cautiously silent about ether ships and in some instances have joined or led the popular course of derision. But these scientists are obviously not among the borderland scientists.

BEHIND THE FLYING SAUCERS

Chapter 6
Hoaxers and Saucers

LOWEST in the list of air-minded persons, and therefore likely to be unworthy of the compassion of even the Air Force checkers, were those Machiavellians who have joined the secret manufacturers of hoaxes. Suspects on the lunatic fringe might presumably be cured of their personal hallucinations or participation in a mass hysteria, but the fabricators of hoaxes belonged understandably on the cold side of the moon, the side we never see.

Such a sentence would be mild enough, but did the cloistered characters who knew life almost exclusively in terms of the five walls of the Pentagon know a hoax from a hot potato? They picked up at least one such hot potato and described it as a hoax and haven't heard the end of it yet.

A bomb that refuses to explode is called a dud. In other words, a hoax. Does that make the Air Force believe less in bombs? Many hoaxes have been perpetrated in the name of flying saucers, but like the duds among bombs, that shouldn't lull people into believing there are no such things as bombs or flying saucers.

Anything as lively as a flying saucer is bound to excite lively imaginations, and among such imaginations one has emerged now and then with a story that seemed almost foolproof. But founded on fiction, reared on faith, it invariably died, if it were a hoax, of overexposure.

It is generally believed that to be any party to a hoax spells ruin, once the hoax is exposed. Nothing is further from the facts. The exposure of the Locke hoax did not ruin *The New York Sun*, any more than Lincoln Colcord's exposure of Joan Lowell's *Cradle of the Deep* ruined Simon and Schuster or Orson Welles's realistic broadcast of H. G. Wells's *The War of the Worlds* destroyed either C.B.S., Trenton, N. J., or Orson Welles.

Nevertheless, no one wants to be either a collaborator or a dupe in such a literary lollypop if he can avoid it.

In general a fair backlog of believable data has to be accumulated before a hoax can be tried with hope of any degree of success. You just can't pull off a practical joke about something no one ever heard of before. That's why Richard Adams Locke's hoaxes in the Sun back in 1835 were so successful. They not only were well written but they dealt with men on the moon and were supported by the best astronomical data of the era. They claimed, moreover, to be reprints of articles from the Edinburgh Journal. They supposedly reported the findings of Sir John Herschel, a British astronomer busy at the time making observations at the Cape of Good Hope, South Africa.

There actually was such an astronomer. He was the son of Sir William Herschel, the man who in 1787 discovered Titania and Oberon-the last two satellites to be identified with the Planet Uranus.

The telescope that presumably revealed habitation on the moon was described by Locke as a 288-inch job. As the much advertised mirror at the Palomar Observatory near San Diego is only 200 inches, you can get some idea of how far ahead Locke's imagination was of present-day facts.

In subsequent installments to his first article, which appeared on August 25, 1835, grass, trees, animals, and eventually bat-men, and of course their female counterparts, began to circulate on the pages of the Sun as well as the surface of the moon. The paper climbed to a circulation in excess of 19,000, giving it pre-eminence over all Anglo-Saxon newspapers of the day. The articles were subsequently printed in pamphlet form.

Two Yale professors played the main roles in the eventual expose, but the Sun didn't suffer in the least by their proofs of fraud. It grew in stature and died in 1950 at the ripe old age of 117, tending to support the theory that a reputation however acquired ("If you read it in the Sun it's so") tends to become hallowed if held on to long enough. Like all old Sun men, I have a copy of the first issue published in 1833, but I have never seen any issues of the days of its greatest notoriety.

At the close of the Civil War there was another outburst of strange tales from skies. Most of them, like Jules Verne's *From the Earth to the Moon* and *Around the Moon*, and Achille Eyraud's *Voyage To Venus*, were frankly science-fiction pieces, but in *Rockets* Willy Ley recorded one that came nearer to the Locke format. It was called *Beyond the Zodiac* by Percy Greg. It was printed in German in four volumes, presumably as a translation.

Ley, a zealous research scholar, claimed he never was able to find the "original" and naturally fell back on the suspicion that the German translation was actually the original, following the lines of Locke's "reprints" from the *Edinburgh Journal.*

Of course much of the early astronomical literature shows a recklessness with facts that leaves the scientist walking a tight rope and frequently falling into what amounts to a hoax of his own making. Franz von Paula Gruithuisen, for example, started out by discovering a walled city on the moon. Then he moved into discovering a moon for Venus. After that he was sure he detected life on Venus. He traced

BEHIND THE FLYING SAUCERS

a particularly bright period of the planet's life to a festival in honor of a newly-crowned Emperor of Venus.

It turned out the walled city was at best some dead mountains; the moon of Venus, a distant star; and the Emperor of Venus, hardly more than a musical-comedy character.

That contemporary arts, sciences, and professions are free from hoaxes, I would be the last to contend. While deep in this opus in the spring of 1950 I received a telephone call from Jack Paar of radio fame. It was on the night of March 29. He told me that KTTV, a West Coast television outlet of the Columbia Broadcasting System, had just cut in on a program to announce that big news would be released at 9 P.M., Pacific Coast Time. That would be an hour later.

Unable to bear the strain, he called the television station and said it was an outrage to do that with news. But the station manager said he could do nothing about it, not till 9 P.M. anyway.

At the appointed hour Roy Maypole, public service director of the station, flashed photographs of a saucer-shaped aircraft which was claimed could start and stop like a polo pony. Fired by turbojets, it could hover at zero or scoot to 550 miles per hour.

It was suggested that possibly these ships were the saucers people thought they saw flying around and if so the pilots in the disks were Navy men-a branch of the service which doesn't cater to men 23 to 40 inches tall, even when it employs disk jockeys for public work.

Jack Paar reported to me as soon as the telecast was over and I was able to calm him by telling him that the flying saucer in question sounded like a Chance Vought job originally designed by Charles Zimmerman in 1933 and tried out in 1942 under the description of V 173. When the Navy first announced it had the ship its spokesman said it was the only plane that offered both extremely high speed and extremely low speed in one machine.

At the time only one had been made and thereafter not much was heard of it. It is now listed in Jane's as XF5U.

The next day the Los Angeles Times, which has an interest in KTTV, made no mention of the sensational news of the night before, but an afternoon paper, the Los Angeles Mirror, which is owned by the same company, turned over its whole front page to a ballooned-up photograph of the ship and asked its readers across five columns:

THIS NAVY PANCAKE IS REAL
COULD IT BE A FLYING SAUCER?

It referred its readers to page 3 where a story began and ran over to page 12. All the previous suspicions were borne out by the story. It was just one of those things. It was our old friend, XF5U, alias V 173.

Now, this comes perilously close to a contrived hoax. It is designed to sell pa-

BEHIND THE FLYING SAUCERS

pers and nothing else. As of that day, March 30, 1950, it sold 195,000 copies, according to Virgil Pinkley, the Mirror's editor and publisher.

V-173 Prototype

XF5U

Somebody deserved a bonus, possibly the poor readers. If further speculation is not closed, the Mirror's editors might try a much more plausible follow-up. The Nazis had a squat little job, which by stretching the word a little here

and there, could be described as a "saucer." It was jet-powered, and was believed to be capable of a speed of 1500 miles per hour. What became of it?

By April 3, XF5U, alias V 173, was revolving out of Washington, D. C. under imprime' of both the A.P. and U.P., which in turn leaned on an article in the *U.S. News and World Report* for support. They should have credited the *L. A. Mirror,* the originator of the story.

The news dispatches stated that these flying saucers were real aircraft of revolutionary design. They were developed in the United States by the Navy and were a combination of helicopter and fast jet plane. The models were built by engineers of the National Advisory Committee for Aeronautics.

Everybody printed this story, including *The New York Times* and the *New York Herald Tribune*. David Lawrence in his syndicated column quoted freely from the original too-without making reference to the fact that he was publisher of the *U.S. News and World Report.*

But the Navy and the Air Force reduced the "pancakes" or "saucers" to a lot of baloney. They denied that they had any such secret missile in operation, and said

BEHIND THE FLYING SAUCERS

it must have referred to an old thing they bought years before, tried out, found it anything but a success, and stored it in Maryland as a curiosity for a subsequent museum of aviation.

This was almost charging David Lawrence with manufacturing a hoax. Almost but not quite. In one of its official releases the Air Force listed several hoaxes about which it had no doubt.

It claimed the month of July, 1947 as a banner month for the practical jokers. A Seattle woman reported to the police that a flaming disk had landed on her roof. Quickly extinguished, the object was turned over to federal agents, who in turn had it checked by Navy electronic experts. They discovered it to be a twenty-eight-inch circular piece of plywood held in position by wire. The letters USSR and EYR were painted on the disk in white. There was of course a hammer and sickle on the disk as well. Two radio tubes and a cylindrical-shaped oil can, mounted on pieces of bakelite, were inside the object. There was also a cloth saturated with an inflammable fluid. The final consensus among Air Materiel Command Intelligence officers was that the disk could not fly and was the work of practical jokers.

The next one came from Shreveport, Louisiana. A saucer, whirling through the air, shooting smoke and fire, landed in a downtown street. This one was seemingly solved without recourse to either the FBI or Air Force Intelligence. The Shreveport police said it was the work of a prankster, who had launched the homemade disk from the top of an office building. The saucer had a fluorescent light starter and two electric fan condensers. It couldn't fly either.

Black River Falls, Wisconsin, was next in line among the hoaxes of 1947. Fashioned from plywood, this flying saucer was seen in flight. An electrician found it lying in the deep grass on the town's fair grounds. He proceeded to make it a side show at fifty cents a peek.

The police stepped in and put the gadget in a bank vault. It was subsequently analyzed at Mitchell Field. The report read "This contrivance is patently a hoax. It will be held for a reasonable time and then disposed of in the nearest ash receptacle."

Next in line in the July platter parade, was a disk from Danford, Illinois. This one had burned the weeds in the area in landing. It was revealed to be composed of plaster of Paris, bakelite-coiled form wrapped in enameled copper wire, an old-fashioned magnetic speaker diaphragm, parts of an electronic condenser and of a metallic magnetic ring.

But the big joker of July, 1947, according to the Air Force report of April 27, 1949, was one which involved Fred Crisman and Harold A. Dahl, previously respected citizens of Tacoma, Washington. According to the Air Force they rated number one among the nation's practical jokers and publicity seekers, at least as far as Project Saucer was concerned.

BEHIND THE FLYING SAUCERS

A few days after Kenneth Arnold had reported about the nine saucers he saw flying above Mt. Rainier, Dahl reported sighting six disks while he was patrolling off Maury Island, Washington. He said one of the disks fluttered to earth and disintegrated, showering his boat with fragments. The fragments killed his pet dog and caused other damage.

According to the government document, Dahl and Crisman then attempted to sell the story to a Chicago adventure magazine which in turn asked Kenneth Arnold to check it for errors. Arnold went to Tacoma with Captain Emil J. Smith, a United Airlines pilot, "who had also received saucer publicity," according to the Air Force digest, "when he reported seeing disks on the Fourth of July while on a routine flight out of Boise."

Arnold, a businessman who flew his own plane, arrived in Tacoma and there asked two officers of Army A2 Intelligence to help screen the claims of Dahl and Crisman.

"Thus," to quote the Air Force report again, "began a story of secret hotel meetings and mysterious anonymous telephone calls which ended in death for two of the participants and exposed the Tacoma disk story as a hoax."

All parties met at the Winthrop Hotel. There Dahl produced some fragments "which he alleged came from the disk which damaged his boat." He repeated the story in detail in the presence of Arnold and Smith and the identified Army Intelligence men.

The next day the A2 officers left to return to Hamilton Field, California, taking some of the fragments with them for technical analysis. But tragedy struck en route. The plane crashed, killing both officers. On board also was the crew chief and a hitchhiker. These parachuted to safety.

On the heels of the tragedy, Tacoma newspapers began receiving telephone calls informing them of the fallen ship which had been carrying flying disk fragments and that the plane had been shot down with a 20 mm cannon by saboteurs. The papers went along with the saboteur idea but the official Air Force opinion was that the crash revealed no indication of foul play.

On the day of the crash Captain Smith went with Crisman and Dahl to check on the damage the boat had suffered from the falling disk. Smith saw some repairs, but was not convinced that they were the result of the claimed incident of a falling disk.

"Later under questioning," the Air Force report concluded, "Crisman and Dahl broke and admitted that the fragments they had produced were really unusual rock formations found on Maury Island and had no connection with flying disks. They admitted telling the Chicago magazine that the fragments were remnants of the flying disks in order to increase the value of their story. During the investigations Dahl's wife consistently urged him to admit that the entire affair was a hoax, and it is carried as such in Project Saucer files."

BEHIND THE FLYING SAUCERS

Now, to check on the checkers. According to Fred L. Crisman, the Air Force report was so garbled and twisted as to bear no resemblance as to what actually happened. He said he had told Roy A. Palmer, editor of Amazing Stories (which seems to be the name of the publication the Air Force report bypassed), that he refused to write the story. He had been made an offer, but he had refused it as he had offers from several other publications.

As to the Air Force report that he and Dahl broke under questioning and admitted that the fragments they had secured were really unusual rock formations from Maury Island, "This," said Dahl, "is a bald-faced lie."

What, he wanted to know, became of the fragments aboard the ship that crashed? What became of the analytical reports that Palmer received and why did a West Coast check differ from that of the University of Chicago if they were the same substance? Why did the Air Force refuse to allow pictures of the crash? Why if he and Dahl were such blackguards as to deliberately cause the death of two Air Force pilots and the loss of a $150,000 plane did not some government agency clink them for damages in the courts?

"I was at the time active in reservist affairs of the Air Force," Crisman reported. "Why did not the Air Force call me to account for my dastardly actions? You know as well as I do that they would not take such shenanigans from a junior officer of the reserve without some form of punishment."

He had other things to say and he was telling the world if anybody perpetuated the Air Force version, he would institute legal action.

Editor Palmer of Amazing Stories confirmed what Crisman said. So did Kenneth Arnold, and the general verdict (the Air Materiel Command dissenting) was that Crisman did not perpetrate a hoax to sell an adventure story.

In fact, there was testimony that after the tragic crash which killed the two Army fliers, Crisman was ordered to take a flight to Alaska in any army plane, and the Air Force would hardly be reposing that trust in a reserve pilot, listed in their records as a perpetrator of a hoax, if they believed their own literature told the whole truth and nothing by the truth.

Instructed verdict for Defendant Crisman. But what happened to Dahl and the flying pieces from a flying disk? Up to April, 1950, nobody knew.

BEHIND THE FLYING SAUCERS

Chapter 7
The Air Force Reports

THOUGH THERE WERE stories printed to the effect that the Air Force had released just about everything it had gathered in the two years it operated Project Saucer, the nearest most peasants like ourselves came to such a feast of reason was a seven-thousand-word digest of preliminary studies released on April 27, 1949, by the Air Materiel Command at Wright- Patterson Air Force Base, Dayton, Ohio.

Project Saucer was officially activated on January 22, 1948. It released its digest of preliminary studies fifteen months later. It declared itself officially "discontinued" on December 27, 1949. But on April 4, 1950, it admitted that it had continued and would continue to receive and evaluate "through normal field intelligence channels any substantial reports of any unusual aerial phenomena."

This was the first official admission of a charge I made in January, 1950 that "Project Saucer had not closed down but only had dummied up." Its April 4 release admitted it had decentralized the chase.

As a further example of how badly synchronized these top level characters can become, on April 4, in a statement from Key West, wherein the President was dragooned into blowing down David Lawrence's story about flying saucers, Charles G. Ross, White House Secretary, told correspondents he would take their morning questions and report back with answers in the afternoon. He did so. He quoted Rear Admiral Robert L. Dennison as saying he knew nothing of the flying saucer. Then he had Brigadier General Robert B. Landry, the President's Air Force aide, explain that the Air Force had set up a project in December, 1947, and had "carried on this project until last August, 1949 when it made a final report there was nothing to these flying saucers."

The fact that the project did not cease until four months after General Landry said it was closed down and the further fact that it had opened a month after he said it had opened in December, 1947 are samples of how little team work or accuracy there is between the members of this team.

94

BEHIND THE FLYING SAUCERS

While it would have been nice to have had all the cards on the table, especially since the Department of Defense insisted it was not conducting experiments "classified or otherwise" with disk-shaped flying objects, nevertheless I suppose we should be thankful for the crumbs that have been allowed to drop from the banquet table.

In the first place let me say for a report of this character that the Air Materiel Command's Digest was supremely well-written, and aside from such typographical errors as the spelling of Henry Holt and Company as "Holte," Mt. Rainier as "Ranier," splitting infinitives, and such trivia, the report had a feeling of substance. It begins with the famous case of Kenneth Arnold, who on Tuesday, June 24, 1947, looked from his private plane and spotted a chain of nine saucer-like objects playing tag with the jagged peaks of Washington's Mt. Rainier.

Arnold's report set off what the Air Force's literary arm described as "a veritable celestial chain reaction." Flying saucers were followed by reports of chromium hub-caps whirling through space, flying dimes, flying teardrops, flying gaslights, flying ice cream cones, and flying pie plates.

It seems more fantastic than the fantastic reports that the Air Force could set up a Project Saucer if it had no more than this sort of fluff to begin with. Nevertheless, as it rounded the turn toward the home stretch in the spring of 1949, it revealed that it had looked into 240 domestic and 30 foreign incidents. With the assistance of government and private agencies and the entire facilities of Wright Field laboratories, the Project Saucer personnel said that in fifteen months they had identified about thirty per cent of the 270 cases under survey as being nothing more than conventional aerial objects-such as weather balloons, guided missile research activities, astronomical phenomena, commercial and military aircraft in unscheduled flights, migratory birds, shots from flare guns, practical jokers, victims of optical illusions, and phenomena of mass hallucinations. The official prognosis was that equally commonplace explanations would take care of at least another thirty per cent of these riddles of the sky.

But as of that spring day of 1949 Air Materiel Command Intelligence still admitted there were question marks in the saucer story. The possibility of technical development far in advance of the knowledge available to American engineers and scientists had been widely considered. That the saucers might be visitations from Mars, Venus, or distant planets attached to other star systems was looked upon by Air Materiel Command Intelligence as "an almost complete impossibility."

That, you will observe on re-reading, is not quite the same as saying "an impossibility." "Almost" is a little loop-hole, but if a flying saucer slipped through it, Air Materiel Command Intelligence could point to the fact that it had never quite closed the door.

Another cautious summary was this:

BEHIND THE FLYING SAUCERS

"While Project Saucer evaluation teams report that no definite and conclusive evidence is yet available to either prove or disprove the existence of at least some of the remaining unidentified objects as real aircraft of unknown and unconventional configuration. Exhaustive investigations have turned up no alarming probabilities."

As thin as that line was between life or death for flying saucers, thirty-four cases were left dangling in space, unidentified, unexplained, unburied when Project Saucer was officially closed December 27, 1949.

From the Digest of Air Materiel Command Intelligence, it is not possible for a detached observer to tell whether they believed they had identified Kenneth Arnold's nine flying saucers or not. At least three years after Arnold first reported the flying saucers he still maintained his position and has probably been more overwhelmed with reports of like character than any other civilian on earth.

His story is simplicity itself. He dealt in fire-control equipment and covered the Northwest in his private plane. On June 24, 1947, he saw the reflection of a bright flash on his wing, he looked around and caught a chain of nine peculiar aircraft approaching Mt. Rainier. They flew like geese in a diagonal line as if they were linked together. They flew close to the mountaintops. He judged them to be about the size of a DC-4. They were approximately twenty or twenty-five miles away, near enough for him to see if they had tails, but he couldn't see a tail on any of them. He watched them for about three minutes. They were flat like a pie pan and so shiny they reflected the sun like a mirror. He clocked their speed at about 1,200 miles per hour.

"I never saw anything so fast," he told investigators.

Air Materiel Command Intelligence put Professor Joseph A. Hynek, head of the Ohio State University Observatory, to work on the Arnold report. Dr. Hynek was under contract with Air Materiel Command to check on the astrophysicist phases of Project Saucer. Dr. Hynek thought the objects were traveling at subsonic speed and were therefore some sort of known aircraft.

Arnold had stated that they were traveling at 1,200 miles per hour, which would make them definitely supersonic.

I take it that Air Materiel Intelligence screens even its astronomers. Had it found itself saddled with Dr. Walter Lee Moore, astronomer of the University of Louisville, instead of Dr. Hynek of Ohio State University, it might have got a different story about flying saucers. Dr. Moore reported that he personally focused his telescope on several flying disks. They headed straight toward Venus. Venus was nearer to the sun-in its perigee phase. The day was clear. In fact the planet could have been seen that day during the daytime with the naked eye.

According to Dr. Moore the disks headed straight toward Venus on the return trip. This led him to suspect that as little as we know of what is going on behind those Venusian cloudbanks, Venus was the point of origin of those flying saucers which he saw and those which Kenneth Arnold saw.

But Aero-Medical Laboratory men instead of Dr. Moore were called in by Air Materiel Command Intelligence to needle Arnold's story. They stated that an object traveling at 1,200 miles per hour would not be visible to the naked eye.

But Arnold didn't say he looked at them with a naked eye, and the Aero-Medical Laboratory men, who of course were not up there with Arnold, never reported how fast Arnold's eyes might be at spotting objects twenty-five miles away and possibly scooting by him as he jogged along at 200 miles per hour. They never checked on Dr. Moore's either. In fact as far as I could find, Air Materiel Command Intelligence never evaluated, and, if so, never released Dr. Moore's report at all.

Among the filed-and-forgotten of Air Materiel Command Intelligence's "Unidentified File" was the Captain Thomas F. Mantell case, which everybody tried a hand at explaining until the scientist at the University of Denver came up with the real answer-magnetic disintegration at the hand of some intelligence which understands both magnetic propulsion and magnetic destruction.

Other cases which I presume Air Materiel Command Intelligence never solved-at least they were not solved in the unclassified handout which gentlemen of the press, ladies of the evening, or anybody could have for the asking-run to quite a formation, but the following few give you the general idea.

Listed as perhaps their most fantastic saucer story, the Air Materiel Command gave its version of the space ship reported by two Eastern Airline pilots in the skies near Montgomery, Alabama, in July, 1948. The same object was reported by ground observers at Robins Air Force Base at Macon, Georgia, about an hour before the commercial pilots sighted it above Montgomery. All the reports agreed the space ship was going in a southerly direction, that various colored flames were trailing from it and that it maneuvered with great speed.

The Eastern Airline pilots were Captain C. S. Chiles and John B. Whitte. They described the object as "a wingless aircraft a hundred feet long, cigar-shaped, and about twice the diameter of a B-29, with no protruding surfaces."

They both saw it at the same time and asked each other what in the world was this? It flashed toward them and they veered to the left. It veered to its left and passed them about 700 feet to their right. At this point it was above them.

"Then, as if the pilot had seen and wanted to avoid us," Chiles testified to investigators, "it pulled up with a tremendous burst of flame from the rear and zoomed into the clouds, its prop wash or jet wash rocking our DC3."

Captain Chiles said the illumination inside the craft itself reminded one of the brilliance of a magnesium flare.

From the side of the craft came an intense blue glow that ran the entire length of the fuselage-like a blue fluorescent factory light. The exhaust was a red-orange flame, which extended thirty to fifty feet behind the craft and became deeper in intensity as the unidentified ship pulled up into a cloud. The commercial pilots judged its speed to be about one-third faster than a jet's, which would mean about 800 miles per hour.

In their investigation of the Chiles-Whitte story Project Saucer personnel screened 225 civilian and military flight schedules and found the only other aircraft in the vicinity at the time was an Air Force C-47.

At this point came one of those impressive but bewildering contributions from Air Materiel Command Intelligence.

"Application of the Prandtl theory of lift to the incident indicated of the fuselage of the dimension reported by Chiles and Whitte could support a load comparable to the weight of an aircraft of this size at flying speeds in the subsonic range."

What in heaven's name does that mean? This is a digest of a report from one branch of the people to another branch of the people, but it certainly doesn't sound as though it were written by the people. The only possible clew as to what all this has to do with the case is that remark about "subsonic range," and even that doesn't seem quite bright. The commercial pilot said that the space ship was traveling about one-third faster than a jet. Jets can go faster than sound. Certainly a ship traveling one-third faster than even a common jet would be doing at least 800 m.p.h., and that's not subsonic; that's seventy miles per hour faster than sound.

But Prandtl, his theory, subsonic or supersonic to the contrary, Air Materiel Command left the object on April 27, 1949, as "still considered 'Unidentified.'"

Those southern skies in fact seem to have had almost as many reports of flying saucers as Oregon and New Mexico. Early in August, 1947, two pilots from Bethel, Alabama, told investigators that they spotted a huge black object which seemed bigger than a C-54. It stood out against a brilliant evening sky.

To avoid collision, the pilots had to pull up to 1,200 feet. The object crossed their path at right angles. They swung in behind and followed at 170 m.p.h. until it left them far behind and about four minutes later disappeared from sight.

Though described as resembling a C-54, this was a very general and somewhat erroneous classification. The two pilots further qualified the description by saying it was "without motors, wings, or visible means of propulsion, and was smooth surfaced and streamlined."

By way of closing the case, Air Materiel Command Intelligence concluded not without anticlimactic humor, "No balloons were reported in the area."

The famous case of Lieutenant George F. Gorman of the North Dakota National Guard, and his twenty-seven-minute dog fight with a flying saucer above Fargo, is recapitulated in the Air Materiel Command Digest of its preliminary studies, but this one doesn't even come out with the consoling words "still considered unidentified."

Gorman, a solid character, manager of a Fargo construction company was preparing to land at the Fargo airport on the night of October 1, 1948, after a routine F-51 patrol flight. Cleared by the tower to land, Gorman asked if there were any-

BEHIND THE FLYING SAUCERS

thing in his way, because he saw what appeared to be the tail light of another plane a 1,000 yards away. The tower told him there was a Piper Cub below him, and that was all. He could see that clearly enough, but that was not what he was alluding to.

He decided to close in and take a look at the mystery light a 1,000 yards ahead of him. It was small, clear and white, and it kept blinking on and off. As he approached, however, the light became sharp and steady and pulled into a sharp left bank.

"I thought it was making a pass at the tower," Lieutenant Gorman reported. "I dived after it and brought my manifold pressure up to 60 inches, but I couldn't catch up with the thing. It started gaining altitude and made another left turn."

Lieutenant Gorman put his F-51 into a sharp turn, and tried to cut the light off in its attempt to turn. By then they were 7,000 feet up. The light made a sharp right turn, and they were headed straight at each other. When they were about to collide, Gorman guessed he got scared.

"I went into a dive," he said, "and the light passed over my canopy at about 500 feet. Then, it made a left circle at about 1,000 feet above, and I gave chase again."

It looked as if they were headed for another collision, when this time it was a case of the light that failed. The object shot straight into the air. Lieutenant Gorman went after it to 14,000 feet, when his plane went into a power stall, and the lighted object turned to a northwest direction and disappeared.

The lieutenant reached his home field pretty worn out after that twenty-seven-minute chase, at speeds varying from 300 to 400 m.p.h.

Had the lieutenant come with this story on his own, he probably would have found it subsequently explained away by some psychiatrist consulted by Air Materiel Command Intelligence as just another man with another hallucination. But it so happened that the airport traffic controller at Fargo, L. D. Jensen, reported that he had watched the mystery light through a pair of binoculars, and while Gorman and Jensen could possibly both be wrong, two don't quite make a "mass hysteria."

Jensen said he was unable to distinguish any form other than what appeared to be the tail light of a very fast moving craft. Lieutenant Gorman, who was a pilot instructor for French military students during the Second World War, said he was sure there was an intelligence behind the maneuvers, and that it was limited by intelligence, too, because it was unable to make turns beyond the natural curves. That it could out-turn and out-speed the F-51 was also conceded. He doubted if many earth-born pilots could have withstood the turn and speed affected by the light without blacking out.

Except for raising a psychological question-Is it possible for an object without appreciable shape or known aeronautical configurations to appear to travel at variable speeds and maneuver intelligently?-Air Materiel Command Intelligence left Lieutenant Gorman and his light pretty much in the dark.

Again the answer to this one may be in the hands of the magnetic research engineers, scientists who seemingly were not consulted in the manufacture of this brochure.

From saucers six or eight inches in diameter, to those seeming to have the bulk of B-29's and the speed three times that of jets, the Air Force had its troubles clearing up that "Unidentified" file.

One more incident and I am done with Air Materiel Command's unsolved mysteries. This one took place 5,000 feet above sea level in the Cascade Mountains, where one Fred M. Johnson, a prospector, told of spotting five or six disks about thirty feet in diameter. He grabbed his telescope and watched the disks for fifty seconds while they banked in the sun. While the disks were in sight, the hand of his compass watch "weaved wildly from side to side."

Here was another magnetic clew, but like the solution of its other mysteries Air Materiel Command Intelligence, was leaning heavily on astronomers or psychiatrists and having no part of the Velikovskys, Einsteins, or Newtons, who had decided that this earth and all other planets in our solar system were just big dynamos governed by electromagnetic energy.

"To sum up," Air Materiel Command Technical Intelligence Division stated, "no definite conclusive evidence is yet available, that would prove or disprove the possibility that a portion of the unidentified objects are real aircraft of unknown or unconventional configuration."

The Digest concluded: "There are scores of possible explanations for the scores of different types of sighting reporters. Many of the aerial phenomena have been positively identified. However, the correct tagging of the remaining percentage is still the job of Project Saucer. The saucers are not a joke. Neither are they a cause for alarm to the population. Many of the incidents already have answers. Meteors. Balloons. Falling stars. Birds in flight. Testing devices, etc. Some of them still end in question marks. It is the mission of the Air Material Command Technical Intelligence Division's Project Saucer to supply the periods."

There must have been a high priority on punctuation marks between 1947 and 1950, because as late as May, 1950, months after Project Saucer was officially closed (but still operating unofficially on local levels), nobody in the Department of Defense, from the unidentified spokesman of Air Materiel Command Technical Intelligence up to Defense Secretary Louis Johnson himself, ever supplied those periods.

BEHIND THE FLYING SAUCERS

Chapter 8
From Fort to Fate

ALL THROUGH the saucerian sky-writings the Forteans must have sat around in their seminars grinning like contented cats. Thanks to the painstaking researches of their dead master, they could claim they foresaw Project Saucer and the reign of error.

In the *Books of Charles Fort* (Holt, 1941), which consists of *The Book of the Damned, Lo, Wild Talents*, and *New Lands*, all merged into one monumental volume of 1,125 pages (indexed), Fort has recorded thousands of examples of wild talents in our skies, some running back as far as three hundred years.

As Fort held that "if it's plausible, accept it at least temporarily" and that "nothing is of itself complete but is part of a continuous operation," this should make space ships from another planet very easy for the Fortean Society to accept-at least temporarily. For did he not say also if one temporarily accepts their existence one facilitates their arrival?

He listed strange tales which pure science rejected from 1597 to 1932. But he really didn't get going at his best until 1819. From there on the reports increased in numbers until they hit their top stride after the Civil War and in 1883 reached a peak of 32 listings—a record, incidentally, smashed to smithereens in the first four months of 1950 when 109 airborne oddities were listed.

By 1931 the depression had hit strange bodies in the skies as well as starved bodies on this lowly earth. Fort listed only 19 that year. The next year he tabulated a mere half dozen, and after that no more was heard from this amazing statistician of the sandlot sciences.

He died on May 3, 1932, at the Royal Hospital, the Bronx, and presumably sent no more reports from where he went from here. But in his 58 years on this earth he gathered a lot of odd flowers from the field of science and some were surely daisies.

That he could not have lived to have listed some of the reports that followed in the wake of each rumor of a flying saucer as the first half of the twentieth century whirled into the second must be recorded with great regret. His commentaries would have deflated even the Pentagonic witch-hunters who were detached temporarily from grand strategy and assigned to Air Force Intelligence, there to flay every citizen who thought he saw what he saw.

As for the scientists the military hired to evaluate what neither quite understood, Fort would have had a better time with them than he ever had with their forebears who explained everything unusual in terms of the commonplace. "The Wessex Explanation" he used to call it.

Before science admits a flying saucer has been found on earth and proved up all the gossip that has gone before, it probably will do what it did with the stories of stones from the skies, which Fort reported early in his parade of scientific novelties.

These were reported to have belted the earth shortly after the Prussians took their cannon home from Paris in 1877. Through Monsieur Lavoissier, a member of the French Academy, it was absolutely proved that a stone had not fallen, because there are no stones in the sky; therefore one could not fall from there. What had happened, according to M. Lavoissier, was that a flash of lightning had struck a stone on the ground and the peasants had assumed the stone had fallen.

In time, meteorites, stones, and space ships were reported to have fallen, and, like the stones, some scientists thought they might have been debris dropped by a hurricane from elsewhere and possibly hit by lightning when tossed out of the cyclone.

This was in line with the Wessex Explanation. By that Fort meant any attempt to interpret the enormous in terms of the minute, to localize the universal, to give a cosmic cloud absolute interpretation in terms of "little dusty roads and lanes of Wessex."

What rest and satisfaction Air Force Intelligence would have found if it could have cleared up all its cases, with the expression "absolutely identified," was not a yen unusual to the Air Force. To many minds, according to Fort, absoluteness, or the illusion of it, was the universal quest. When chemists identified substances that had fallen in Europe as sand from the African deserts, this put minds at rest which would otherwise have been disturbed by interplanetary prowlings and invasions.

"The only trouble is that a chemist's analysis," wrote Fort, "which seems so final and authoritative to some minds is no more nearly absolute than is identification by a child or description by an imbecile."

That he described electricity as "born as a parlor stunt," did not mean he was against Dr. William Gilbert or electricity. When Dr. Gilbert rubbed a rod with the skin of a cat, and made bits of paper jump from a table, he thrilled perhaps forty per cent of his seventeenth-century listeners, and set up an opposition of sixty per cent. The majority, as in all ages, did not look on this magic for what it was so much as to where it might lead. "Witchcraft," to quote another Fortean proverb, "always has a hard time until it becomes established and changes its name."

He did not look upon all scientists as beneficent beings. He knew too well that every scientist who upheld a new idea brought upon himself abuse from other scientists. Or to use his own words: "Science has done its utmost to prevent whatever science has done."

He was partisan to the industrial scientist and the good he had done as opposed to the academic or aristocratic scientist who was living on the repute of industrial science. He compared them to a good watch dog and the fleas upon him.

"If the fleas too could be taught to bark," he wrote, "there would be a little chorus that would be of some tiny value. But fleas are aristocrats."

Throughout his works, you will find scores of observations upon cylindrical-shaped bodies that have appeared in this earth's atmosphere. Some too were torpedo-shaped or cigar-shaped. He suspected that many of these, traveling super-geographical routes, had been driven into this earth's atmosphere.

He wrote: "From data, the acceptance is that upon entering this earth's atmosphere these vessels have been so racked that had they not sailed away, disintegration would have occurred: that, before leaving this earth, they have, whether in attempted communication or not, or in mere wantonness or not, dropped objects, which did almost immediately violently disintegrate or explode. Upon general principles we think that explosives have not been purposely dropped, but that parts have been racked off, and have fallen, exploding like the things called `ball lightning.' "

He exposed, more than berated, people like Professor Lawrence Smith and Sir Robert Ball, who stated that nothing could fall to this earth unless it had been blown up from some other part of the earth's surface. These, in brief, belonged to the same school which among Air Force Intelligence today believe there's no such thing as an object having external origin. The notion of things dropping in upon this earth from without is as unsettling and as unwelcome to them as children blowing fish horns during a symphony concert.

Fort offered for acceptance, "as something concordant with the spirit of the twentieth century," the expression that beyond this earth are other lands, just as one time beyond the Mediterranean were other seas, and, though the minds that run Air Force Intelligence would have denied it if they had formed a part of Caesar's imperial guard, far to the west of the Roman Empire were other lands. Some of those other lands have since become the Americas, where men who fly planes at 1,000 miles per hour scoff at men who suspect others from other lands can fly 186,000 miles per second. This, oddly, is slower compared to Air Force jet planes than Air Force jets are to Caesar's marching legions, for if his centurions could do 30 miles per day a jet could do 8,000, and that, in a month, would be 240,000 miles, while Caesar's soldier was walking off his first 1,000 miles. It is therefore

BEHIND THE FLYING SAUCERS

more plausible to believe in 1950 that flying saucers can travel 186,000 miles per second than it would have in Caesar's time been to believe anybody could ever travel 1,000 miles per hour.

Fort thought, as to most of his data concerning things flying throughout atmosphere, that the super-things really had no more interest in this earth than have steamship passengers in the bottom of the sea. Now and then there may be a passenger with such a keen interest "but circumstances of schedules and commercial requirements forbid his investigation of the bottom of the sea."

This concession to the curious traveler naturally led Fort to concede that there may have been super-scientific attempts to investigate phenomena on this earth from above, "perhaps by beings from so far away that they never even heard that something somewhere asserted a legal right to this earth."

I had intended to bedazzle doubters by trotting out Fort's first, second, third, fourth, and fifth teams, just as Notre Dame on the gridiron has overwhelmed many opponents by the show of mere numbers, but I have decided to transfer his kind of impressive chronological parade to an appendix.

Well, one measures a circle beginning anywhere, according to Fort. That I suspect does not conflict with the Hollywood saying, "Let's drop the romancing and cut to the chase."

This chase would take us from Fort and 1932 up to Kenneth Arnold and June 24, 1947, when the story of super-vehicles that have traversed this atmosphere really got down to cases.

Arnold is the young man who saw nine flying saucers, flying in formation at 9,.500 feet and going from north to south, heading toward Mt. Rainier, Washington. He was flying from Chehalis to Yakima. He was married, had a wife and two children, and his own landing field which adjoined the Bradley Air Field, Boise, Idaho. His pilot's license was 333487; his plane's national certificate, No. NC-33355. It was a single-engine job, designed for high altitude performance.

While en route to Yakima, he looked around for a lost Marine transport, believed to have disappeared on the southwest side of Mt. Rainier. He didn't find it, though subsequently it was found.

The weather was crystal clear and as he headed back to his course a bright flash reflected on his plane. He turned and observed nine odd-looking aircraft, moving in a diagonal line as if linked together. For a moment he assumed they were a new type of jet planes, but then he observed they hadn't any tails. They dipped in and out among the mountain peaks at terrific speed. He deduced that the chain was about five miles long, and the time it took the formation to pass from the southern edge of Mt. Rainier to the northernmost crest of Mt. Adams was one minute and forty-two seconds.

The objects held almost constant elevation. They flew like geese, the fastest geese he'd ever seen. He estimated their speed at 1,200 miles per hour.

BEHIND THE FLYING SAUCERS

Disturbed, he went back hunting for the lost Marine plane. After fifteen or twenty minutes he became so disturbed al the thought of those flying disks that he took a last look at Teton Reservoir and then headed for Yakima.

When he landed, he reported to the general manager of the Central Aircraft Company, who, Arnold felt, didn't quite believe him. Then he talked to Sonny Robinson, a former Air force pilot, who later employed his talents in "dusting operations" around Pendelton, Oregon. That's a job of spraying fruit trees from planes.

"What you observed," Robinson said, "is some type of jet or rocket-propelled ship that is in the process of being tested by our government, or it could even be by some foreign government." As soon as his story became public knowledge, Arnold received telephone calls, letters, telegrams, and communications from all over the world, and not one person transmitted ridicule.

"The only disbelief," said Arnold, "was what was printed in the papers."

He invited open investigation by the FBI and the Army. Up to the time he presented his findings to Fate, the little magazine which opened its first number in the spring of 1948, with Arnold's insistence that he did see the flying disks, he said that no interest was evidenced by either the FBI nor Air Force Intelligence at the time. The subsequent interest of the Air Force is a matter of record, for Air Materiel Command Intelligence admitted in its preliminary report that Project Saucer really began with the interest aroused by Kenneth Arnold's story.

Fate really went all out on flying saucers in its Volume 1, Number 1, and if anybody was in the field before the little pocket magazine from Evanston, Illinois, I have not been able to find any evidence of it. The scientific manner in which it checked its own accepted data was in the highest tradition.

As Arnold's flying saucers were thought by some to resemble a military craft known as a doughnut, Fate's editor, Robert N. Webster, turned John C. Ross lose on the Arnold report. Ross had access to military research bases, notably the Guided Missile Center at Point Mugu, California, and the two rocket testing centers at Muroc, California.

At that time, which was the winter of 1947-1948, Ross didn't believe we had an aircraft that ever reached the speed of 1,200 miles per hour. Nor did he believe we had a power plant capable of propelling any aircraft that fast. Nor missiles that could keep a close formation, and certainly none that were doughnutshaped. In fact he didn't believe that there were any supersonic aircraft in this country or any other at the time.

But we did have missiles which had attained a speed in excess of 1,200 miles per hour, Ross admitted. In fact, the bazooka and the German V-2, he said were capable of 3,000 miles per hour.

We had at the time aircraft that were manned by pilots, and even missiles, that roughly resembled a doughnut in shape, but these had no speed approaching sound, which at sea level is 760 miles per hour. One was the rocket-propelled Bell XS-1 and another was the Douglas D-558, a transonic jet plane.

Three other types might be mistaken for doughnut-shaped craft, if seen from a distance, but they too lacked the speed indicated by Arnold. One was the NIM, built by Northrop, but it was propeller-driven, which automatically limited it to subsonic speeds. Another, N9N, which were designed to carry one person, had a sixty-foot wing spread, and was limited to training pilots for B 25's. A third, was an MX-324. This was rocket-driven, but was a failure because it could not develop enough thrust. A fourth was the XP-79. This was jet-driven, and closely resembled the Northrop planes in that it had big and broad wings with no tail. This one was called the Flying Ram and could do 500 miles per hour. The subsequent B-25's and B-49's were propeller-driven, which would take them out of circulation when it came to traveling 1,200 m.p.h.

As for the Vought V-173 and the XF5U-1, these too were propeller-driven and looked like huge, flat saucers. They were the ones previously discussed in this volume (see Chapter 6) as the source of David Lawrence's subsequent "discovery" in 1950.

The nearest to Arnold's description in speed was a Jaeger P-13 designed by Alexander Lippisch, for the Luftwaffe. It was intended to fly at 1,500 miles per hour, and Lippisch estimated it might reach 2,200 m.p.h. It was powered with a ram jet engine and had no moving parts. The air entered the front of the engine, was run into the combustion chamber by the terrific speed of the plane itself, mixed with air and fuel in the combustion chamber, ignited, and blasted out of the rear. The wings went so sharply back that it could easily be confused with a saucer, but so far as we, the people, beyond the confines of Air Force classification are concerned, this plane has never been announced as completed and flown. Nevertheless, it is the only one that fitted Kenneth Arnold's description as to speed and configuration.

In subsequent articles Fate covered just as thoroughly the case of Lieutenant George Gorman, who had a dog fight with a flying disk over the Fargo, North Dakota, airfield. To Lieutenant Gorman's story, it added those of Lloyd D. Jensen,

BEHIND THE FLYING SAUCERS

and H. E. Johnson, both CAA controllers at the control tower of the Fargo field, and Dr. A. E. Cannon, an optician who saw the object, and watched the dog fight from a private plane through his binoculars.

This is a more elaborate report than the Digest offered us by the Air Materiel Command Intelligence and left us with the conclusions that the F-51 which Lieutenant Gorman was piloting was outdistanced at 400 miles per hour and also outmaneuvered, that he attempted to crash the object which might have resulted in his own death, but fortunately failed.

In that spring, 1948 issue Fate carried another article. It was entitled "The Mystery of the Flying Disks." From reading it, the only conclusion to be arrived at is that the mystery was no mystery except to the fabricators of mysteries attached to the Air Force. The article contained a more elaborate presentation of the Crisman-Dahl controversy. This was a year before the Air Materiel Command's Digest portrayed these men as perpetrators of a "hoax." In fact, for one dollar, taxpayers could have got far better reports from Fate than they ever got for the millions expended on Project Saucer. Not only that, but they could have got the desired information a year sooner.

BEHIND THE FLYING SAUCERS

Chapter 9
Added Starters

THE UNANIMITY with which magazines of larger format sought to brush off little Fate's claims to priority in the matter of being the first to record the presence of disks flying above our native land has been little short of a conspiracy in restraint of credits.

The Saturday Evening Post ran two articles in the spring of 1949. They were entitled "What You Can Believe About Flying Saucers," and they were signed by Sidney Shallet, an old New York Times Washington correspondent.

A year later Roy Palmer, who had acquired control of Fate and had once edited Amazing Stories, wrote a piece entitled "Space Ships, Flying Saucers And Clean Noses." In it he told how he had fed Sidney Shallet material for Shallet's Post articles. He also told of an interview with Stuart Rose, associate editor of the Post, some time after the Post articles had appeared.

I asked Rose about this. He replied he didn't know Palmer and had never heard of Fate.

I checked the references to Fate in the Post. There they were: on page 139 of the April 30, 1949 issue of the Post. What's the score now? Don't editors know what goes into their own magazines any longer?

In his articles Shallet accepted the assurance of the highest officers of the Air Force that they had nothing concealed up their sleeves. He quoted General Hoyt S. Vandenberg, then chief of staff, General Carl Spaatz, retired chief, Lieutenant General Lauris Norstad, Lieutenant General Curtis E. LeMay and Colonel H. M. McCoy, all high among the Air Force brass at that time.

Their opinions bunched together and their evaluations reevaluated, the substance of this parade of desk pilots was that they did not believed flying saucers existed. Most of them had noticed strange objects flying around, which turned out to be, according to them: (a) a reflection of a ground light, (b) reflection of a star on a cloud, (c) a glint of sunlight from the canopy of one P-51 into the eyes of a pilot of another P-51, (d) a certain type of aluminum-covered radar-target balloon then in use and (e) an "iffy" remark from General Spaatz to wit: "If the American people are capable of getting so excited over something which doesn't exist, God help us if anyone ever plasters us with a real atomic bomb!" In brief, an answer to logic and observation with a fright wig, and a ridiculous non sequitur if I ever read one.

Among the scientists only two of any substance were quoted. One was Professor Joseph A. Hynek, the Ohio State astrophysicist who was back in the subsonic age of propulsion, and may still be there for all I know. The other was Dr. Irving Langmuir, a Nobel Prize winner in physics and, like most Nobel Prize winners, immediately thereafter an authority on everything. He was the assistant director of General Electric's research laboratory at Schenectady, New York. He was also a member of the Air Force's scientific advisory board, according to Shallet, though not announced as such in any Air Materiel Command press handouts I ever saw. Shallet said Langmuir had "spent a lifetime debunking what he called pathological science." Asked what he would advise the Air Force to do about flying saucers Shallet said Langrnuir snapped, "Forget it." The snapper sounded as if Langmuir had picked up even his dialogue from the high command. I could almost see, in my pathologically scientific way, the two civilians ending their interview with a snappy salute.

Do you think the Post was paid off in gratitude by the military for telling its millions of readers at the end of ten thousand words to forget the whole thing? Au contraire. It was crossed up in the tradition of the Pentagon which seemingly holds all Americanos as Prussian Junkers used to hold their peasant class, except when its officers come around for a congressional handout.

Between the two issues of the Post, which in substance said there was nothing to the flying saucer story, the Air Materiel Command released a digest of its preliminary report, which in substance said there were a lot of things still unexplained about flying saucers and it would try to explain them before its next report came out. Nice teamwork. What happened to Combined Operations? It worked well among press, radio, and the high command on D-day. Too bad the combination was lost in the postwar era.

Next among the added starters after the Post was Variety. But perhaps it would be a mark of politesse to make way for the claims of others on the theory that guests should be served first.

On April 7, 1950, David Lawrence in his nationally syndicated column struck back at the White House and the Pentagon for their repudiation of his United States News and World Report feature, which revealed the Navy had flying saucers. In his column Lawrence quoted Ken W. Purdy, publisher of True for added support.

"You are correct in saying that flying saucers exist," Purdy told Lawrence. "Of course they do and I think no one can properly write this story without reference to the fact that we made the first statement in December, 1949."

BEHIND THE FLYING SAUCERS

The "of course" is that no one can properly write the story who says anything of the sort. Weeks before True got on the newsstands with its Donald E. Keyhoe feature, Variety had run two features of mine-the first as early as October 12, and the second on November 27. Mine, however, contained material never before released, though frequently used and garbled since.

But using similar source material, which Fate, the Post, and True did, it's incredible that the last two could be ignorant of the prior scoops of the first.

True deserved a lot of credit for bravery under ire. It must have known that in going out on a limb with the simple declarative sentence "Flying Saucers Are Real" it would annoy the Pentagonic party liners no end. The magazine had to employ a retired Marine pilot to front for the story, because obviously no Air Force member would touch it with a ten-foot pole. True tapped Donald E. Keyhoe, a Naval Academy graduate who had flown in active service with the Marine Corps and had been a balloon expert for a while. Between wars he had aided in the exploitation of the plane which Admiral Byrd used to fly over the North Pole, as well as having a hand in Charles Lindbergh's public relations after the latter returned from his solo flight to Paris in 1927. For a period Keyhoe also had been chief of information for the aeronautics branch of the Department of Commerce.

True said Keyhoe's article was the most important it had ever published, was "utterly true" and "could document every occurrence reported." Eight months of investigation were claimed to be behind the contribution. Among its conclusions were:

1. That our planet has been under systematic observation for 175 years, with a greater intensification since 1947.

2. That three types of transports have been used: Type I, a small pilotless, disk-shaped job, equipped with some form of television or impulse transmitter; Type II, a large disk-shaped ship, perhaps 250 feet in diameter operated on the helicopter principle; and Type III, a cigar-shaped wingless craft "operated in conformance with the Prandtl theory of lift."

True didn't believe the ships were operated by any means of propulsion unknown to us but that the operators were 225 years ahead of us in their thinking even so. This ruled out the likelihood of their being designed by today's aerodynamic engineers.

"An important magazine," Keyhoe wrote (obviously referring to the Post) "published two strangely inconclusive and contradictory articles, stated to have been prepared with the cooperation of the Air Force purporting to dismiss disks as of no basic significance."

Keyhoe then sought to give his own interpretation, at great length, of the Mantell case and from there went into the practicality of building flying saucers on this earth, powered by atomic energy or "the energy that produces cosmic rays."

He also quoted from the Air Materiel Command digest that "the chance of space travelers existing on planets outside the solar system is very much greater than the chance of space-traveling Martians."

A recapitulation of unsolved disk sightings followed, as well as rocket propulsion and such items, ending on an Air Force quotation: "The saucers are not a joke."

Scarcely had Keyhoe's opus, which was "one-tenth inspiration and nine-tenths perspiration," to quote an old phrase of Thomas Edison's, got off the presses when the Air Materiel Command proceeded to follow its regular behavior pattern. It gave True a head start of 24 hours and then slugged not only True but, like an asp biting itself, its own previous preliminary report as well. The saucers were not only a joke to the Air Force by now; they were the product of hallucinations and mass hysteria as well.

Rebuffed from above, True's staff scattered to all parts of the country, seeking aid and comfort and hoping to find some authority superior to Air Force Intelligence, to take the magazine off the limb. By March it had got nothing better than another member of the naval arm, this time a commander on active service, Robert McLaughlin, to support the reality of space ships around this earth. Commander McLaughlin told how he had run across a flying saucer while assigned to getting weather data from the upper atmosphere 57 miles northwest of the White Sands Proving Ground, New Mexico.

A crew of four were checking on a balloon with a theodolite and a stop watch. A strange object crossed their path. It was elliptical in shape, about 105 feet in diameter, flying at an altitude of about 56 miles. It was moving at about 1,800 m.p.h. High powered binoculars showed no exhaust trail, no stream of light, nor other evidence of propulsion as we know it.

"I am convinced," McLaughlin was convinced, "that it was a flying saucer and, further, that these disks are space ships from another planet, operated by animate, intelligent beings."

It didn't seem fantastic to him for earth-born mortals to explore other planets. "Why then should it be fantastic, for Martians, say, to visit us?" he wanted to know.

It may not have seemed fantastic to him but between the time of his observations and their publication in True, the armed forces had been merged under the Department of Defense and naval opinion had been moved far down from the head of the table.

Commander McLaughlin got orders to report for sea duty.

Naive to all nuances as well as the direct rebuffs which had come to those who tried to play ball with the Pentagonic specialists in negation, Henry J. Taylor, an eminent radio commentator heard from coast to coast over American Broadcasting Company's network, thought he would add chapter and verse to the story. He told his listeners that the real facts were good news for the nation. Flying saucers were actually of two types and both were top secrets of our armed forces. The experiments were started on June 25, 1947, and have been expanded ever since.

One type was a disk that whirls through space, Taylor revealed, halts suspended in air, soars to 30,000 feet or more, drops to 1,000 feet and then usually disintegrates. These are harmless, pilotless disks varying from two to 250 feet in size.

The other object is the Flying Phantom, the XF5U, jet-propelled.

These words, said the commentator, are stenciled on the back of every real saucer in case it doesn't disintegrate: "Anyone damaging or revealing description or whereabouts of this missile is subject to prosecution by the U. S. Government. Call collect at once."

The Air Force of course denied the whole Taylor story. So there was no good news that night.

Taylor's revelations and Lawrence's overlapped in fact, but both were slapped down by official denial. In Lawrence's case, however, even the President had to be trotted out to back up the defensive halfbacks in the Pentagon. His press secretary, Charles Ross, said it was extremely unlikely that there would be a secret weapons project not known to the President.

I have pointed out elsewhere that the naval and air force aides of the President issued statements that were so far off in their timing that if they had been directing the atom bomb that dropped over Hiroshima it might have hit MacArthur in Manila. It took Brigadier General Robert L. Landry, the President's Air Force aide, all day to prepare a statement. When released at Key West, the statement miscalculated the official opening and closing of Project Saucer by three months.

But official errors weren't even getting the rebuff of a correction from the major metropolitan dailies in those days. In fact, except for a small town paper here and there, nobody bothered to take the military to task for the kind of slipshod journalism that would get a police reporter fired.

Only the night before Taylor went on the air with what he assured us was only a hint of the good news which some day it would be a joy to tell in detail (because the saucers, he assured us, were 100 per cent American), Walter Winchell told his listeners in North and South America and all the ships at sea that the flying saucers were real all right but they were not the inventions of Uncle Sam. They were uninvited imports from Uncle Joe.

As Russia at that time had no official spokesman other than Uncle Joe and Uncle Joe was not talking to Walter Winchell, there was no official denial of the Winchell "scoop" from the Kremlin.

In fact for a novelty there was no official denial from a Pentagon spokesman either. It was a Sunday night and possibly all the official and unofficial spokesmen were sleeping off the fatigue of a hard afternoon at golf. I doubt if many of them missed Winchell's broadcast because they were at vespers.

Sidney Shallet, reflecting the official opinion in his Post articles, wrote that if the Russians were experimenting with supersonic aircraft and guided missiles Air

BEHIND THE FLYING SAUCERS

Force Intelligence, "which painstakingly sifts all reports," would like to know how they do it and, what's more to the point, how they get home without being seen by more people? Up to that time, Shallet said, Air Force Intelligence "did not have so much as one loose nut off any unexplained object."

If they found one I suspect they would have sent it to psycho instead of to the magnetic research engineers.

In the main the United Press played up the saucers and the Associated Press played them down. Ed Creagh, AP staff man operating out of New York, released a long one on April 2, 1950, that was so full of holes he might have done better if he had stayed in bed.

It was entitled "Things In The Sky." Whether they were myths or military secrets, optical illusions or invasions from Mars, Creagh said he didn't presume to judge but as his story developed he seemed inclined to take the party line of the armed forces and dismiss the subject as so much moonshine.

Creagh didn't identify any member of the armed forces by name and a spokesman for the other side, using the same cloak of anonymity, said it was about time the military identified themselves and took the war-of-words out in the open. "Otherwise people will hang it on to Creagh and say he is the one who is passing out so much moonshine."

One of the irate opposition closely identified with the magnetic research engineers who had examined at least three grounded flying saucers gave me a tape recording which chided Creagh plenty for being chumped by some faceless spokesmen of the Air Force. He particularly took Creagh to task for taking one state highway patrolman's word against 5,000 citizens of Farmington, New Mexico. The copper said that the hundreds of saucers 5,000 persons reported as flying over Farmington were pieces of cotton.

"If Mr. Creagh," the tape-recorded statement in my possession revealed, "had ever been in the vicinity of Farmington, New Mexico, he would have known there is no cotton grown within a thousand miles of that town." Instruments checked the cop's "pieces of cotton" as they scooted across the sky from horizon to horizon in three seconds. That's at the rate of 100 miles per second or 6,000 miles per hour. No piece of cotton about the size of a quarter could travel that fast, even to a person suffering from hallucinations. To put 5,000 persons in that category is placing too much faith in a cop's untested sanity or vision."

Then Creagh related what he called "an exploded yarn" about a space ship from Mars, manned by little men.

"When was it exploded," the spokesman for the magnetic research engineers wanted to know, "and who exploded it? Come on, Mr. Creagh, let's have your facts. Don't just make statements of this kind without naming the explosive and who set off the fuse."

There were at least 3,000 words to this recording, but I'm afraid I'll have to get on to the rest of the added starters without using them.

Edward R. Murrow, ace commentator of the Columbia Broadcasting System, though a late starter, supervised a roundup on flying saucers that had all the documentary believability, though none of Westbrook Van Vorhee's sepulchral tones, of time marching on. He covered the controversy from Kenneth Arnold to President Truman, which means he covered it from 1947 to 1950.

Murrow prefaced the roundup by saying that none of the CBS staff had ever seen a flying saucer, though a large percentage of sane and reliable persons reported they had. He talked with Kenneth Arnold in Boise, Idaho, by telephone and recorded Arnold's testimony on tape in New York. Arnold, remember, was the businessman who had been flying his own plane for six years and was the first to report nine flying saucers near Mt. Rainier.

"The slight `beep' you will hear," Murrow said, "is required by law to let both parties know the conversation is being recorded." This put the wire tapping on an honorable level.

Murrow's version of Arnold's story cleared up one point. It revealed how the objects happened to be called "flying saucers" in the first place. It was all due to a misquotation by the press.

"When I described how they flew," Arnold explained to Murrow, "I said they flew like you'd take a saucer and throw it across the water. Of course the newspaper misunderstood and misquoted that too. They said I said they were saucerlike. What I said was they flew in a saucer-like fashion."

The press reduced all this to "flying saucers" and thus began a phrase that may never die.

After recording Arnold's story, Murrow cut in everybody from the top brass in Washington and astronomers at Harvard down to the man and woman in the street. Some of the voices were real, some were simulated, but the things they said were quoted from their own statements.

Murrow, soft voiced and assuring, revealed a few things about the Captain Mantell story that were new, too. It had been often recorded than Mantell was a Kentucky National Guard pilot, which of course is no disgrace, but actually he was a combat veteran of the Normandy invasion, with 3,000 flying hours behind him, before he chased either a flying saucer or the planet Venus to the disintegration of his ship and himself.

Paul Kerby, commenting on the catastrophe, remarked that a pilot of that experience represented a terrible loss to the nation and certainly somebody should be held responsible if he lost his life chasing a craft known to the Pentagon but unknown to Mantell. If he died chasing a space ship from another planet, the only ones (with the exception of the crew of the space ship itself) who could be held responsible would be those who denied such things existed without knowing at all what they were talking about.

BEHIND THE FLYING SAUCERS

Murrow of course didn't go into the thing as deeply as this. After all, radio survives by skating very deftly over rather thick ice, and hardly scratching its surface. He touched on Project Saucer and said its findings, compiled in two thick volumes, had been "declassified" and released for public study, though most of us have never seen anything beyond a 22-page Digest released by the Air Materiel Command. He had some voice from the Pentagon giving the old tired trinity-hallucinations, mass hysteria, and hoaxes. Was that the same voice that told California newspapermen that we had no supersonic jets, long after everybody had got tired of seeing them whiz around in excess of 800 miles per hour?

But the cutest cut-in on Murrow's program was a woman who was interviewed near the end of the program. Asked what she thought of flying saucers, she replied that there must be lots more to the story than the people are getting. She said it all reminded her of the New York World correspondent who telegraphed from North Carolina back in December, 1903 that Wilbur Wright had just flown 250 yards in a plane near Kitty Hawk. The reporter got fired for wasting telegraph charges.

Murrow made no such direct statements about flying saucers. He left a vent in his saucer, however, and in consequence was not fired for wasting wire charges. Time, as they say around Rockefeller Center, marches on and as it marches commentators become convincingly cautious.

So far none of the added starters had done much more than march the various stories up the hill and march them down again, and then exit, noncommittal and smiling. It remained for Time to assume the role of dragon slayer.

An old hand at biting the hand that feeds them, Time's course on flying saucers could be charted in advance. Dynasties have descended from dragons. In fact in many places it's still a mark of aristocratic pedigree to have descended from dragons. The same is true of course of dragon slayers.

In Iran, Verethraghna slew Verethra. In India, Vritrahan slew Vritra. In England, St. George slew the dragon. In New York, Time slew the flying saucer.

Sometimes in these myths a descendant slays the sire. Is it too much to expect that in the Luce dynasty that Life or Fortune, children of Time, may one day do as much for the well-cloaked snipers of Time?

The Time formula is to pick the brains of original researchers and then, by snapping a sarcastic whip in the last few paragraphs, slay the dragon of the week. It had its whole staff out as a sort of collection agency on the flying saucer story in April, 1950.

Fritz Goodwin, chief of its Los Angeles news bureau, came to see me on April 7 to see what I could contribute to my own liquidation. As I was deep in this book at this time, and rushing to meet a deadline myself, I wasn't very keen about joining a cannibalistic feast where crows fed on crows. I asked him what angle Time was going to take on the roundup story? He said he didn't know. Maybe he didn't, but

BEHIND THE FLYING SAUCERS

I knew. I told him they would build the whole thing up and just before the end they would blow it all down; which is just about what they did in their April 17 issue.

Not quite sure they were big enough to slay the dragon alone, they called on Rear Admiral Daniel V. Gallery, who at one time had been in charge of the guided missile program operating at the White Sands Proving Ground. It was from there, remember, that Commander Robert McLaughlin reported to Admiral Gallery that he had seen a flying saucer. The Admiral, 3,000 miles away in Washington, thought a proper answer was to ask McLaughlin, what kind of whisky he had been drinking in New Mexico? Between two graduates of Annapolis this sort of humor didn't seem too far off protocol. But McLaughlin persisted, wrote pieces about it and in time found himself in command of the destroyer Bristol, where apparently he hasn't seen a flying saucer since.

"If you look back about 500 years ago," said Admiral Gallery, by way of dismissing the whole subject to the aid and comfort of Time "you will find that the people of England had a period of hysteria when everybody was seeing flying dragons in the sky. We are now going through the modern version of flying dragons."

Admiral Gallery should have gone further back than 500 years. Didn't St. George have it out with the dragon, and St. Michael with Satan? And how about the old serpent of the Apocalypse? The Chinese could fill any book with such combats. He may not believe anybody slew a dragon anytime in recorded history, let alone 500 years ago in England, but in Africa in the spring of 1950, Howard Hill, drew an arrow that went 27 inches through the hide of an elephant. Anybody who could kill an elephant with such a weapon could have killed a dinosaur and a dinosaur is not far removed from a dragon.

I was not burned by the hot breath of a dragon, nor ridiculed by the Time dragon slayers, as were David Lawrence, Henry J. Taylor, and, by implication, Walter Winchell. In quoting the Department of Defense as saying: "None of the three services or any agency in the Department of Defense is conducting experiments . . . with disk-shaped objects, which could be the basis for the reported phenomena." Time was fellow traveling on the old party line. This has been the Pentagon's story for a long time. Nobody believes it, least of all those who release the handouts. But the statement was supposed to take care of Taylor and Lawrence at any rate. In another sentence the release added: "There has been no evidence to the activity of any foreign nation." That took care of Winchell who said they came from Russia.

Thus three top journalists were brushed off by some unidentified Pentagonic personality in one swoop. Time joined the wolf pack of official scoffers.

As for myself, though interviewed by their Hollywood manager, and photographed by one of their staff, I came out practically unscathed. All the roundup said of me was: "Henry Holt announced a `serious' book on flying saucers by

BEHIND THE FLYING SAUCERS

Variety's columnist Frank Scully."

Under the circumstances, you'd think I would be discreet enough not to go around slaying dragon slayers. But I'm looking into the future, and I don't need a crystal ball to tell me that I won't come through the next occasion unscathed. Like the moon, I'm due for capture. But like the prophet, who was not without honor, save among his own kind and his own kin, I'm not missing at least this opportunity to say: "I told you those birds couldn't be trusted."

Did it ever occur to Time or the Pentagonians to ask each other this question: The Navy is sure that the saucers observers saw were not theirs. The Army was sure the disks weren't theirs. The Air Force knows they have none in the skies. The Department of Defense doesn't believe they are the work of a foreign power. All three ridicule the idea that they are from another planet. But they are around. Doesn't that strengthen the suspicion that either somebody, is lying, ignorant, or both?

Little Quick in its May 1 issue threw the harassed high command a hint. In its predictions it said:

"The high command will have to make its denials stronger to stop flying saucer rumors. The Pentagon is full of officers who don't know what to believe."

The only amendment I could offer would be the substitution of *whom* for *what* to believe. Long ago I wrote, "If the Pentagon tells you flying saucers are here, don't believe them. If they say they are a myth, don't believe them. Just don't believe them. Believe me."

I find I have been so hospitable to the wayward and conforming members of the press that there is practically no space left for Scully's heretical findings as published in Variety in 1949 and 1950.

Well, that's the price a good Samaritan has to pay for granting asylum to strangers and maybe truth is served better that way.

BEHIND THE FLYING SAUCERS

Chapter 10
As Astronomers View Them

UP TO THE SUMMER SOLSTICE of 1950 practically no "name" astronomer had come out as an eye witness to flying saucers. Indeed such eminent astrophysicians as Dr. Donald Menzel of Harvard, Dr. Gerard P. Kuiper of Chicago, and Dr. Joseph A. Hynek of Ohio State all swore on their loyalty oaths that except for some crockery caught in a cyclone, flying saucers were nonsense. Here and there of course an astronomer gave a positive-maybe sort of testimonial, but most of them would as leave have been photographed as a man of distinction clinking glasses with Mae West or taking a Chesterfield from the proffered hand of a convicted spy as to have taken issue with the Air Force's unwritten law against the proximity of space ships.

But away from their observatories, their loyalty oaths filed away for the night, and protected by home ties, many of them confessed that space travel from elsewhere held "considerable possibility." This wasn't much, since anything which can be considered, a pin point for instance, is "considerable" and anything possible is a "possibility." Napoleon once said: *"Impossible? Ce mot West pas francais!"* It isn't English either.

Dr. Walter Lee Moore, astronomer of the University of Louisville, felt sure he had sighted a disk and watched it head toward Venus, and Professor George Adamski of Palomar once said he thought there was something to them. William Lamb, Wyoming's eminent astrotheologian, was as certain of them as he was of St. Michael's wings. Younger astronomers, amateurs like Stanley P. Higgins and Edward Coffman, had done a great deal of extracurricular activity in the field. Higgins retained an open mind, but Coffman insisted he had seen one over Van Nuys, California, and brought three witnesses who corroborated his findings.

But in the main astronomers of established rank and position followed the request to keep their traps shut please about any visitations from Mars, Venus, Russia, or anywhere else. True, few had seen behind the clouds that envelop Venus, so it was easy for them to declare that no life existed behind that inconvenient curtain. To expect them, therefore, to confirm that a space ship adequately propelled could hop from such a planet to this earth and back in an hour was equivalent to reversing the current of an electric shock treatment and splitting their previously disturbed personalities as wide open as a schizophrenic's.

To condition people into an acceptance of interplanetary travel, I can think of no better route than those blazed long ago by Oberth and Hohmann and their present-day disciples, Bonestell and Ley.

Before taking their trips to the moon, Venus, and Mars, perhaps it would help if we rounded up the currently accepted findings of astronomers concerning our solar system. As of 1950 the accepted planets revolving around our sun numbered nine; their satellites in turn, 31. Three planets presumably had no moons. Jupiter had 11; the Earth, one.

Only 14 astronomers were credited with the 31 satellite discoveries. Of these discoveries, Galileo, Cassini, and Herschel were credited with four each. Kuiper, a latecomer, when pickings presumably were few, managed to get two as recently as 1948 and 1949. His telescope had to reach out 5,000,000 miles to get one of them. That is a long way from Chicago.

Of the moons, Jupiter's are the largest, those of Mars the smallest. In fact, Deimos of Mars, is supposed to be only five miles in diameter, as compared to our moon, which is 2,160 miles in diameter.

Mercury, Venus, Earth, and Mars seem a neighborly little group in the solar system (if you disregard the millions of miles as you would disregard millions in a national budget, and think of them instead as well within one hundred units of each other). Under such a simplification, Mercury is 36.0, Venus 67.2, Earth 93.0, and Mars 141.5, units from the sun. That way they all seem within a day's ride of each other, and the climatic changes do not seem much worse than sunshine in one town and rain in another in almost any county in America.

The time it takes them to complete an orbit is not too diverse either. Mercury and Venus takes little less, Mars a little longer than ours. The orbital velocities are pretty close too. We travel at 18.5 per second, Venus at 21.7, Mercury at 29.9, and Mars at 15.0. Their gravities are not too diverse. Taking the Earth as equal to one, Venus would be 0.85, Mars 0.38, and Mercury 0.27.

The period of their rotation is guesswork in the case of Venus, but Mars is known to rotate at 27 hours and 37 minutes as compared to the Earth which magnetically is 23 hours and 58 minutes, and sidereally 23 hours, 56 minutes.

Their mass volume and density show not too great a discrepancy, and their diameters are even closer. The Earth is 7,900 miles wide, Venus 7,700 miles, Mars 4,200 miles, and Mercury 3,100. Their percentage of light shows the widest discrepancy. Mercury has only 7 per cent, to the Earth's 50 per cent, and Mars has only 15 per cent. Venus, however, has 59 per cent.

The size and position of these planets has not been upset by anybody in a long

BEHIND THE FLYING SAUCERS

time. Pluto is the nearest to the Sun, and the others move outward in the following order: Neptune, Uranus, Saturn, Jupiter, Mars, Earth, Venus, and Mercury. In size they range from Jupiter, which is the largest, through Saturn, Neptune, Uranus, Earth, Venus, Pluto, Mars, and Mercury, which is the smallest.

Uranus, Neptune, and Pluto have all been discovered since Johannes Kepler's time. Nearly all the planets in our solar system are in the same plane, and they move in ellipses rather than circles around the Sun. That brings them sometimes nearer and sometimes farther away from not only the Sun, but each other. Their maximum orbits are called their apogee; their minimum, their perigee.

The Earth has one moon, Mars 2, Saturn 10, and Jupiter 11. Venus, Mercury, and Pluto do not seem to have any. Moons, however, have been discovered as early as Babylonian times and as late as 1949. So it is possible that other planets may have moons which no telescope or spectroscope has detected as yet. Venus in particular, because of the clouds surrounding it, may have a moon which defies detection. After all, Mars has a moon which is only 5,800 miles from its surface as opposed to one moon of Jupiter which is 14,880,000 miles from home. There is an observable law governing all this. Kepler laid it down.

As there are 23 solar systems which so far have been checked as having satellite planets, is it unreasonable to assume that given similar conditions in the universe no other sun would have a planet 90,000,000 miles away, and therefore, like ours, capable of supporting intelligent life. In fact many astronomers believe that in addition to our sun there must be at least one habitable planet for each of the other 22 stars.

In the Air Materiel Command Digest of April 27, 1949, there was reference that the nearest eligible star which might have a planet comparable to our Earth, was one called Wolf 359. But this is eight light years away from the Earth. Even if a space ship traveled at 18,000 miles per second, which is as fast as an Air Force mind could go in 1950, it would take such a space ship 80 years to travel from the earth of Wolf to the earth of the Sun. If nuclear material could be converted into jet energy, the time, the Air Force engineers believed, might be cut to 60, or, at the shortest, to 16 years.

With a sigh, their engineers and astronomers decided to let go of Wolf 359 and try their hand at Mars. Orson Welles tried his hand at bringing these people in, and Kenneth Arnold is still referred to by some people as "the man who saw the men from Mars." The general opinion of astronomers, however, is that Mars is even more desolate and inhospitable during its best moments than the middle of the Sahara during a sandstorm. Such people, the Air Force astronomers contend, would be more occupied with survival than with air travel. To survive against the loss of atmosphere of oxygen and water, they would have had to protect themselves by some scientific control of diminishing natural resources. By the construction of homes and cities underground they might reduce the arctic temperatures of their nights. It is possible, of course, that a race faced with diminishing assets might go out on the hunt for another place to live. Certainly on this earth when faced either with plows which have destroyed their plains, or atom bombs, people have either migrated by covered wagon, jalopy, or plane, or have gone underground.

Contrary to the Air Force astronomers, others do not believe that Mars is so much colder than our arctic areas, being nearer 50° F. at noon on their equator. The terrain being flat and featureless, there would certainly be plenty of landing fields, though all agree that even the snow at the polar ice caps can hardly be more than a foot deep, and water scarce at all times. There is a vegetation much like arctic moss. Certain types of plants grow on the windswept tundras. There is very little weather, as we know it, but dust storms are frequent.

Kuiper has detected no oxygen in the atmosphere. The density is very low. The canals or surface markings which have been estimated up to twenty miles wide and three thousand miles long, have been credited to everything from supermen to cracked telescopic lenses. As the ice caps shrink, the canals begin to become apparent. Shortly afterward, green vegetation develops.

Back in 1939, when Mars was close to us, various astronomers came in with various reports of what they had seen. Some saw as many as forty canals, some didn't see any. But the consensus remained, at least through the first phase of the flying saucer era, that the canals did exist, though the diggers of them didn't.

As we are between 35,000,000 and 63,000,000 miles away, it is hard for us to adjust our sights on those canals. They sometimes wriggle and sometimes seem straight. They interlace, and at intersections give the appearance of oases.

Surely if there is any intelligence on Mars, and that intelligence observed the loss of humidity, it could not be a very high intelligence if it didn't look around for another planet, when life was found to be no longer supportable on its own.

Obviously, if such people hadn't been killing each other off through wars, they might have moved much farther ahead in their arts and sciences than the human race on this planet. But it would be only fair, if it were at all possible for us to do so, to tell them not to settle down here until we can stop intimidating each other with bigger and more horrible explosives. Surely as innocent bystanders they'd get the blast first.

If astronomers don't think much of life on Mars, they think even less of it on Venus. This despite the fact that Venus is nearer to the earth in its physical characteristics than any other planet. Barring the moon, it is our nearest neighbor; but because of its dense cloud formations, astronomers have succeeded in seeing Venus on only a few occasions, and even then, they were in such violent disagreements as to what they actually saw, whether mountain chains or volcanic eruptions, that the revelations so far have had practically no value.

The planet Venus at the present time revolves around the sun in 288 days, which is the sidereal year of the planet. However, seen from the earth it revolves around the sun on a longer orbit and at a lower speed.

Venus returns to the same position with respect to the earth, after 584 days, which is its synodical year. It rises before the sun, earlier every day for 71 days, until it reaches the western elongation, or its westernmost point away from the rising sun. Each morning thereafter this morning star rises lower and lower and for 221 days approaches the superior conjunction.

About a month before the end of this period, it is eclipsed by the rays of the sun, and for over 60 days it is not seen because of the sun's rays. It is behind the sun, or in superior conjunction. Then it appears for a moment after the setting sun, being now the evening star, and east of the western sun.

For 221 nights, beginning with the evening on which it first appears as an evening star, it appears farther from the setting sun, until it reaches the eastern elongation. Then for 71 nights it approaches the sun. Finally it enters the inferior conjunction, when it is between the earth and the sun. It is usually invisible for one or two days, and thereafter appears west of the rising sun and is again the morning star.

These movements of Venus, and their exact duration, have been known to the people of the Orient and the Occident for more than two thousand years. Actually a Venus year, which follows the synodical revolution of Venus, was employed in calendars of the Old and New World alike. Five synodical years of Venus equals 2919 6/10 days, whereas eight years of 365 days equals 2,920 days, and eight Julian years of 365 1/4 days equals 2,922 days.

In other words, in four years there's a difference of approximately one day between the Venusian and the Julian calendars.

Since the latter part of the eighth century before the present era, Venus has followed an orbit between Mercury and Earth which it has maintained ever since. It became the morning and evening star seen from the earth. It is never removed more than 48 degrees, when at its eastern and western elongation, or three hours and a few minutes east or west of the sun.

All planets revolve in their orbits in the same direction, counterclockwise, if seen from the north, around the sun. Most of their moons revolve counterclockwise in direct motion, but there are a few that revolve in the opposite direction in retrograde motion. No orbit is an exact circle. There is no regularity in the eccentrical shapes of the planetary orbits. Each elliptical curve verges in a different direction. Information obtained by different methods of observation of Venus is contradictory. It is not known whether Venus rotates so slowly, that its day equals its year, or so rapidly that its nightside is never sufficiently cooled.

Air Force consultant astronomers, strangely, do not consider the possibility of intelligent life on Venus as completely unreasonable. No oxygen or water has been found as yet, though this does not mean there is none. It could mean that the water vapor has not reached the outer cloud banks where it could be detected by us.

There is a quaint astronomical opinion that a cloudy atmosphere around Venus would discourage astronomy and hence discourage space travel. Spectroscopic analyses have shown that there are large quantities of carbon dioxide on Venus.

Lee Bowman, who has made half a million dollars on patents, worked up a plane run on CO_2 gas, which is way ahead of even the drawing boards of those engineers who weren't even beyond hydrogen, a highly inflammable gas, on paper by 1950.

The idea that people behind a cloud would not be curious to know what transpired on the other side of the cloud is the sort of thinking that went out with Columbus. Handicapped in his desire to reach India from Spain by travelling west, we had to overcome the ignorance of those who held that if he insisted on it his ships would fall off the flat earth beyond the horizon and disappear forever. But he took an egg and convinced certain backers at least that if he went on long enough he would come back to where he started from.

It is therefore possible that some early Venusians, having come on CO_2 as a means of propulsion long before Lee Bowman, may have been outside those cloud formations for untold centuries. And it is the opinion of the best authorities on electromagnetic energy that some intelligent beings from somewhere have got far beyond CO_2 as a means of propulsion, despite the bookies in the Air Force, who quote odds on such space travel at 1,000 to 1.

The best of our aerodynamicists can do to date is to think in terms of rocket ships from this earth to Mars or Venus along narrow Keplerian ellipses.

Willy Ley and Chesley Bonestell deserve no end of credit for softening us up so that we can believe in space travel and though I believe the time will come when their means of propulsion will seem like selling us oxcarts in a day of hot rods, their travelogues will still be exciting reading when our day becomes known as the prehistoric period of space travel.

In *The Conquest of Space* they use the homeopathic approach. They start us out with an actual, factual report of a rocket taking off at the White Sands Proving Ground. Next they talk us into a rocket trip from New York to California. Next they take us from Long Island to Europe and around the world.

Since we have weathered all those trips safely, they next take us to the moon. I have never been trapped more alluringly into a trip I never intended to take.

Bonestell's paintings and sketches look more real than color photographs or even black and white prints. On a transcontinental trip from a Long Island airport to California, he "photographs" (presumably from another rocket) a rocket which has climbed to ten miles above Manhattan. Tilted at a 45-degree angle, we see star-spangled Manhattan below and the next thing we know we are twenty-five miles above New Jersey where all of Long Island and Manhattan are visible behind us.

Next we are 125 miles above Williamsport, Pennsylvania, and in the distance we can see Lake Erie, Detroit, and Buffalo. It was dark when the rocket left Long Island, but our speed is fast overcoming that disadvantage. By the time Nebraska is reached the rocket is 500 miles up and everything as far north as Hudson Bay and the Aurora Borealis is visible.

That was its high point. The rocket started to slip after that and by the time it reached Nevada it was down to 250 miles above the earth's surface. From there to Baja, California, the descent was rapid-good thing, too, or all of us would have drowned in the Pacific Ocean.

Having made that trip with such ease, nobody unless he were a chicken-hearted Pentagonian would balk at a rocket trip from Long Island, across the Atlantic and around the world. He might have to climb 4,000 miles high to make it, but it would be a nice conditioning for that inevitable trip to the moon.

The moon by rocket, we are assured, as if it had already been tested (which of course it has as much as that rocket trip we took from New York to Los Angeles), takes four days and nights. The moon is that little thing-253,000 miles away from us at its maximum (apogee) and 222,000 miles away at its minimum (perigee). Its average density is 3.3 to our 5.5 and its gravity a good deal less than ours, from one-fifth to one-sixth of 1.0, which is the unit used for gravity on this earth. Its albido, or whiteness, is only seven per cent as compared to our fifty per cent.

Assuming that the pilot of the moon ship has been conditioned to withstand acceleration up to 4 g., and assuming further that such a rocket would have to have a velocity of seven miles per second to get out of this atmosphere, it would take 300,000 seconds to reach zero velocity. By then nine-tenths of the distance between the earth and moon would have been covered. The main task at that point would be to get across the frontier because in interplanetary travel, as on this earth, there are customs problems and they involve adjustments and delays. Our rocket would have to be turned around so that it could back down to the moon.

Most interplanetary travelers shoot right by these difficulties, but there is a dividing line between the earth and its satellite, and how to get out of the gravitational grip of one and into another pulling in the opposite direction, is as difficult as swimming down with one tide, trying to cross over in midstream and swimming back on another. At one point you are likely to be pulled under and disappear.

If you overcome this, the next job is to see that the gravitational pull toward the moon doesn't increase your speed the nearer you get to the satellite. Without brakes you might hit your target at 7,200 m.p.h. It would take powerful rocket motors working in reverse and braking to bring that velocity down to zero.

As for that little matter of turning the ship around when between the earth's pull and the moon's, so that the rocket can back down to the moon, the rocket engineers have this all worked out, and since you've already traveled from New York to Los Angeles and from Long Island around the world, why should you doubt that they would be stumped in getting from neutral into reverse? Fifteen years ago you surely would have believed that a trip to the moon was more feasible than the atomic bomb, and since you've accepted that there is such a thing as atomic energy, why doubt that such masters in the field of industrial science would be stumped by the problem of getting you over the frontier, from the earth's gravitational pull to the moon's?

The job of getting you back from the moon, of course, would be easier than leaving this earth, provided (1) you had fuel and (2) you had oxygen. Astronomers say that there is practically no air on the moon, and nobody has ever claimed they had filling stations. But it would be easier than leaving here, say the rocket engineers, because of the fact that the moon's gravitational pulls is about 16 per cent of what the earth's is.

Then, too, once you passed that frontier again on the way home, you'd be in the earth's gravitational field for the next 215,000 miles. In the last eight minutes coming down I suppose you would have to decelerate at about the same speed you accelerated on the way up-so by the time you reached the earth's surface the pull would be zero on the ship and no more than 4 g. on you. Otherwise you would be hitting the earth at 7,200 miles per hour, which would be a mess.

But just as Ley and Bonestell convinced you it was easy to travel around the world, they present a series of color and black and white "photographs" of a trip to the moon on weekly schedule. Actually it would be eight days without even stopover privileges, but thanks to the realistic paintings of Bonestell, there will be few surprises for tourists there. The various craters, promontories, and dried-out bays will also be there for those who would step on them, and thanks to the reduced gravitational pull they would enjoy a spring in their step such as has never been experienced on this earth.

Thermal erosions which have filled up valleys, including the great valley of the Alps, will be there to be studied by earth-light as well as sun-light, for just as the moon reflects its light on our planet, so we reflect ours on our satellite.

While the trip to the moon (now that it's over) was comparatively easy, one to Mars or Venus would require much wider ellipses. The longest one to Venus might be the easier because it would be more economical in the use of fuel. A ship to Venus would start out counterclockwise moving as our earth does.

Like the trip to the moon the Venus-bound ship would have to drift outward into the solar system and of course into the orbit of the planet. If that were Venus the orbital velocity would be about 21.7 miles per second. If everything were timed right, the space ship would meet the planet at the right point at the right moment. If they missed it would be a case of "whoops!" like the man on the flying trapeze whose timing was off.

But assuming everything were mathematically correct it would be easier to go to Venus than to Mars because of fuel requirement. In fact in one of these trips it was worked out that the easiest drain on gas and oil would be to Venus, then to Mars, and then back to Earth from Mars. But either direct trip or a round trip seemed well within the textbook skills of contemporary rocket engineering.

All this is based on the theory or error (vote for one) that the only way to conquer gravity is by superior force. The idea of harnessing magnetic lines of force and riding on them as one would on a scenic railway has not occurred as yet to the rocketeers.

Ley in *Rockets, The Future of Travel Beyond the Stratosphere* gives an excellent example of the difference between flying in this atmosphere and another. Traveling in a rocket in this atmosphere is liking moving from one seat to another in the same car of a train. Flying to the moon is like moving from one car to another car of the same train. Flying to Venus is like moving from one train to another on an adjoining track moving in the same direction. If you miss it you may fall flat on your face on the tracks and may never be heard of again.

A trip to Venus, according to partisans of the rocket propulsion, would take two years, one month, and three days. (According to those on the side of magnetic propulsion it would be about half an hour.)

Willy Ley used as his authorities for the rocket trip Oberth and Hohmann. Dr. Walter Hohmann, who wrote *The Attainability of the Celestial Bodies,* was the city architect of Essen-on the-Ruhr. His book dealt with departure from this earth, return to this earth, free coasting in space, circular orbits around other celestial bodies, and landing on other celestial bodies.

Professor Hermann Oberth was a mathematician who published a book in Munich in 1923 on the theoretical possibility of space travel. He believed that technological knowledge was sufficient to build machines that could rise beyond the limits of the atmosphere of this earth, and that further development would give them sufficient velocity so they could continue in space and not fall back to earth, that they could be built to carry men and that within a few decades they could be manufactured on a profitable basis.

The earth's atmosphere is variously argued to extend from 40 to 500 miles but most scientists agree that after 40 miles the density is nearer a vacuum and the gravitational pull pretty nearly academic.

As our armed forces have admitted propelling rockets 70 miles in atmosphere (which is about 40 miles this side of what some rockets have actually done unofficially), it does seem that in the "classified" information on file in the Pentagon somebody somewhere already knows whether there is any gravitational pull above 40 miles.

Of course the speed of rockets is not the problem. The human body is the thing that has limitations. It is supposed not to be able to travel at a velocity in excess of

BEHIND THE FLYING SAUCERS

four to six gravities which is far in excess of what it normally has to withstand on this earth. Actually the human body is traveling at 72,000 miles per hour without even knowing it, because that's the speed which the earth has to maintain to complete its orbit around the sun on time. What the human body can't stand, apparently, is the sudden change of pace, though in May, 1950, a pilot at Edwards Air Force base riding down a track at 150 m.p.h. and strapped in a seat had his speed cut in half in .2 seconds, the equivalent of 35 gravities, and lived to say it blurred his vision, but didn't black him out.

The questions asked about rocket-propelled space ships are equally applicable to flying saucers.

How are you going to land? How are you going to return? What are you going to use for fuel? How do you expect passengers, pilots, and co-pilots to stand the strain? What about food, water, oxygen for breathing, fuel for heating the cabin?

In *Consider the Heavens* Forest Ray Moulton said that there was not the slightest possibility of such a journey, that there is no way of getting off this planet and no way to guide us through interplanetary space to another world if we could propel our departure from this. Moreover, no ship could carry the large amount of oxygen, water, and food for such a long voyage and there was no known way of easing an ether ship down on the surface of another world if we could get there.

Willy Ley, fortified by Oberth and Hohmann, thought Moulton had more fears than intelligence and recent disclosures of submarines traveling 5,000 miles without surfacing, manufacturing their own oxygen en route and eating food concentrates, tends to support Ley and dismiss Moulton.

When I was young and twenty there was a song entitled, "The Longest Way Round Is The Sweetest Way Home." It must have given Dr. Hohmann an idea, for he worked out ingenious trips from this planet to some others and finally ended with a triple-play from the earth to Mars to Venus and back to earth as a faster trip than to any one planet alone. To Venus alone he figured it would take two years and one month; to Mars, two years and eight months, and from the earth to Mars, to Venus and back to this earth, he figured could be done in eighteen months!

There were five possible orbits to travel on. But two crossed orbits and therefore had to be ruled out, because that involved a change in direction. That would be contrary to the general rotation of the solar system. Space ships have to float with the currents, not fight them.

A trip to Venus could be made in 146 days, but since Venus travels faster than the earth that would involve a stopover on Venus till the earth was again in position for the return trip. That would mean a stopover of 470 days on Venus. Another 146 days to get back and 762 days would have passed before the traveler would be returned home with his version of *Two Years Before The Mast.*

Mars moves at a slower pace than the earth. But a trip to Mars and back could not be made without a stopover any more than it could to Venus, for the simple reason that the earth would not be where we left it and we would have to wait until it came around again. That would mean 455 days waiting and another 258 days to get home. This, with the 258 days needed to get to Mars, would make a grand total of 971 days for the round trip.

But the most exciting of Hohmannic maneuvers was a nonstop flight from the earth to Mars where the pilot would not land. Instead he would drift around on the orbit that touches the earth and Venus until he found the orbit of Venus. In doing so he would have passed the earth's orbit en route but the earth would have been nowhere in sight.

He'd find Venus where he expected and would circle around Venus for a while until he was caught in the orbit of the earth. That would draw him home in less time than if he had taken stopover privileges on either of the alien planets. He wouldn't have had much to report about life on Venus or Mars, but he would have passed their way and got home in eighteen months, and as all fast travelers will tell if you save time you save money.

The whole trip would prove a little confusing to clock watchers because the planets all travel counterclockwise.

The fuel expenditure for such a trip is already solved but other factors are far from solved. In fact even under the rocket ship method of travel, moonships are considered twenty-five years in the future and those to neighboring planets much farther away. It comes as a shock therefore to hear that while we are dithering around with nuclear fission, jet propulsion, cosmic rays, and rockets, trippers riding the magnetic wave bands on disks may have been looking us over for centuries and not sure even yet if they should shake hands with us.

BEHIND THE FLYING SAUCERS

Chapter 11
An Aerodynamic Correction

THERE'S an aerodynamic proverb, or if there isn't, there ought to be, that everything has an end-except a flying saucer, which has neither a beginning nor an end.

Exceptions to this might be taken by Leo Bentz, George de Bay and Jacque Fresco, all of whom have either seen or designed flying saucers many years ago. Bentz, an old-time builder of automobiles, said he saw a confidential demonstration of a flying saucer in Griffith Park, California, as long ago as 1928. It was designed by George de Bay. It skipped through the air like a flat stone, or better, a saucer with its curved side toward the earth. Thus it worked on a vacuum principle, which de Bay explained would require ten times less power for propulsion than what was used at that time. It was not, however, designed to carry a pilot or crew. Bentz lost sight of de Bay before the war and believed he had gone to Russia.

In 1938 Jacque Fresco designed a flying saucer but at that time the aircraft companies said the model was too far ahead of anything they could handle and it was shelved while he worked on a more conventional job, which he did at Pearl Harbor, just before the war, and some Buck Rogers contributions which were his lot at Wright Field during the conflict.

A small dark man with the eyes of a fox terrier and a mind as sharp as an arctic wind, Fresco belongs to the "believe only what you can measure" school of science. Flying saucers might be mirages reflecting from round-shaped aluminum-painted oil tanks, he suggested. "They might seem to move in the sky as the sun moved, thus confusing people either on the ground or aboard planes."

But, even so, disk-shaped aerial ships he thought had a sound aerodynamic future. But he wouldn't go beyond hydrogen gas and turbojets as a means of propulsion. In fact when he heard somebody was offering $25,000 for a saucer that would fly he said that would be like taking candy from a baby. "I can build one for $15,000 and make it fly fast enough to pull a pilot out of his skin," he said, "and I'm

BEHIND THE FLYING SAUCERS

working on a way to make even him survive the experience."

The first time I hinted to him that the flying saucers under examination were in all likelihood powered by magnetic energy, the remark stopped his stream of speech and turned him for a moment into a mute, inglorious Milton.

"No aircraft engineer will go that far," he warned. "Mind, I am not stressing flying saucers in the first place, for the simple reason the industry doesn't want them, but if they're made in the future, they will have to be along conservative lines." I leave it to readers to judge what he considers conservative lines.

In the aircraft industry Fresco is known as the man who is forever twenty years ahead of his time. Up to the day I consulted him on flying saucers, hoping to use him as a possible control factor, he had been working on what he said would be the forerunner of space ships. These pre-space ship models, he said, would have to be constructed to handle problems within reach of the earth's gravity. They would have to get rid of the nuisance of static electricity, which most ships do today by the use of a tail wire which discharges extraneous electricity picked up by the skin as the ship cuts through the air. His ships of the future will use that static electricity for added propulsion.

The next problem that must be solved is to stop stalls or spins, especially at low speed. Fresco has designed a system of electrostatic controls which would not let the ship stall even if the pilot lost control. A stream of electrons fanning out from the wings will control a banking ship. Electrostatic action will not only control the ship but increase its speed. An electronic rain baffle will keep vision clear and send a positive charge of electricity through the canopy, thus creating a resistance-free passage for the craft. Raindrops would never hit the canopy, thereby giving the pilot clear visibility, rain or shine.

As for Fresco's regular planes of the near future, they will be rocket types, with snug wings for use if and when needed. Shock wave eliminated through the use of electrostatic power, air can be made to flow in any direction. Resistance thus reduced, 3,000 miles per hour will be commonplace, fast service between Los Angeles and New York a matter of perhaps minutes, interplanetary travel, 100,000 miles per hour.

Conventional motors will be used to start a ship and to bring it in. Between times it will use polarized field motors. These will change the polarity of matter and offset the effect of sudden acceleration, which would otherwise kill pilots.

In fact Fresco is of the opinion that the less you give a pilot to do the fewer people are apt to be killed. He is a great believer in a push-button war on the overworking of pilots.

I told him, according to the flying saucers my informants had researched, that had already been accomplished. The ships examined were completely run by push buttons, had no visible motors and apparently could land safely even with dead pilots.

130

BEHIND THE FLYING SAUCERS

He insisted that any such talk would only annoy aerodynamic engineers. I told him that Hall Hubbard, vice president and chief engineer of Lockheed, was already annoyed. Hubbard conceded that it was possible to build and to fly a ship that looks like a saucer but he didn't believe it possible with our present knowledge to make them fly with the speed that everybody is talking about.

Fresco wanted to know how fast the magnetic research men said that was. I said as fast as light, 186,000 miles per second. In fact, some argued that 282,000 miles per second was possible, despite Einstein's contention that nothing can travel faster than the speed of light. Fresco took a middle position between Hubbard and Einstein. "I believe we will hit 100,000 miles per second outside this atmosphere in the not too distant future," he said, "but I balk at anything faster than that, and you'll only make yourself appear ridiculous if you go beyond that even on paper.

To show me how far it would be safe to go he sketched some saucers that could be built even now. He started out with a modest job that was his model of 1938. It had eight jets spaced around the rim of the saucer like a pinwheel firecracker. The center rotated on a turbine held in position like a helicopter, while the outer rim revolved on a turbine. It was before turbojets and hence considered impractical at the time.

Since then, however, he has gone beyond turbojets in an effort to meet space ships from another planet at least half way. He has designed a hydrogen-powered turbine disk which has ten essential parts. The canopy for the crew is of transparent metal. In the center is a sphere containing liquid hydrogen. Three tubes from the sphere convey hydrogen through a nuclear reactor. The upper tube feeds the hydrogen to the upper turbine. This sets the turbine revolving. The hydrogen is then fed back through a duct to the lower turbine. This turbine moves in the opposite direction to the upper turbine. Between them they neutralize the torque in the center as would a helicopter.

A series of blades are turned so as to propel the air from the upper surface of the disk to the lower. The result would be decreased pressure on top of the disk and increased pressure below, lifting the disk vertically to any desired altitude.

The vents are then closed and a cyclic pitch actuator controls the flight direction of the disk as desired. When flying forward the disk would be tilted nose downward. This would cause the air underneath the disk to slip backward, thus propelling the disk forward. Its speed thereafter could be propelled by the use of interstellar radiation, such as the field polarizing type of motor or the harnessing of cosmic rays, thus forcing the saucer to travel in a manner similar to the way meteors travel through space.

I asked him if he knew what meteors are composed of. "Nickel and iron, mostly. Some cobalt."

"Do you know what makes the best magnet?"

BEHIND THE FLYING SAUCERS

"Sure. Steel."

"What about manganese and aluminum?"

"They're nonmagnetic. In fact an electromagnet repels aluminum."

"True, but did you know that 61 per cent copper, 24 per cent manganese, and 15 per cent aluminum when combined as an alloy are strongly magnetic?"

He wanted to know what I was hinting at. I told him the magnetic engineers say a meteor travels on magnetic lines of force and the reason they land here now and then is because they have struck a magnetic fault zone in our atmosphere. In fact they say the same thing must have happened to the flying saucers.

"People will never believe it," he said.

I told him when we got through with them they would.

BEHIND THE FLYING SAUCERS

Chapter 12
Inside Flying Saucers

IT IS an accepted practice in jurisprudence to give the plaintiff enough rope in the hope that he will hang himself and thus spare the defendant the task of doing it by way of rebuttal. On occasion when such a procedure may have left some doubt in the minds of jurors it is up to counsel for the defense to spring a surprise witness, and this I propose to do.

In the summer of 1949, while consorting with men engaged in magnetic research on the Mojave Desert, I met a man of science whose contemporaries rated him the top magnetic research specialist of the United States. He had more degrees than a thermometer and had received them from such diverse institutions as Armour Institute, Creighton University, and the University of Berlin. He is the scientist I have called Dr. Gee.

He had been assigned to direct a division of top scientists during the war. Their task was to knock submarines out of the seven seas and directed-missiles out of the skies by other than the slow and disheartening methods then in use. They conducted 35,000 experiments on land, sea, and air on this defense project. They worked out of two laboratories and had a budget of one billion dollars at their secret command. Their work has never been publicized, as was the two billion spent on creating the first atomic bomb, first, because defense is never as spectacular as offense and, second, because so much of their work was still uncompleted by the war's end that it has remained top secret to this day. Suffice it to say that it was of magnetic origin.

Long after other scientists were discharged and back in their industrial and scholarly laboratories, these men labored on. The director in fact didn't get even a conditional release until July, 1949.

I met him shortly afterward. He was the man who told us the whole story of the first flying saucer that had landed in the United States. Another had landed in the Sahara before this, but that one was more cracked than a psychiatrist in an auto wreck. But the one he had worked on had gently pancaked to earth like a slow

BEHIND THE FLYING SAUCERS

motion of Sonia Henie imitating a dying swan.

Two telescopes caught this unidentified ship as it came into our atmosphere. They watched its position and estimated where it would land. Within a few hours after it landed, Air Force officers reached the flying field at Durango, Colorado, and took off in their search for the object.

When they found it, it was in a very rocky, high plateau territory, east of Aztec, New Mexico. They immediately threw a guard around it. Then Dr. Gee and seven of his group of magnetic scientists were called in to examine this strange ship. When they arrived on the ground they decided that the best thing to do was not to touch it or try to get into it. They studied the ship from a distance for a matter of two days, bombing it with Geiger counters, cosmic rays, and other protective devices.

"Finally, we decided that it was probably safe," the doctor said, "as nothing had transpired inside the ship to indicate that there was life therein. Apparently there was no door to what unquestionably was the cabin. The outside surface showed no marking of any sort, except for a broken porthole, which appeared on first examination to be of glass. On closer examination we found it was a good deal different from any glass in this country. Finally, we took a large pole and rammed a hole through this defect in the ship.

"Having done this, we looked into the interior. There we were able to count sixteen bodies, that ranged in height from about 36 to 42 inches.

"We assumed that there must be a door of some kind, unless these people had been hermetically sealed in a pressurized cabin, so we prodded around with the pole which we had used to push through the opening made through the broken porthole, and on the opposite side from the broken porthole, we hit a knob; or a double knob, to be exact. When we pushed against that double knob, to our amazement and surprise, a door flew open. This enabled us to get into the ship.

"We took the little bodies out, and laid them on the ground. We examined them and their clothing. I remember one of our team saying, 'That looks like the style of 1890.' We examined the bodies very closely and very carefully. They were normal from every standpoint and had no appearance of being what we call on this planet 'midgets.' They were perfectly normal in their development. The only trouble was that their skin seemed to be charred a very dark chocolate color. About the only thing that we could decide at the time was that the charring had occurred somewhere in space and that their bodies had been burned as a result of air rushing through that broken porthole window, or something going wrong with the means by which the ship was propelled and the cabin pressured."

They then began an examination of the ship itself. First they decided to take complete measurements of the ship from the outside. The skin was aluminum colored.

"Reports that had appeared from time to time in the papers about these strange

134

visitors," continued Dr. Gee, "had always been to the effect that 'they looked like flying saucers.' With this ship on the ground we could not help but be aware of the fact that it looked like a huge saucer, and you might almost say that there was a cup in it, because the cabin set in an insert in the bottom of the saucer. The over-all dimensions of the ship were found to be a fraction short of 100 feet in diameter. To be exact it measured 99 99/100 feet wide. From the outer tip of the wing, which was entirely circular, to the bottom of the saucer, measuring in an imaginary line vertically, was 27 inches. The cabin which was entirely round, was 18 feet across, and 72 inches in height. Exactly 45 inches of the cabin was exposed above the outer rim of the saucer. The portholes were located in this area."

On getting into the ship, the doctor said, their first objective was to decide, if they could, how the ship was propelled. He was the first to suggest that it probably flew on magnetic lines of force. Some of his staff suggested pushing some of the buttons on what appeared to be the instrument board to find out if his suspicions were true. But all agreed after some discussion that that would be about the worst possible thing they could do, because if the ship started, nobody would know which button to push to stop it again.

"So the result was," said Dr. Gee, "that none of us pushed any buttons on the instrument board."

There were two "bucket seats," as the doctor called them, in front of the instrument board and two of the little fellows were sitting there. They had fallen over, face down, on the instrument board.

Now, it appeared that this ship, if flying on magnetic lines of force, must have had an automatic type of control, so that when it came into danger or when its occupants were not in a position to operate the ship, it simply settled quietly to earth. Obviously it had already flown into our atmospheric area, either on intelligence or instruments.

"None of us could arrive at any conclusion as to when or how this window had broken," Dr. Gee remarked, "or at what possible point in space these occupants must have been killed. The simple fact was that there they were, dead from either burns or the bends, and we proceeded with the further examination of the interior of the ship.

"We found some pamphlets or booklets, which in all probability dealt with navigation problems. However, we were unable to decipher any of the writing, which we judged to be a pictorial type of script. All of these booklets were turned over to certain officials of the Air Force, who in turn reported that they were going to have them placed in the hands of men experienced in translating work of this kind."

I asked the doctor if he had heard if the handwriting experts had much success. He said as far as he knew no headway of any kind had been made in working out a translation of the written subject matter of the booklets. He said there were not

BEHIND THE FLYING SAUCERS

any maps, and so far as they could determine the ship carried no instruments of destruction, nor the crew any firearms of any sort.

In studying the matter further, the doctor pointed out that this of course was entirely unnecessary, because if the ship had been operated magnetically, it unquestionably had the means by which it could demagnetize any object, from an asteroid to a F-80 that might cross its path. The demagnetization would destroy or disintegrate the obstacle. This of course would equally be applicable to human beings on this earth, or any form of matter which they came in contact with on this planet.

I said, "Doctor, what do you make of this whole thing? Where do you think these ships are coming from?"

He said, "Of course we don't know, but our best guess at this moment, astronomers to the contrary, is that they have flown here from the planet Venus."

I asked him why they had decided this.

"Well," he said, "in all the latest research regarding the possibility of life on other planets it was fairly well agreed among quite a school of thought in astronomical research, that there was more likelihood of human habitation on the planet Venus than on the planet Mars."

The size of the men, too, was a factor in his decision. He went so far as to say that if there were any human beings on the planet Mars they would probably be three or four times as large as human beings on this planet, and since the people on the grounded disk ship ranged in height from about 36 to 42 inches, that, in his judgment, ruled out Mars.

Day after day over a period of the next ninety days following this first talk about this first space ship, or as we came to talk of it, this "flying saucer," one of our number, made it his business on all sorts of occasions, most of them when alone with the doctor and in the midst of research in magnetic work, to ask him for more details. The questioner came up with questions at the most inopportune times, because, it must be understood, that he felt that he owed it to himself as well as to us, to run this thing down to where we could finally decide as to whether or not this was all true.

On one occasion he asked, "Doctor, how were these ships constructed?" He said, "The outer skin of the ship was what looked like aluminum, but on all the tests so far made, there was nothing that had been found by the scientists who had checked into it, to indicate that this was any form of aluminum that we know."

He said that on the big ship two or three men could lift one side of it, it was that light. On the other hand, as many as a dozen of them had crawled up on top of the wing and it was so strong they made no impression on it whatever.

He said that the Air Force, in wanting to move the ship, decided to dismantle it because it was too big to move otherwise. This began a most interesting study. There were no rivets. There were no bolts, no screws. There was nothing on the

136

outer skin that would indicate how the ship was put together.

After a long study it was found, however, that the ship was assembled in segments. The segments fitted in grooves and were pinned together around the base.

When the cabin was lifted out of the bottom of the saucer, they found a gear completely encircling the bottom of the ship and this gear fitted into a gear that was on the cabin.

The whole thing was very ingeniously put together, and there had to be a lot of care taken in breaking it down.

After it had been broken down, it was moved to a government testing laboratory and there it remained while parts were being tested for a considerable period of time.

When Dr. Gee next saw it, the instrument board, to his amazement and chagrin, had been broken up and all of the inner workings torn apart. This, he said, prevented any further study by them as to the magnetic operation of the ship itself.

He regretted this dismantling very much, because he said that had they been able to keep it intact long enough, there might have come a time when they might have worked out a plan whereby they could make certain tests as to the different push buttons on the instrument board. These, he was certain, held the clews to the magnetic form of combustion developed on the ship itself.

One of us asked, "What has been done with the people that were on the ship?" Dr. Gee said that some of them had been dissected, and studied by the medical division of the Air Force and that from the meager reports he had received, they had found that these little fellows were in all respects perfectly normal human beings, except for their teeth. There wasn't a cavity or a filling in any mouth. Their teeth were perfect.

From the characteristics and physiology of their bodies they must have been about 35 to 40 years of age, judged by our standards of age.

As to clothes, he said they all wore the same type of uniform, a dark blue garment, with metal buttons. He said it was significant that there was not any insignia of any kind on the collars or on the sleeves or on the caps of these people. So, to all intents and purposes, all of them had the same rank.

He said it might of course be possible that they had different ranks among themselves but that by our standards of military ranking there was nothing to indicate who they were nor what they were.

Going into the matter of physical possessions on the bodies of these people, Dr. Gee said that so far as he saw himself, they were very limited, but that there were two or three pieces to which he had had access that might have been timepieces.

He said it was very interesting to study these timepieces, because they seemed to do their work, or functioning, without any attention. The timepieces were about the size of a silver dollar in diameter and a little bit thicker. They had four markings, one at the top, and one at what would be 3 o'clock, another at 6 o'clock, and a fourth at 9 o'clock.

It was discovered that the inside part of what he and his staff called a timepiece, actually moved, but that it took a full magnetic month for it to complete its circle.

"Now," said Dr. Gee, "you know of course that a magnetic day is 23 hours and 58 minutes. We found that the time it took for the timepiece to make this complete circumference, was over 29 days. Figured out in hours and minutes, that totaled exactly the number of magnetic days in a magnetic month."

He said that there was what appeared to be food on this ship and that these were little wafers. They fed them to guinea pigs, and they seemed to thrive on them. On one occasion one wafer was put into a gallon container of boiling water and it very quickly boiled over the sides of the container.

This was the only evidence of food on the ship. He added that there were two containers of water on this particular ship, and on checking the water they found it to be normal in all respects to our water, except it was about twice as heavy. The doctor pointed out that there was a water in Norway that was about the weight of this water.

One day Si Newton, who was closest to Dr. Gee and felt he was in a position to act as a sort of buffer state, since he was both a partner in geophysical research and independent of any Pentagonic ties, past or present, was surprised to hear the doctor say, "I want you to see these ships and judge for yourself whether we are on the right track and not guessing at their point of origin. I'm trying to get clearance right now."

Newton asked, "Did you say *ships*?"

"Oh yes," responded Dr. Gee, "we have had three and we saw a fourth. But that one got away," he added with a laugh. "The second one landed near one of the proving grounds in Arizona, as opposed to the first which landed near a proving ground in New Mexico. When we got to the second one we found almost the same conditions of the first, except that the door was open and the sixteen dead people in it were not burned nor browned. In fact medical opinion was that they had not been dead more than two or three hours. Our conclusion was that they had died in our atmosphere when the double knob of the door was opened and our air rushed into their cabin which was probably vacuumed or pressurized for their atmosphere but not ours."

Newton asked, "How do you determine the presence of these particular ships. Do you stumble on them or know the moment they come in our atmosphere?"

Dr. Gee replied, "In the laboratories and also at Alamogordo and Los Alamos and at different parts of the country we have tenescope observers who spend 24 hours a day watching for evidence of objects or ships flying in the sky. Everything that comes within the range of these tenescopes is noted. If it is unfamiliar and lands, the Air Force is aware of it almost immediately, and if it presents scientific problems we or other groups are consulted."

He said that the second ship was smaller, 72 feet in diameter, but otherwise similar to the 99 $^{99}/_{100}$ foot ship. He and his fellow scientists had decided that the mathematical system of the operators of these ships was in all probability the same as ours, "because mathematical law should follow for all the planets in this solar system." Their reason for thinking this was because they were struck with the fact that when the measurements of the ship in all its parts were broken down they found that it followed what he called "The System of 9's."

He went to considerable length to explain the mathematical system of 9's, and added, "We concluded from this clew that in all probability they used a system of mathematics similar to ours."

The third ship he and his staff examined landed right above Phoenix in Paradise Valley. "We happened to be in Phoenix, so we got out to it in a hurry."

One of the little men was half out of the escape door or "hatch," as the doctor called it. The little man was dead. The other little fellow (there being only a crew of two on this ship) was sitting in his seat at the control board. He also was dead. This ship was 36 feet in diameter and the size of the cabin and all the rest of dimensions balanced out on the same system of 9's, that had been found in the other ships.

Asked if they had any sleeping quarters or toilet facilities, the doctor explained that on the 72-foot ship there was a very ingenious device which when they discovered how to operate it, turned out to be the sleeping quarters. Pushed back into the wall was what turned out to be a collapsible or accordion type screen, and as it was pulled out, it moved around in a half circle, so that by the time it reached the wall of the circular cabin little hammocks had dropped down from this screen or accordion-like wall, and there were the sleeping quarters for these men.

He said there were toilet facilities inside the sleeping quarters. The smallest ship, however, had no such conveniences, from which the doctor deduced they were making round trips so fast they didn't feel the need of such facilities any longer.

Newton asked, "Where is the little ship?"

"We have that one in the laboratories at the present time," replied Dr. Gee. "As soon as I get your appointment through I will be authorized to let you inspect it."

In time Newton's appointment came through, but by then the ship had been dismantled and reported shipped to Dayton, and all comment thereafter proscribed, denied, or ignored.

All the doctor had to show for his labors was a tubeless radio, some gears, some small disks, and other items that could be carried in one's pocket. He was granted these baubles for research.

I saw and examined these. More than 150 tests had failed to break down the metal of the gears. The gears themselves were of a ratio unfamiliar to engineers on this earth; had no play, no lubrication.

As for the radio, it was not much bigger than a pack of cigarettes. It had been torn from a corner of the cabin, which was in all likelihood its aerial antenna. It had no tubes, no wires, and only one dial. Dr. Gee built a special antenna for it, about 4 inches high, and was able to catch a high C sort of note at 15 minutes past every hour. It wasn't radio as we know it, but it was a means of communication with somewhere.

Asked what possible reason there could be for keeping all this a secret, Dr. Gee couldn't imagine, "unless," he added, "fear of a panic or the upsetting of certain religious beliefs, or just plain brass exercising its authoritative powers to keep their powers from atrophying. The government wants to keep people away from that area of New Mexico, as this could very well start a stampede of curiosity seekers as well as a panic among certain types of people who are easily frightened. I've talked to religious leaders and they ridicule any idea that this would upset theological concepts. So I can't imagine what the Air Force had in mind. All I know is they ruined our chances of working on 'live' models and have left themselves groping and guessing ever since. I think we have some of the answers by now, but they are derived from our side not the visitors, who, my guess is, are 500 years ahead of us-in their knowledge of propulsion at any rate."

Whether we can soon return the compliment and visit the Saucerians, with or without permission of the Pentagonians, even with nothing more than the charred body of Orson Welles, depends, Dr. Gee believed, on how fast we can step up our knowledge of magnetic propulsion and the whole subject of magnetic energy generally. That the visitors showed improvement in each ship they sent out, the doctor didn't doubt. He pointed out a three point landing gear which was on the smallest ship. It held steel balls in vacuum cups which permitted the balls to revolve. While the balls were moving in one direction, nothing could tilt or tip the ship, but when they were motionless a child could tilt it. To solve that secret alone, Dr. Gee contended, would be worth years of research. Maybe others in the vast interdepartmental structure of the Pentagon are doing it and keeping it a secret from those who worked on some other phase of it. The whole procedure tends to make a man hoard what he knows instead of sharing it, lest he be clinked for giving away the nation's security, or what some fallible and unidentified authority has decreed for the moment is the nation's security.

We asked the doctor what in his opinion were the chances of the Air Force's eventually admitting that the flying saucers have come from another planet. He replied that as nearly as he could judge from all the work that he and his associates had done, the Air Force was not interested in admitting the discovery of a new method of flight. Jet propulsion was their story and we were stuck with it. Then he launched on a technical explanation concerning the creation of motive power by the breaking of magnetic lines of force. He called to my attention that there are 1,257 magnetic lines of force to the square centimeter. These are counted on a tenescope as one would count strands of wire at the cut end of a cable.

He said that the crossing of two or more lines of force made it possible in effect to permit movement in a manner hitherto unknown in aerodynamics.

"Of course, you understand," he added, "the saucer-like construction is the most ideal type of vehicle to move in the air. The fact that the saucer whirls is only for the purpose of balance, because there is not any thrust insofar as the wing surface is concerned. There is not any thrust by reason of any propeller, either, because there are no propellers.

"What actually happens is that, even though the wing part is whirling, the saucer actually crawls forward from one crossed magnetic line of force to another.

"Now, when you consider there are 1,257 lines to the square centimeter and no two cross. We have the problem of combustion or propulsion, or power created when they are crossed under control. The successive crossing of these magnetic lines of force under control makes possible the speeding up of the whirling action of the plate or wing part of the saucer, because the saucer is attempting to get to the next succeeding line of force; or, perhaps we could say, seeking to get back in balance.

"In other words, the ship is trying to get away from itself, or trying to get away from the position it finds itself in, when combustion power is created by the crossing of magnetic lines of force.

"We think in terms of electric current, when it is produced in a wire, as traveling in the wire itself, or as some scientists put it, flowing through a wire. This has never been conclusively proved. But we do know that where the electric energy is created at its source, the dynamo, it is transmitted through the wire, and the wire of course becomes a magnetic field and at its various termini we have the use of it, as electric light or in other forms."

Asked if he didn't consider that the motive power of the saucer was what one might say, in reverse as to electric energy in a wire, Dr. Gee explained, "What we have here is energy existing and created without a wire and actually in the lines of force themselves. The saucer being so regulated magnetically is eternally trying to get away from its disturbed magnetic points, as a person prodded from behind by a needle might try to get away from the disturbance, and thereby movement is created.

"When the saucer moves out of our atmospheric area, or control, then, of course, we have no weight and we have no resistance. And all we have left is magnetic lines of force, which are in an undisturbed state, out to where they approach magnetic lines of force from another planet. Since these magnetic lines of force are identical, they act similar to the two north poles of any magnet. In other words, like poles (which is the first law of magnetism) repel. Therefore, the planet Venus,

BEHIND THE FLYING SAUCERS

for example, and the planet Earth, is each held in position by reason of its magnetic repulsion. All are in universal balance and all move in their orbits in the same fashion.

"We do not understand how these magnetic fields are created from the sun; we only know that they exist, and when we learn something about how they are created, or how they evolved, then we can begin to learn something about how they act."

His reason for appraising the interplanetary visitors who have flown in here as being 500 years ahead of us, is based on the fact that they now appear to come and go at will. Somehow they can cross from their magnetic lines of force on to ours, despite the fact that the two planets involved are positive and would therefore repel any object's effort to move from one to the other. It is as easy to conceive of them traveling in their zone and we in ours as it is to conceive of traveling up and down on a scenic railway once given sufficient push. But hopping from one scenic railway to another going in the opposite direction represents a triumph of magic over experience. This the Saucerians appear to have achieved. They fly singly, and in groups and, as reported at Farmington, New Mexico, during the month of March, 1950, they even appear now and then in groups of hundreds. It is as if they were demonstrating that where one, two, and even three of their number had failed, they later corrected the faults that caused the failures and came over in strength, flying over the very area where their pioneers had died trying.

Those whose doubts exceeded those of the Pentagonians have harped on the size of those piloting the flying saucers. It has seemed to them like a rewrite of Gulliver's Travels. These scoffers should not be allowed to forget that Jonathan Swift's little friends measured six inches high, whereas these Saucerians measured three to three-and-a-half feet tall and are therefore at least as believable as Mickey Rooney.

BEHIND THE FLYING SAUCERS

Chapter 13
From Lodestone to Einstein

TO UNDERSTAND at all how magnetic energy could be the quiet one behind all the current sound and fury concerning the presence and propulsion of flying saucers, it may be necessary to point out historically how this primary force got lost in the shuffle.

The Pentagonians obviously were ignorant of it. Otherwise they would have included references to it in their various communiques to us, their paymasters, before closing down Project Saucer. Scientists in related fields may know a little more than the Pentagonians, but because the former no longer enjoy the free exchange of ideas under the bugaboo of "security" they are either reluctant to give the devil his due or ignorant of his activities. The cell-by-cell method of research, further sealed off by the military's forceful phobias, has developed modern science into a self-limiting disease, as physicians would call it.

Thus it would be as fruitless to ask Vannevar Bush, Robert Millikan, Harold C. Urey, and possibly Albert Einstein to check on these findings as it would be to ask them to check on the end results of a hydrogen bomb which fortunately hasn't been detonated as yet. So they as well as the lower orders of idealists, may find a briefing in the other man's field as not too gratuitous.

They know of course that the first law of magnetism is that like poles repel and unlike poles attract, that William Gilbert (1544-1603) was known as the father of magnetism (despite the fact that Thales of Miletus, the first Ionian physicist, had discovered the phenomenon of frictional electricity and hence of magnetism 2,000 years before Gilbert and Peter Peregrinus, 1269, discovered magnetic poles) and that it might have been better if Benjamin Franklin were known today as the patron of both these pioneers instead of as "the father of electricity," for without a knowledge of magnetism we would have had no knowledge of electricity.

The word magnet, according to Lucretius, was derived from the hills of the Magnesians where he thought it was first found, though Pliny credited it to a shepherd named Magnes who one day raised his iron crook on Mount Ida and found to

BEHIND THE FLYING SAUCERS

his amazement that his staff stuck to a ledge which projected above his head. Centuries before this, however, the Chinese used a lodestone, which was as much of magnet as the stone Magnes contacted in the second century B.C.

Around the year 1000 Mediterranean navigators were using suspended magnets to help them home. These lodestones or "lead-stones" were the guides for Peter Peregrinus who by converging lines like meridians toward two points on a sphere's surface found that he had worked out the idea of magnetic poles. In fact he called them that.

From the open sea, magnetism next moved into the parlor where in the sixteenth century we find William Gilbert entertaining Queen Elizabeth with his parlor tricks. He rubbed two bodies together (one of them amber) and could pick up pieces of paper, thanks to the generated magnetism. This came close to black magic and witchcraft, but Gilbert was a court physician instead of a female on a broomstick and thus was spared the rod, which if whacked hard enough on a wool-covered gluteus maximus would have generated more "static electricity," not less.

If Gilbert had not been so familiar with Greek and had not called bodies which, when rubbed, attracted lighter bodies to themselves, electrics (after elektron the Greek word for amber) a lot of the later confusion between electricity and magnetism never would have arisen. Between Gilbert's electrics and non-electrics developed what is today known as insulators and conductors of electricity.

The next great step away from simplicity was when Stephen Gray (1729) electrified two wooden cubes-one hollow and one solid. He showed they produced the same effects and concluded that the electrification is identified with the surfaces and not the volumes of objects. Thus began two hundred years of new discoveries, most of them wrong, because if Gray had realized that however you cut an object, its magnetic qualities remain the same, he would not have gone off on a tangent about electrification being the surface not the center of things.

After Gray came Du Fay, who developed the positive and negative phases of electricity. Franklin came on this discovery sometime later independently.

Then there was Von Kleist, Von Musschenbroek, Grallat, and finally Leyden, whose jar permitted the concentration and storage of electricity.

Of course everyone remembers Benjamin Franklin's famous kite and the key that drew off fire from the cloud, but few remember Coulomb (1785) who introduced a quantitative basis into the study of magnetism. Previously research had been exclusively qualitative. Coulomb showed that electric charges exert forces on each other inversely to the square of the distance. The same was true of magnetic poles.

This law of Coulomb's was merely a restatement of Newton (1680) who had applied the inverse-square law to the gravitational field. The two (gravity and magnetism) though obviously stemming from the same parent, remained unrelated until Einstein, as late as 1950, sought to bring them together again, where in

BEHIND THE FLYING SAUCERS

fact they had been from the beginning.

Around 1800, Volta made the first voltaic pile and found that by closing the circuits, he could get a continuous electrical effect. This differed from the Leyden jar which like a modern storage battery had to be re-electrified after each discharge.

Nicholson, Carlisle, Humphry Davy, Berzelius, and others moved into the physical field of electricity behind Franklin, Coulomb, and the pioneers. Berzelius advanced the theory that every compound contained two parts, and that the chemical combination resulted when oppositely charged ions united, thus giving stability to the compound and neutralizing the electricities therein. This is so close to the modern theory that everything is kept in magnetic balance, that it's fantastic it should have been lost sight of for 150 years.

Researching in the same general period were Ampere (the Newton of Electricity), Faraday (who had worked under Humphry Davy), Sturgeon, (who worked out the first electromagnet), and Ohm after whom Ohm's Law was named. Of this group perhaps Michael Faraday would be most worthy of long-time recognition because he worked out the principle on which present-day alternating currents are based. This particular discovery of his, however, lay dead for fifty years.

Another one of his researches might bear further study today. That is a study of the intervening space or substance subjected to electric or magnetic influence. Before Faraday's time, as of today, most people were interested in the end-results. That is to say, the phenomena themselves. But Faraday decided to find out what went on between the electricity and/or the magnetism which caused certain phenomena, and the phenomena themselves. Thus, if he were alive today it could be fairly well predicted that he would be neither fronting for the Air Force (denying such things as flying saucers), nor off in space somewhere trying to find what causes that, but would be right in the middle examining every part of the ships themselves.

After Faraday came Lord Kelvin, who got his title because he was a distinguished physicist, not because somebody of the same name died. Kelvin did a great deal toward the accurate measurement of physical matter, and was largely responsible for the electrostatic and electromagnetic systems of units based on the point electric charge and the point magnetic pole, referred to in scientific circles as CGS.

In 1856, Weber and Kohlrausch worked out the unit of measurement between electrostatic and electromagnetic units and found it to be three times ten raised to the tenth degree. This in itself reads just like another algebraic figure, which ought to be avoided in a book of this sort at all costs, but actually it contains a secret that might be most revealing, if it ever penetrates the caverns of the Pentagon. Because $3 \times 10^{1°}$ is very close to the velocity of light, and as all know, light travels at 186,000 miles per second.

BEHIND THE FLYING SAUCERS

By 1905, Einstein had concluded that nothing traveled faster than light. Today magnetic research scientists deny this, but rather than project their heresy into the discussion at this point, let us limit all speed to the speed of light. An object that could travel at such speed would make transportation between this planet and another no more time consuming than a commuter's trip from New York to New Haven. In fact a trip from Venus to this earth and back would take 42 minutes.

To return to our muttons, however, in 1852, Kelvin and Clausius laid down two laws of thermodynamics which still hold good. The first was that energy may be transformed from one state to another, its total amount remaining constant. This law of the conservation of energy was followed by a second law, which stated that wherever energy was transformed from one state to another some of it appeared in the form of heat, which was considered the lowest form of energy (to which in time it was feared all energy would degenerate).

Lenz contributed a law following the statement of the principle of the conservation of energy. He declared:

"Whenever a current is induced by the relative motion of the magnetic field and a conductor, the direction of the induced cur- rent is always such as to set up a magnetic field which opposes the motion."

In other words, the electrical energy (EMF) is gained in this case at the expense of mechanical energy.

Clerk Maxwell (1873) was the next pioneer in the field. I fact it was he who cleared up many of the obscurities of Kelvin, Weber, Kohlrausch, and Faraday. In Maxwell's equations, he asserted that electric and magnetic fields, if changing in time, generate each other and by their combined action, propagate energy as waves out into space with the velocity of light.

From here to the assertion that light was nothing more than an electromagnetic wave was but a short step, but it nearly got Maxwell's legs blown off. Today it is as accepted as the presence of the electric light itself.

After these great men came many whose names are known to the present generation. But one not so well known was Max Planck, who discovered that Maxwell's marvelous definitions failed to explain certain facts about radiant energy. It was assumed that light was propagated through space in the form of continuous waves. Planck said it wasn't so, that the radiant energy was transmitted from the originating source in "clusters" or "quanta" and thus began the quantum theory, the beginning of the belief that all matter is atomic in nature. Of course, some argue that Maxwell's old theory was better able to explain the interference of light than Planck or the quantum theory, but the modern magnetic scientist believes that both can be gathered under one canopy because everything is magnetic in its origin.

From Planck to Einstein was a short walk but it involved a great change of scenery, and from that great change in 1905 to today has seen all science moving further away from Gilbert's original error in calling matter electric and Newton's error in calling the law of magnetic balance gravitation.

Early in the career of science there was only one godhead and that was magnetism. But by the time the twentieth century got really going the physical world had been split into as many parts as an automobile. Chiefly they were electricity, physics, chemistry, and light, with poor old Father Magnetism shoved off in the attic somewhere. The electronic theory sought to unite them by holding that all matter was essentially electrical in its constitution, but, as I have pointed out, this was Gilbert's original error in associating the word with the Greek word for amber.

The wars brought them all under one roof again, but the injection by the military of secrecy, security, and such unscientific jargon broke them into unrelated cells again. Their postwar efforts to get together have been stamped as proof of disloyalty by one political division or another.

Einstein's Special Theory of Relativity was another step toward an attempt at unity, and further attempts, such as the dropping of electromagnetic term for the simpler magnetic term may bring the whole inquiry back to where it began.

The electron theory rests on the belief that all matter is electrical in its constitution. It isn't much to admit that magnetism and electricity are one and from there to the acceptance that all matter is magnetic in its constitution is but a step.

Einstein briefly, stripped of 24 pages of equations, was trying to prove the following points:

1. His objective in formulating his Unified Field Theory was to prove that all forms of nature-stars, planets, light, electricity, and possibly the tiny particles inside the atom-obey the same basic universal laws.

2. Practically all the phenomena of nature arise from two basic forces: the electromagnetic force, the basis of light and all radiant energy, heat, etc.; and the gravitational force, the force which guides the movements of material objects as well as celestial bodies. (There is one other force which tends to operate in a sphere of its own. Nuclear force, as personified in the atomic bomb.)

3. There has been speculation for years as to whether the gravitational force described by Newton wasn't really electromagnetism. The bug was that all past efforts to establish gravitation as a form of electromagnetism has met with failure. Either Newton or Maxwell was wrong.

4. What the Unified Field does is to show that gravitation and electromagnetism are inseparable.

5. Einstein stated in 1905 that all matter is "frozen" energy, and that matter differs from energy only temporarily.

6. He said in 1916 that all measurements of time are actually measurements in space. (Space-time concept, the fourth dimension).

Only one person was supposed to have understood Einstein's Special Theory of Relativity when he advanced it in 1905. That was when he handed down a decision that nothing exceeded the speed of light. His exception to the general law of travel, however, was that whereas two automobiles traveling at 30 miles an hour would meet head on at 60 miles an hour, two light waves traveling at 186,000 m.p.h. would meet head on at 186,000 m.p.h. That would be their relative speed in space.

By 1916 when Einstein released his General Theory of Relativity the number who understood him had increased to 12. The rest of us had to be satisfied with the suspicion that it meant that parallel lines eventually meet, that a fourth dimension (the time-space factor) would have to be accepted to understand the theory at all, and that for average men it would be only necessary to understand that if they were on a train, which was standing at the station, and a train on the next track moved, confusing the passengers in the first train as to whether they or the people in the other train were moving, all parties had got all they needed to know about the Theory of Relativity.

By now maybe more people understood Einstein's latest theory, the Unified Field Theory, which is the last of his many attempts to integrate Newton's law of gravity with modern theories of radiation, light, and magnetic energy, generally classed under the head of electromagnetism.

But for all who may claim to understand Einstein's latest attempt to simplify the law of the universe, from theologians who may rejoice in gathering the once professed atheist into God's pastures, to fellow scientists who may feel he bit off more than he could chew if he lived another hundred years (which he readily conceded), there is grave doubt if there are a dozen persons, Einstein included, who have a thorough grasp of electromagnetic energy.

Even those scientists from the magnetic field, who supplied Einstein with a good deal of original material, don't quite know yet after thousands of years what makes a lodestone work, or why. If they did they could power planes on this earth and send them spinning to Venus and back like perfectly controlled boomerangs.

Einstein's twenty-page resume of his latest theory left the conflict between two kinds of physics unreconciled. What happens to an atom and what happens to the universe at large still don't match, and they won't match, magnetic scientists contend, until all accept the theory that there are things faster than light, that in this atmosphere it is possible for an object to travel on a magnetic wave at 282,000 miles per second and that beyond the magnetic forces of this planet, travel at a million miles per second, is not only possible but routine.

Just as Einstein was positive that nothing exceeded the speed of light and that all energy was "frozen" energy and that matter differs from energy only temporarily (as, for example, a ball on a shelf and the same ball falling to the floor) so are the magnetic scientists positive that everything from a pencil to a flying saucer has its magnetic frequencies and that any force which can disturb or break (for even a split-second) these frequencies, can disintegrate the object so disturbed. This moves us ahead of atomic fission, into, in fact, magnetic fission.

It explains why our concern need no longer be about enemies on this earth, but

BEHIND THE FLYING SAUCERS

what protection we have from visitors from other planets who may have mastered the means of moving from their magnetic field on magnetic lines of force into ours and disintegrating our whole planet while we are working out ways to disintegrate cities of earthbound "enemies" by atomic or hydrogenic bombs. We could of course give some serious thought to the use of countermagnetic disintegration as a perfect method of shielding this fair land in case of air invasion, but since the observers have shown no belligerence unless positively threatened perhaps the emphasis should be on politesse rather than pugnacity.

The Air Force as well as scientists and people generally need to be trained to politeness on an interplanetary level. This may be as difficult as it is for strangers to make friends with babies. Some of our scientists are reported to have whistled at a group of grounded Saucerians and when the Saucerians ran, the scientists ran after them, only to have the Saucerians disappear in the blue.

Felix Frazer tells me that in discussing the question with Air Force pilots, colonels no less, they said they had no instructions as to how to act if they met a saucer above our mainland. The procedure, they informed him, is let the ship have it first and ask questions afterward. If met on the ground the procedure is to take the aliens into custody, by force, naturally, if necessary, and to shoot them if they attempted to run away.

Of course the proper procedure is not to lay hands on them, any more than you would on a wire carrying a current of 2,000 volts. An act of friendliness might change the world at such a time. Since the Saucerians are obviously so far ahead of us scientifically, it would be utterly silly for us to try to outsmart them. We are really where the Japanese in Hiroshima were in defense against the A-bomb in 1945. Whatever way we could learn from the Saucerians as to how they got on without blowing each other to pieces would be welcome information to us. It is quite possible that in many ways we may have developed techniques in civilized living which would be helpful to them, for we have done many good things in peace as well as bad things in war.

The worst feature of our present predicament is that the military has first crack at everything and is the poorest equipped for handling such delicate matters as the birth of communication on an interplanetary level. For this work we should be training an army of Emily Posts instead of trigger-happy bombardiers.

I hereby turn this suggestion over to the Nobel committee for consideration before they award their next peace prize.

BEHIND THE FLYING SAUCERS

Chapter 14
Some Magnetic Definitions

DESPITE THE BACKGROUND they now possess of a capsule history of magnetism, our readers, unless strapped in with a more technical briefing of the mysteries behind magnetic energy, may fly off into space as we move inside, around and behind the flying saucers at 90-degree angles.

Even when granted asylum among these mysteries, as St. Francis of Assisi or Androcles might grant protection to wild animals, the Pentagonian wolf pack may find the chase too much for them and drop dead of exhaustion. For those who hang on it is only fair to warn them that, as in Dante's Inferno, they should abandon all hope who enter here, for cynicism, skepticism and negative approaches generally will never knock down the magnetic lines of force which were set up millions of years ago to disintegrate them if they carried their pursuit of ignorance this far.

Enough hints have been dropped at intervals through this monograph to have warned all dissenters with an I.Q. above 102 as to what would happen to them if they persisted in following the Air Force's party line to the effect that flying saucers do not exist anywhere in this solar system and that believers in their presence are victims of hallucinations, mass hysteria, or hoaxes. Unfortunately those who persist in following party lines, and even fellow travelers, are almost to a man unsusceptible to nuances, hints, suggestions, and sometimes even to shock. But now and then you find an exception.

As an example of last-minute conversion I quote Harry von Zell. Up to May, 1950, he was in the doubters' camp. But after he returned to Hollywood from New Mexico, where he had been on location with a picture company he asked to be stricken from the list of Doubting Thomases. He said that anywhere within fifty miles of Los Alamos the air was so full of magnetic charges that he had to ground his house key to keep the static electricity from giving him a perpetual hot-foot. "Everybody's hair stood on end. Don't tell me that we're not fooling around with the stuff or that somebody somewhere doesn't know how to use it to propel objects through the air."

Only a week before this plausible dispenser of radio commercials hit the magnetized trail, I had twenty men listen to a personal history of one man's experience with flying saucers. The group contained former Air Force pilots, former G-2 men, aerodynamic engineers, physicists, astronomers, and specialists in the field of magnetic energy. The seminar took five hours and all agreed it was an evening such as they had never previously enjoyed in their lives.

They were made privy to such inside stuff as is known to no one outside the inner circle dealing with magnetic phenomena. Much they could not understand because the technical language was as alien to their ears as Sanskrit. As more is about to be revealed, perhaps it would be sensible to pause for a moment while certain terms are defined.

Since it would only produce confusion worse confounded to go into matters of conductivity, flux linkages, inductance, potentials as distinguished from permittivity, demagnetism as distinguished from diamagnetism, definitions will be limited to:

Magnetic Analysis. The separation of a stream of electrified particles by a magnetic field in accordance with their mass, charge, or speed. This is the principle behind the mass spectrograph.

Magnetic Declination. The angle between true north geographical and magnetic north, the direction of the compass needle. This angle is different for different places and changes continuously with respect to time. Magnetic Dip. The angle that the magnetic field of the earth makes with the horizontal at a particular location. Also called magnetic inclination.

Magnetic Field. A vector field magnetizing force as generally used in magnetic field indicates the region throughout which the magnetizing force values are of significant magnitude with respect to the conditions under consideration. In effect a magnetic field is in a region in which the magnetic forces created by a permanent magnet or by a current carrying conductor or coil can be detected.

Magnetic Figures. A pattern showing the distribution of a magnetic field, made by sprinkling iron filings on nonmagnetic surface in the field.

Magnetic Flux. Magnetic lines of force.

Magnetic Flux Density. The magnetic quantity. Number of magnetic lines of force that determines how much voltage will be induced in a conductor that moves in a particular point in a magnetic field. It is the number of magnetic lines of force per unit area at right angles to the lines. More generally called magnetic induction.

Magnetic Hysteresis occurs when a ferro magnetic substance is subjected to a varying magnetic field and causes the magnetic induction to lag behind the changes in magnetizing force.

Magnetic Lines of Force. Imaginary lines used for convenience to represent the direction in which magnetic forces are acting in a magnetic field and to represent the strength of the magnetic field.

Magnetic Map. Map indicating (a) isogenics, which are lines of equal declination and (b) isoclinics, which are lines of equal dip.

Magnetron (a) A vacuum thermionic tube in which a magnetic field externally produced by a coil surrounding the tube is used to control the unidirectional current flow. It is used for generating microwaves, radio waves below one meter in wave length. (b) In a split anode magnetron the cylindrical anode that surrounds the cathode is divided longitudinally into halves between which the oscillations are produced. (c) Enlarged magnetrons handling powers up to about a thousand kilowatts in continuous oscillation are produced in the plate circuit at twice the frequency of the high frequency alternating field provided by the filament without the use of a grid.

Magnetic Particle. A small but relatively long and thin portion of a magnetizable medium, possessing equal poles of opposite types at the ends.

Magnetic Pole. (a) Either of the two poles of a magnet, north pole and south pole, near which the magnetic intensity is greatest. (b) Either of two locations on the surface of the earth toward which a compass needle points. The north magnetic pole is near the north geographic pole and hence attracts the south pole of a compass needle.

Magnetic Storm. Rapid and erratic changes in magnetic field of the earth believed due to the activity on the sun. It seriously affects both radio and wire communications.

Permeability. The ability of a material to become magnetized when placed in a magnetic field. The same as the dielectric constant in the electric field.

Unit Pole. One that repels a like pole of 1 dyne when they are placed 1 cm. apart in a vacuum.

Magnetic Zero. The magnetic zero station in America is at Gary, Indiana, which is on the agonic line of our isogenic map as prepared by the U.S. Geodetic survey.

Albert Wallace Hull, research physicist, born April 19, 1880, a graduate of Yale, invented the magnetron and in co-operation with Dr. F. R. Elder, developed oscillators, which produce 10 kw. at 50 kilocycles. The magnetron came into renewed prominence in 1928 with the discovery that magnetrons having split anodes can generate very high frequencies.

Since: then the magnetron has had many important applications. It depends on the fact that electrons can be ordered in their path by a magnet. In ordinary electron tubes, the flow of electrons from the filaments to the plate is regulated by the change on the grid. In the magnetron there is no grid, but the tube is in a magnetic field. As the intensity of the field increases, there comes a stage at which the electrons are curled back into the filament and never reach the plate. At this critical point a slight change in the field produces a large change in the current carried by the tube.

BEHIND THE FLYING SAUCERS

The magnetron is especially valuable for producing high frequency oscillations used for generating ultra short waves. The magnetron is a diode or thermionic tube having a strange axiol cathode surrounded by a cylindrical anode. Its use as a magnetic prospecting instrument derives from the fact that in the presence of a magnetic field the electrons do not travel regularly from the cathode to the anode; instead they spiral around the cathode in circular paths and after a critical magnetic field intensity is reached, the electrons will return to the cathode without reaching the anode. At this field strength the plate current will drop abruptly. The procedure in operating the instrument consists in decreasing the plate voltage on the diode until the voltage is reached at which the current falls off rapidly. The place voltage at which this occurs is related to the critical field strength H by the relation H-6/7200 V/R where R is the radius of the anode.

In practice a compensation procedure is used wherein the field to be measured is nullified by a known field produced by Helmut's coil arrangement. The magnetron is affected by the component of the earth's field which is parallel to its axis. The instrument theoretically may be used to measure any components of the earth's field by suitable orientation.

The sensitivity of the tube may be increased through regeneration by passing the plate current through an additional solenoid. Interesting experimental results have been obtained by using magnetic alloy field pieces to increase the affected magnetic field.

The earth being simply a huge magnet, a dynamo wound with magnetic lines of force as its coils, tenescopically counted to be 1,257 to the square centimeter in one direction and 1,850 to the square centimeter in the other direction (eddy currents) indicates that natural law has placed these lines as close together as the hairs on one's head. And yet they never touch or cross each other if let alone. If done so by accident the catastrophe would spread like a searchlight and destroy everything in its path. An original error of say, a foot, at its source would burn everything in its path up to 20 miles and a mile and a half wide in a ten-thousandth of a second. If left to encircle the world the original flash would have banded the globe ten times in one second. Fortunately, as a weapon of defense, this destructive force has been mastered.

The spectroscope shows that there is an enormous magnetic field around the sun, and it is the present conclusion of the best minds that magnetic lines of force from the sun envelop this earth and extend to the moon, and that everything, no matter what its form on this planet, exists by reason of magnetic lines of force.

We do not understand why certain forms of matter, referred to as being nonmagnetic by themselves, but when placed together in combination become strongly magnetic. The combination of 61% copper, 24% manganese, and 15% aluminum-all practically nonmagnetic separately, but strongly magnetic when combined as an alloy of these three component metals, is an excellent example of this

BEHIND THE FLYING SAUCERS

mystery.

It is common to refer to electric current as "passing through a wire," but we already know that there are magnetic lines of force surrounding every wire through which an electric current is passing.

It is impossible to study electricity without realizing and recognizing the close connection between magnetism and electricity, the two go hand in hand if they are not one and the same thing. The present is known as the electrical age, but it will be known to the future just as much as the magnetic age, because the two are inseparable.

The more we learn about magnetism, the greater the opportunity we have for an understanding of the source of electrical energy, which was given a great impetus at the beginning of the present century by the development of the electronic theory of matter.

The simplest of all mechanical motions is that of rotation, and whenever we utilize magnetic lines of force in cutting across the loop of the coils so as to cut the lines of force at right angles to their flow, we have the dynamo in its simplest form, and the current then picked up from the rotating coil becomes electricity as we know it.

Millikan, Gale, and Coyle teach this even to schoolboys. They say in their elementary textbook on physics: "All the various kinds of dynamos or generators are fundamentally nothing but devices for moving a conductor through a magnetic field and drawing off the current thus produced. However, the electrical energy is produced only when the motion takes place in such a manner as to cut the magnetic lines of force."

When referring to magnetic fields and lines of force, we must recognize that at all points about a magnet a compass needle is affected by magnetic forces. This means that a magnet is surrounded by a region in which there is magnetic force everywhere. Such a region is called a magnetic field of force.

Referring to magnets themselves, as we know them, every magnet, regardless of its size, when broken up, reforms itself into additional magnets and no matter if the magnet were cut into pieces as small as those of an atom, we would still have a magnet with a north and south pole.

As to the isogenic and isoclinics, the isogenics are lines of equal declination; the isoclinics are lines of equal dip. An isoclinic is a line connecting points on the earth's surface that have equal dip angles. Maps are available that show the light lines or isoclinics for the United States.

The dip in the United States increases toward the north from about 55 degrees at the south end of Texas to 75 degrees at points on the line through Maine to Montana.

At a point of the Boothia Peninsula, north of Hudson Bay, and about 20 degrees from the earth's north geographic pole, the dip becomes 90 degrees. A dip needle

154

there stands vertically; that is, the north pole points downward. This is the earth's north so-called magnetic pole.

At the south magnetic pole, about 18 degrees from the south geographic pole, a dip needle again stands vertically, but the north pole points upward.

The magnetic equator is an imaginary line through two points on the earth's surface where the angle of inclination equals zero. That is where the lines of force are horizontal.

Since the magnetic and geographic poles are not coincident, neither are the magnetic and geographic equators. One may think the geographic equator as a great circle drawn about the earth halfway between the geographic poles. But the magnetic equator is not just halfway between the magnetic poles. One reason for this is that our imaginary earth magnet does not extend through the center of the earth. A straight line connecting the north and south magnetic poles, would miss the earth's center by some 800 miles.

A compass needle usually is pivoted so that it can swing in a horizontal plane only. Consequently, it is only the horizontal components of the earth's magnetic field that has anything to do with the needle's orientation. At the poles where the dip is 90 degrees, the horizontal component is zero.

At the magnetic poles, then, there is no tendency for a compass needle to point at any particular direction. Therefore, we find a proper explanation for what we call the Aurora Borealis. That is, we have magnetic lines of force that are crossing one another at or near the geographic and the magnetic poles, and as a result we see those beautiful colored lights. The directive force on a needle is greatest at the magnetic equator where the dip angle equals zero and the horizontal component is a maximum. The angle of declination at a point is the angle between geographic north and south and the direction taken by a compass needle at the point. In other words, it is the deviation of a compass needle from geographic north and south.

An isogenic is an imaginary line connecting points on the earth's surface having the same magnetic declination. Agonic is an imaginary line connecting all points on the earth's surface when the declination is zero.

Referring again to the Aurora Borealis, it must be understood that what causes the magnetic lines of force to cross in the area of the magnetic poles, is the fact of the change in the magnetic field of the earth. We have evidence of these changes and we attribute them to the changes in the magnetic field on the sun, usually referred to as being caused by sun spots. The disturbance sometimes is so great that even all our electrical systems, our telephones, our radios, our telegraph lines, and all communications which rely on this source of energy, are affected.

The more we delve into the question of magnetic propulsion as to flying saucers, the more we become convinced that this method of transportation or travel has been developed by people from an unidentified planet and have reached a

BEHIND THE FLYING SAUCERS

high point of excellence due to the fact that they are able to travel from one planet to another. They are probably doing research work as to the magnetic conditions of this earth.

Time variations in the earth's magnetic field in all likelihood have drawn the attention of these people in their flights over this planet. The secular variation, that is the systematic change of the earth magnetism over long periods of time, is of slight importance in any study of applied geophysics, but the diurnal variation, which appears to be a terrestrial phenomenon varying chiefly with the position of the sun above the horizon, is ordinarily of such magnitude that it must be taken into account in nearly all applications of geomagnetic theories. Variations produced by magnetic storms (those violent disturbances which last hours and on occasion days) must be taken into account because they may change the earth's total magnetic field by as much as one per cent. Naturally, this could disturb fliers using magnetic lines of force for propulsion, too.

But these are small accidents to a small planet, which in the main is beautifully taken care of by the sun. The earth appears to be hung to nothing, held up by nothing. It has no tracks like the rails that guide a speeding train, and yet its movements are more precise and more predictable than those of the best Diesel-driven train driven by the best engineer. Obviously, if the earth is a magnet, the sun from which it is derived is the master magnet. We are a substation of the great dynamo. So are the other planets. To travel on the main line does not seem beyond even our intelligence. But how people can get across town, that is, from one planet to another, still has us mystified.

The people who have flown the space ships are unquestionably of a higher order of intelligence, because of the fact that they have done what man on this planet has not been able to do. The fact that they are little is of concern only to police reporters, sports writers, and draft boards. Only persons of very little brains believe size has anything to do with brain power.

Magnetic scientists, many of them big men, physically as well as mentally, have tried to put themselves in the position of these brilliant Tom Thumbs from elsewhere. They have tried to reason out why the visitors seemed to appear at certain preferred places over this country. The consensus is that the space pioneers are making a study of the magnetic lines of force that encompass this earth, checking discrepancies and disturbances, and making, in brief, a geodetic survey.

Assuming that these ships are traveling from the planet Venus, a maximum distance of approximately 161 million miles, the terrific distance may give us cause to pause, but it must not be forgotten that once outside of the atmospheric pressure conditions of a planet, ships move into space, where there is no weight, where there is no resistance, where there are only magnetic lines of force. And since circular motion is one of the most ideal of all aerodynamic methods of travel, which has been proven over and over again, we're not surprised at the saucer-like shape

156

BEHIND THE FLYING SAUCERS

of these ships of the air.

Actually there is no thrust in regard to these saucers, nor is there any needed, because what actually happens is that the ship, once in motion, moves forward at whatever speed is desired on magnetic lines of force.

In other words, the ship is trying to get out of its own way, having crossed one or more lines of force. We find that the ship is whirling as to its wing, which of course is circular. Therefore it is trying to get away from itself, which it actually never does.

Now that we have learned that these ships from another world fly magnetically, it is my opinion that our own magnetic engineers will solve the problem of magnetic flight and match the ships of the visitors with saucers made on this earth.

But until that day comes, we shall have to remember that the greatest exhibition of magnetic flight that has ever happened in this universe, insofar as we know, came on the second day of the memorable three-day circus over Farmington, New Mexico, when the sky was filled with flying saucers which to date at least have not been credited to any agency on our planet.

BEHIND THE FLYING SAUCERS

Chapter 15
Why Saucers Landed Here

HAVING GIVEN about every devil his due, I have been debating the next step. Should I Tell All? Or am I, too, bound to exercise discretion? The bugaboo of security may enter here on much more plausible grounds than in the field of atomic fission, for the simple reason that the making of A-bombs and H-bombs are not secrets of American scientists exclusively. How to make them on a mass production basis and not bankrupt our capitalist system is the problem and that's still being kept a secret. On the other hand, much of magnetic action is a secret to all but perhaps a few scientists, and the rest is a secret even to them.

Raised in a school of journalism that believed that the only secret that shouldn't be told to the people of a democracy was that told in a confessional I have small patience with private pacts on any level.

Secret weapons and surprise attacks are narcotics that may lull the military for a while, but a secret weapon must one day be brought out in the open, and a surprise attack is over once it's made. After that, the better man wins, as the blitzkrieg in Russia and the bombing of Pearl Harbor proved.

Every nation has been the victim of this sort of self-hypnosis. But if you believe that God is on the side of the more virtuous, not merely, as Napoleon said, on the side of the biggest armies, you must believe that virtue and competence, unlike mushrooms, do not grow better in dampness and darkness.

For my part I prefer a civilization run as Rube Waddell used to run a ball game. He called outfielders in when about to strike out a third man. He told the outfielders to shift when he was going to make a batter hit to right or left field.

Once I was a member of a group which was delousing a city of its iniquities. The police were on the side of the underworld. They had a special squad whose job it was to harass and intimidate all those on the side of civic virtue. These goons in uniform would even bomb a kitchen of a civic leader at night. That would not kill anybody, but it would scare hell out of all the occupants sleeping in another wing of the house.

BEHIND THE FLYING SAUCERS

One day while discussing the state of things over a tapped phone with our attorney, I said it didn't really matter that the goon squad knew our plans from day-to-day because they were not smart enough to profit by the knowledge. "If you were at bat," I said, "and the chief demolitionist were playing in center field and you shouted to him that you were going to hit a Texas leaguer right back of second base, it wouldn't do him any good because he'd be too dumb to act on the revelation."

With that the chief demolitionist, listening in on the conversation, let out a raucous Bronx cheer. We all laughed, he loudest of all.

But within two months he bombed the car of an ex-police chief who was on our side. The bombing was meant to kill, but the ex-chief survived 186 slugs and the police captain who engineered the bungled job got 20 years at San Quentin.

What does this tend to prove? That secrecy and incompetence go hand in hand and should never be tolerated in a free world, or even in any corner of a free world. They are the other fellow's secret weapons and contain his certain defeat. America should drop the whole ridiculous business, because when you get down to brass tacks as distinguished from brass hats, a secret is something shared by one person. Even two is a crowd. When three are in on it you have an agent whose business it is to buy and sell other people's secrets. No secrets, no sale.

That's my philosophy, but as Bernard Shaw said to the man who hissed his play, "I agree with you, young man, but what can we two do against so many?" So I guess I can't tell all. But I can tell you that by men who know tenescopes best it's saucers 2 to 1. Let the Air Force scream it's not true. They may have their reasons for doing so but truth is not among them.

I don't believe the magnetic research scientists had hallucinations. I don't believe they were participants in a mass hysteria. I believe the military had hallucinations and I believe they certainly were participants in a class hysteria-the Junker class against the rest of us. They don't want us to know what they know. They trust us even less when we know what they don't know.

They simply knew nothing of the principles of propulsion and destruction discussed in this brief. Their reports prove that. Observe how far off the mark they come in this excerpt of the Air Materiel Command's report:

> *Although visits from outer space are believed to be possible, they are thought to be highly improbable. In particular, detailed reports made on study of individual incidents and the over-all picture of project "Saucer" point to the fact that actions attributed to the flying objects reported during the last two years are inconsistent with the requirements for space travel.*

> *The possibility that the "saucers" were supported by means of rays or beams was investigated and debunked. By "rays" or "beams" are meant either purely electromagnetic radiation or else radiation which*

BEHIND THE FLYING SAUCERS

is largely corpuscular like cathode rays, cosmic rays or cyclotron beams.

Any device thus propelled would have to be fundamentally a reaction device. The basic theory of such devices is that a given amount of energy is most efficiently spent if the momentum thrown back or down is large. This means that a large mass should be given a small acceleration, a theorem well understood by helicopter designers.

Beams or rays to the contrary, a small mass is given a very high velocity, and consequently enormous powers greater than the total world's power capacity-would be needed to support event the smallest object by such means.

Several unorthodox means of supporting or propelling a solid object have been considered, including the fiction writers old standby, the anti-gravity shield, but all have been found impractical. This, in the opinion of investigating scientists, lends credence to the assumption that the unidentified flying objects are supported and propelled by some normal means, or else they are not solids.

This quaint resume was published in 1949-349 years after William Gilbert had told all who could read that the earth was a giant magnet. All of Gilbert's writings were destroyed in the great fire of London, but he did leave some instruments which enabled sailors to find out their latitude without seeing the sun, moon, or stars. If Air Force Intelligence can get back to the Pentagon by means of one of these compasses, perhaps it can scrounge around and find some reports that not only back up Gilbert but the main points of this treatise.

The simplest proof is that magnetic lines of force know no barrier is evidenced by the action of a magnetic compass. Set it up on the south side of Pikes Peak, it still points north. Nothing in the famous peak disturbs the lines of force in any manner. If a magnetic needle is disturbed through usage all you have to do is to place it on the surface of the earth and it immediately rearranges itself. In fact, there's a belief that the same could be done if an electrocuted body (which is a demagnetized body) were placed immediately in the earth. Its magnetic frequencies would be re-established, and life thus restored.

Certainly from the Air Force communiques you would get no inkling that anybody had found a way to use magnetic lines of force or the crossing of them as a means of defense. I mean a literal defense of these shores, not a Department of Defense which is in reality a department of offense.

Can the Air Force be ignorant of a force that if crossed can destroy everything for miles within 1/10,000ths of a second? Are they ignorant of magnetic sequence counters which are capable of 1,000,000 calculations a second?

Don't they know that everything on this planet, and, indeed, in the entire solar system, operates on magnetic frequencies, from a pencil to an Air Force general, and that anybody who has mastered this knowledge could demagnetize and de-

160

stroy anything he desired? If so why didn't the Air Force hit on the suspicion that the simplest way to destroy Captain Mantell's ship over Fort Knox was to demagnetize it? Why all this hocus-pocus about chasing Venus, running out of oxygen, and marking the whole case "an unexplained mystery?"

Has what probably happened to Captain Mantell ever been duplicated by earthborn experimenters? Oh yes, by accident. With what result? Disintegration and fire.

We have certain places where magnetic blow-outs occur, notably around Oregon and New Mexico. If a ship traveling on such magnetic lines of force should hit a blow-out it might be in for trouble. Wouldn't you check on those disturbing factors if you traveled that way? Or are you the sort of chauffeur who gets blow-outs and never looks back to see where you picked up the nail?

On those space ships examined by our magnetic research men no destructive force of any kind was found, except possibly those push buttons which nobody ever pushed. Somewhere on that panel was the secret of their propulsion and their secret weapon. Their weapon wasn't such a secret either, because, as I have hinted, among the 1,600 scientists who worked five to seven years in this field some accidentally fell on the secret of destruction and by changing its direction turned it into a defensive shield for this continent. I know how they did it but I'm not telling. If the Air Force knows too, fine. If not, *tant pis*.

As for those pilots and other observers who thought they saw lights of various colors connected with flying saucers and were listed as crackpots by the military's quackpots, let them rest easy on their beds from this day forth. What they think they saw they saw. White lights, blue lights, yellow lights, green lights, red lights- all can be produced in a laboratory by disturbing magnetic lines of force. In fact, nature has been doing it for thousands of years outside of laboratories. When the earth shifts a fraction there is a magnetic disturbance around the poles and that's all the Aurora Borealis is. These magnetic lines of force go as deep as the skin of the earth, which is 32 miles. It is assumed that the sun supplies its other planets with this energy as it does us. It is assumed they are all positive forces and thus repel each other and so keep in magnetic balance. Anybody who can effect a negative current can get from one positive planet to another positive planet.

In laboratories, our scientists have worked it out so that it is possible to surpass the speed of light by traveling on these magnetic lines of force. One experiment calculated the speed at 282,000 miles a second. It was on such a theoretical calculation that I said in Variety on October 12, 1949, that flying saucers could fly from Venus to here and back in 42 minutes.

But even if their speed were limited to the speed of light, as ours at one time was limited to the speed of sound, the round trip could be accomplished well within an hour. The assumption is that the Saucerians have developed their own ships to where they can create a magnetic flux and move at any speed-from zero to 282,000 miles per second. In fact, once out of their atmosphere, or ours, where no resistance operates, they could move at 1,000,000 miles per second.

But if we stay on the conservative side o£ Einstein, who holds that nothing can exceed the speed of light, where does that get us? At 186,000 miles per second, that's 11, 172,000 miles per minute, or 630,320,000 m.p.h. At one time Venus is 154,000,000 miles from us; at another time, 161,000,000 miles away. Taking the shorter distance; that's 308,000,000 miles for the round trip. Half of 67,320,000 is 335 160 000. In other words, the round trip could be made in less than 42 minutes. It could be made in half an hour.

As for the three space ships that failed to make their round trips (others too have been reported, one in the Sierra Madre Mountains of Mexico with six dead men aboard), the assumption is that their ships were set on automatic float, in case anything happened to the pilots.

On reaching magnetic zero, which is what the skin of the earth would be to such a positive force, the ship having arrived at magnetic balance would stop all motion. Until another button was pushed that would repel it from this earth, it would not move. Since nobody knew which button to push and therefore didn't push any, we will never know for sure of course how that particular ship would have acted, but our magnetic research engineers can make a pretty fair guess.

That the greatest hazard of the visiting Saucerians was decompression, is the best guess as to what killed those found dead on such ships as have been grounded on this planet. The assumption is that they have overcome that, because no ship, with its crew dead possibly from the bends, has been found for more than a year. The suspicion is that numbers still land and leave at will, but that's only a suspicion. Faultings may bring them down against their will, but why couldn't they master those as our navigators have mastered the stormy waters around Cape Hatteras?

These fault zones are not very well understood either. Neither are volcanic eruptions which are the results of them. At the turn of the century it was believed that the earth was a ball of fire which had cooled off on its outer crust. Today we are told that its core is of solid metal and that the crust, or skin which is about thirty miles thick, is of rock, metal, and soil.

The planet Jupiter is a good model. Its core is metallic. Outside that core are thousands of miles of ice. Beyond the ice is a hydrogen atmosphere, and beyond that, methane and ammonia clouds.

To those who raise the question, how come volcanoes if the center of the earth is not a molten mass, modern astronomers and geophysicists both concur that volcanoes are the results of faultings and frictions. These set up fire and continue in their eruptions until the particular faulting is corrected or falls into magnetic balance.

They will point out to you the presence in Mexico of a volcano which looks thou-

BEHIND THE FLYING SAUCERS

sands of years old, and which has been observed as going from nothing to its present eruption in our lifetime. Scientists who have flown over it in various periods and have watched its formation look upon it as something as superficial as a boil on the body-a blemish which doesn't necessarily go to the marrow of the bone, which in this case is not calcium but cold steel-an ideal material for a giant magnet.

Professor George Adamski, in *Pioneers in Space*, holds that all knowledge of space ships is a denied military secret but nevertheless a secret because the military must always have a secret. It will give up this one when it gets a better one. To him America is in the kindergarten scientifically compared to men from Mars. He says the Navy is training men in courtesy against the day when interplanetary calls will follow protocol, which could of course be naval propaganda because all the Air Force ever thinks about is shooting down the sonsabitches.

They can fight their way out but to think their way out seems to be beyond them.

Is it any wonder that the ignorance of the Pentagonians is conceded by all (except the Pentagonians) to be abysmal?

Chapter 16
The Question Box

ON JANUARY 11, 1950, l asked the Pentagonian desk generals twenty questions. They have not answered them to date. This has put me in a unique position. Everybody else has been answered. At least Donald E. Keyhoe, Henry J. Taylor, David Lawrence, Walter Winchell, Ray Palmer, R. B. McLaughlin, and several thousand eye-witnesses to flying saucers have been answered, but I have been left in a deep freeze. They have been either ridiculed or diplomatically heaved on to the huge rubbish heap which divides the sane from the insane.

I may have received a brushoff for violating protocol, because instead of sending the questions to the Air Force chief of staff and delaying all publication until receiving a reply tersely worded "no comment," I caused the questions to be published in Variety, the showman's bible, and sent the military no personal communication whatever. I assumed that those hired for espionage and counterespionage can read and do not need either to have things drawn to their attention or spelled out for them. It was an erroneous assumption.

Others, however, picked up the questions and reprinted them, notably *The Buffalo Evening News, The Christian Science Monitor, Fortnight, The Canyon Crier,* and Dick Williams in the *Los Angeles Daily Mirror*.

One of the editors of the eminent Buffalo daily went so far as to telephone me in California for permission to reprint the questions and, as proof that capitalism is not dead, sent a check on publication, though money had never entered the telephonic conversation. The others took the position, I suspect, that in spreading the saucerian inquest they were doing a public service.

Of the twenty questions, only one has ever been answered, and that not by those to whom it was addressed but by an employee of a privately endowed institution in Chicago. He said No. I could, of course, have then addressed the question to Philadelphia's Drexel Institute, or New York's Museum of Natural History, or Washington's Smithsonian Institution, or Denver's Phipps Museum, and so on. But I was not interested in chasing the Air Force collaborators or indeed Air Force generals themselves, on foot, while they could either hole up in the Pentagon or skip off in a B-29 to check on installations anywhere between Frankfort-am-Main and Indo-China and bill me for the junket, on the grounds that security was involved.

So without even exercising an editorial blue pencil or asking leave to amend, I am submitting the original questions again. I have been charitably explaining to believers in free inquiry that the Air Force closed down Project Saucer with 34 of its cases still unsolved because the desk pilots didn't want to be asked any more questions to which they personally didn't have the answers. Nobody likes to say, "I don't know," though Dr. Samuel Johnson added to his immortality when he explained that a wrong definition in his famous dictionary was the result of "pure ignorance, madam."

As several months have passed since those questions were addressed to the Air Force, it is quite possible that by now they either have the answers or reasonable facsimiles of same. So I'm asking them again:

1. Do you think it such a good idea to close off Operation Saucer at this time when the records show that more saucers fly the skies between December 21 and March 15 than at any other time of the year?

2. Why is it that pilots who have been trained to identify every make, model, and nationality of airplanes all describe these space ships they have seen as "saucer-shaped?"

3. Did the Air Force wrecking crews break up one of these ships instead of letting it in the hands of magnetic engineers until they could study in detail how such a ship, if not put together on this earth, could have transferred from the magnetic lines of force from another planet? In other words, how could they leave on their beam and land on ours?

4. Did the Air Force ever make public what the "Explosives," looking like a dismantled flying saucer, were, which they transported in army trucks from a western research base to Dayton, Ohio?

5. Weren't all the saucers found on the western hemisphere magnetic rather than jet jobs?

6. Wasn't the small one, which was 36 feet in diameter, equipped with landing gear which had steel-looking balls instead of wheels and which when moving could not be tipped over by ten men but when not moving could be tilted by one man?

7. Considering how many of our planes have smash-ups on landing, wouldn't it have been worth while to have studied the secret behind these magnetized ball-shaped landing gears before releasing parts to brass-bound souvenir hunters?

8. Why don't you release the tape recordings of comments and questions asked at the public viewing of one of the men picked up dead from a flying saucer, put in a preservative solution, and placed between human specimens from prenatal to grown man in an exhibit in Chicago?

9. What has happened to the remains of the 16 men found dead in one of the large saucers and the two in a smaller flying disk?

BEHIND THE FLYING SAUCERS

10. Did you ever find the secret of how these flying saucers were hermetically sealed so as to show no outside crack when the door was closed?

11. If you suspect the flying saucers were manufactured and released by a foreign power, don't you know that as late as 1930 the foremost of such nations was happy to get rehabilitated Liberty motors from us (worth $100, and with improvements, $1,100) at $3,000 apiece and hasn't shown any particular genius since in originating devices designed to conquer the air?

12. Have you looked thoroughly into what our own air plants might be manufacturing with or without your knowledge or consent?

13. Did you ever see a radio like the one which was on the flying saucer that landed on a ranch in New Mexico?

14. Why did the Air Force in its report pick Wolf 359 as an ideally habitable planet outside the solar system?

15. What happened to the body of the man 3 $^1/_2$ feet tall, taken dead from a saucer which had landed in New Mexico and exhibited in Chicago? Was that at the Rosenwald Institute?

16. What do you know about magnetic fault zones in certain areas on this earth, notably in Oregon?

17. Do you know how magnetic waves emanate from the sun, revolve around the earth, continue on the earth's moon, come back to the earth, and return from there to the sun? Do you know that magnetic waves following a similar course travel between the sun and Venus? If you don't know much about this, why did you insist on tearing everything open that might have helped the magnetic scientists into determining if a saucer magnetically controlled could hop from one magnetic zone to another?

18. Since the scientists who researched these saucers have never been able to find any evidence of two of the saucer's metals on this earth, how much nearer to the solution has Air Force Intelligence come since taking over the project and now presumably shelving it?

19. Don't you think it was something less than cricket to encourage Donald E. Keyhoe, a former navy-trained balloon pilot as well as a marine corps airplane pilot, into writing that flying saucers are real, only to deny the whole thing after his True magazine story broke?

20. And finally, do you believe we were all chumped by Film Classics and their program picture called *The Flying Saucer*?

The last question of course was facetious and anticlimactic, a Shavian weakness I encourage lest I be charged with taking myself too seriously. Nevertheless, Mikel Conrad who produced the modest little program picture has attested many times that he shot 900 feet of flying saucers in Alaska and had the film confiscated by the military. Nine months later, Conrad said, the film was "declassified" and returned to him. It meant nothing to him in this form, so he whipped up a little number involving conflict between the airborne warriors of Uncle Sam and Uncle Joe wherein Uncle Sam's boys wrested the grounded saucer from their former allies.

As for the query concerning one of the men picked up from a flying saucer, put in a preservative solution and placed between human specimens in an exhibit at Rosenwald Institute, Chicago, Fortnight said: "An old time newspaper man with a strong sense of public obligation, Scully swore his questions were based on good sources, wanted Air Force to answer."

Herb Hildebrand, a spokesman for the Rosenwald Institute, was quoted in Fortnight as replying: "Regarding your question the only specimen we have of a grown man is a plaster model, showing one-half bone and one-half nerve tissue. Dating back to the World's Fair of 1933 is an actual medical exhibit which shows the development of the embryo from conception to the full term."

It was *Fortnight's* opinion that maybe I had stirred up something on one of the biggest stories in history or maybe I hadn't. This two-way escape hatch was followed by the statement: "As usual the Air Force was keeping discreetly silent and-at fortnight end-had issued no denial or answer to the Scully column."

As answers take time and maybe six months was rushing matters, perhaps we might entertain ourselves, if not the Air Force, by asking some more questions.

What about the boy in Appleton, Wisconsin, whose short-wave set hit a magnetic frequency which not only paralyzed automobiles within three miles of his home, but any plane flying over his house?

Chet L. Swital was sent by his paper from Chicago to cover the story and when he reached Appleton he found the place crawling with FBI men. They confiscated the boy's short-wave set and shipped him, his family, and the mystifying radio to Washington for further study. This was in 1941. What happened? Or is that one still "classified" five years after the war and nine years after the reported phenomenon?

What about the reported incidents of pilots who have been terrorized by their motors stopping dead, and then, suddenly, after everything from one minute to five minutes, starting up again? What about the incident specifically, of the two Army Air Force pilots attached to the transport command whose plane was frozen high above the Himalayas?

I have talked with pilots who were in on that one from the beginning. One of them, Charles F. Lane, who has been flying twenty years and is still at it, told me how it happened. The pilots were flying over the Hump. It was a clear day. Something bright whirled and circled around their plane several times. It was traveling at great speed. Suddenly their motors stopped. Their instruments froze. They felt as if they were gripped and suspended in mid-air.

The object circled a few more times and then zoomed away. With its departure, their instrument board began operating again, their motors coughed, their hair which had stood on end flattened down, and they were able to get their destination, though they claimed that they would never feel the same again about our mastery of the air unless someone cleared up that mystery. Did their plane stop its forward motion? Did the law that "a body in motion tends to stay in motion unless impelled by some external force to change that state" meet such an external force? Or did the force merely demagnetize their motor and leave it floating along for a short time, much as the planes flying over that boy's ham radio in Appleton, Wisconsin, were left when a plane got in its way?

What about the young pilot at Muroc who suffered a similar experience in 1950? Was he quizzed by an officer of the Air Force brass who happened to be 3,000 miles from the Pentagonian frontier? Was he ordered to take it easy for a few days? Did he go up with a camera the next day, hoping to get a shot of the flying saucer which had left him suspended the day before? Was he ordered to return to the field and grounded for violating the previous suggestion to take it easy for a few days?

What about another case that Chet Swital reported? This one, according to Swital, took place over an Army airfield in New Mexico. Why do so many happen there? Is it because we are lousing up the atmosphere with our experiments and thus attracting the curiosity of those who fly on magnetic waves? This pilot claimed his progress was intercepted by a flying disk. He said it circled him, killed his motor, and paralyzed all movement of his instruments. The rest of his case history follows the classic formula. As soon as the flying saucer checked him as harmless and swished away, his motor sputtered to life, settled down to a reassuring hum, and, to his relief, his instrument board began telling him that God was in His Heaven and all was right with the pilot's particular part of the world.

Are we going to be told that meteorites tossing off dust caught and reflected in the sun effected the electromagnetic mechanism of these motors, and in doing so, heightened the imagination of the pilots to the point where they were seeing things? If so, it can also be argued that since these forces are in the universe somebody somewhere may be in control of them, and capable of turning them on and off, as easily as we turn on and off lights by touching one finger to a switch.

It can also be argued that they received warnings, like Captain Mantell, but were spared the disintegration of body and ship which were the end-result of his determination to chase a flying saucer and bring it down. But whether Mantell's plane was disintegrated by (a) getting in the magnetic dust of a meteorite, or (b) by having his magnetic lines of force crossed by an intelligence more versed in the laws controlling magnetic energy, the whole thing is still a mystery to the Air Force, though not, I hope, any longer, to our readers.

As to why the skies seem to have a heavier traffic load between December and March, men versed in magnetic research don't quite know, but they did warn me that it was as silly for Project Saucer to close down at that time of the year as it would for the police to vacate Times Square on election night. Ed Coffman, an amateur astronomer of standing, has suggested that perhaps that was the period when the magnetic lines of force between Venus and the earth came closest together.

Question: What is the difference between crossing magnetic lines of force for propulsion and crossing them for destruction?

Answer: Essentially none. In both instances the combustion is controlled but in one it is used to travel onward and in the other it is used to destroy pursuing pests as flit destroys buzzing mosquitoes.

Question: What are eddy currents?

Answer: They are the magnetic lines of force that revolve around the earth laterally. They measure 1,850 to the square centimeter, as opposed to those which run at right angles to the poles and measure 1,257 to the square centimeter.

Question: Didn't the Denver lecturer say that two scientists saw a flying saucer and a live crew on one of the proving grounds in the Southwest?

Answer: Yes he did, but they didn't report it in because (1) it could have been a mirage, (2) because the men and the ship disappeared when they sought to come close to them, and (3) psychiatry is in the pilot seat of the Air Force and it is sometimes easier not to see what you see than to be told to lie down on a couch and let a flock of Freudians psychoanalyze you to see what connection all this had to do with your excessive affection for your mother. Joe Landon, however, advanced the thought that the visitors might have known how to bend light rays which would create a shield till they could get in their ship and sail off. In other words they would be there but couldn't be seen. Magicians can even do this with mirrors.

Question: Doesn't much of this theory of magnetic propulsion violate the conservation of energy principle? In traveling along a magnetic band, much as a package rides along on a conveyor belt, aren't two things ignored: all types of friction and gravity? Isn't more than one set of forces acting on a ship regardless of its shape? Since the saucer has no propellant force of its own, how would it offset the drag of wind resistance, convection of currents, and the pull of gravity? How about obstacles thrown in its path? Wouldn't these knock the package off its conveyor belt? And if the friction forces were constant wouldn't the saucer slow down inversely as the square of the distance, as does a rock thrown by a boy in the air or a rocket shot in the sky by your Air Force?

Answer: Now, here are questions which it would seem might take chapters to answer. Actually the answers can be reduced to a sentence or two. First get rid of the idea that magnetism and gravity are both fighting for control. They are one and the same thing. When an object is traveling on magnetic propulsion it is not fighting magnetic power; it is using it. It is the same thing that makes it possible to lift your arm to wave good-by to a friend. If gravity were so all powerful, you could never lift your arm. Who said the saucer had no propellant force of its own? The contention of the magnetic research engineers is that Saucerians have mastered the greatest propellant force in the universe-magnetic lines of force.

Robert Pike, a former Air Force pilot, acting as spokesman for a group of twenty which included one pilot who had flown everything from the crates of 1918 to modern bombers, listened to a recording of the University of Denver lecture and turned in a report that had much more depth but by no means the length of an Air Materiel Command Digest.

A bit dazed by the whole thing, they found themselves divided on many points, united on others. They all agreed that the obviously high level of intelligence which had applied itself to the solution of what was behind the flying saucers was the biggest single factor in its favor. Without it the solid wall of skepticism which the government had set up through its various Air Force denials would fortify the disbelief of the average person. These were some of their queries:

Question: What about those famous square-cornered turns? Any pilot knows that's impossible in an aircraft relying solely on aerodynamics. Or is this the long sought anti-gravity machine that spares ship and crew alike?

Answer: It is indeed. Once everything is set in magnetic balance and the crew sealed in, say, a vacuum turret with oxygen tanks strapped to their backs, all talk about how many g's a body can stand loses its meaning.

There might be some question as to how fast an ordinary ship could be stepped up without cracking if veered at too sharp an angle but a saucer isn't that sort of ship. It moves at all angles and no angles. We have even now commercial planes which fly at 20,000 feet. Yet the pressure within the cabin remains at 7,000 feet. When that pressure is reduced to sea level even cardiac cases may find flying at 50,000 feet as easy as lying on the sand. This is but an inkling of what is ahead of us and behind those who have mastered old theories of motion and gravity by controlling magnetic lines of force.

Question: What about those dimensions? We seem at odds as to those multiples of nines. When I translated all the dimensions of a saucer I found everything was divisible by three. How would that apply to the metric system?

Answer: Frankly I don't know. That was Dr. Gee's theory not mine. He says everything about the ships worked out in nines or multiples of nine. Typical was the second ship. It was 72 feet in diameter. Its cabin was 18 feet across, and 72 inches high. September has nine letters and is the ninth month. There are nine planets in our solar system. Every ninth wave according to Dr. Gee that beats on every shore on this planet is larger than the other eight. Check on this yourself and see if he's right.

Question: What is the significance of a magnetic month?

Answer: No significance except that it seems a more scientific way to measure time. It takes 23 hours 58 minutes to complete a magnetic day. That makes 28 days 23 hours 29 minutes for a magnetic month. Under this computation the earth completes its orbit around the sun in 13 months, instead of 12 months and 1/4 days.

BEHIND THE FLYING SAUCERS

The Chinese have used a 13-month year for centuries.

Question: Why can't metallurgists analyze any and every metal especially when your scientists say the whole solar system is comprised of blood relations? How could something be present on one planet and not on all, since according to your theory they are all castoffs of the same sun?

Answer: This does seem to present a flaw in Dr. Gee's case. However, he did not say the flying saucers contained two metals which could not under any circumstances be found on this earth. He said they hadn't been found to date. After all, new elements have been found in our lifetime. We are now up to 97. Forty of these have been found on the sun as well. That still leaves a lot unaccounted for. It is quite possible that on another planet an element is on the surface, whereas on this one it is miles below the skin of the earth. What Dr. Gee said was that 150 tests and 10,000 degrees of heat had not been able to break down two of the metals and therefore it was assumed they must have come from elsewhere. They could of course have worked out an alloy unknown to us out of metals known to us.

Question: Is the one-inch square magnetic radio telephone that Dr. Gee and Mr. Newton use okayed by the F.C.C.?

Answer: Yes, I've seen their license numbers.

Question: Are you sure there were no written instructions on the ship? All of us are experienced pilots of from 2,000 to 10,000 flying hours each, and we cannot conceive of an aircraft without written instructions all over the ship, both inside and outside. My brother, convinced that they cannot have a language or it would be printed some place on the controlling mechanism, suggested they might use an advanced form of mental telepathy such as birds and animals, and even ants use. Is that possible?

Answer: Of course. As was said before, anything is possible. But it so happens there were parchments on the ship which Dr. Gee said looked like picture language. These were turned over to specialists in the field who so far have not been able to make anything out of them.

Question: We find any conversation about "little men" is poison. Women are tolerant of the idea but not men. Are you sure they weren't dwarfs or Singer Midgets or something?

Answer: All the Singer Midgets have been accounted for. And as I said before, the fact that the men were small is no more incredible than the fact that little Mickey Rooney is a big star in motion pictures. Climatic conditions have a great deal to do with the size of men's bodies, a good deal less with their brains. The dinosaur weighed 120,000 pounds; his brain weighed a pound. He wasn't very bright. At any rate he's joined the dead dragons and the dragon slayers. It would be nice of course to be able to report that the Saucerians were 6 feet tall, weighed 175 pounds, and looked like members of a varsity crew, but Dr. Gee says they measured between 36 and 42 inches and were 30 to 40 years old. Otherwise he found nothing unusual about them.

Question: Could the facts be withheld on higher grounds than an inability to answer the questions? Say, to avoid panic, or religious controversies?

Answer: Some of the magnetic research scientists have advanced this as a possibility but I doubt it. Panic is a two-way street. Those skilled in public relations could condition the people, "prepare" them, and even work up a stampede of general acceptance of the idea before the facts were released. As to the religious problem, none exists as far as theologians on this earth are concerned. God created this earth. We are descended from Adam. Other planets, other Adams. That God is almighty is best proved by the endless pattern of His creations. The more that is revealed the more almighty He becomes. Even an atheist can find little comfort in infinity or eternity, but those who believe a divinity shapes our ends, rough hew them as we will, must welcome additional proof of this divinity.

Question: What books are recommended on the technical aspects of all this business?

Answer: This one.

Question: Is there any available information about the exact function of the push-button controls in the saucers?

Answer: Ask the Air Force. They may be using the same buttons on their directed missiles, for all I know. Probably listed as "reclaimed war surplus."

Question: These portholes which they can see out of but nobody can see in. Could they be half-silvered to stop cosmic rays?

Answer: Could be.

Question: Did they have any heating devices?

Answer: None that one could see, but of course a complete mastery of magnetic energy would include a mastery of heat, because heat is the lowest form of energy.

Question: How were their clothes. Where were the seams? How were the buttonholes made? How about their shirts? Did they wear ties? Did their pants have pockets? Did their shoes have laces? Were they high or low shoes? Did they have heels? Nails? Did they have stockings? Caps? Were the seats upholstered? Flat, hard, or soft? Did their bunks that disappeared into the cabin wall have blankets, pillows, sheets? Were the beds hard or soft? Was there any floor covering? Curtains? Any first-aid kits? Or drinks other than the heavy water? Any eating utensils? Pictures? Rings? Tables? Were their documents bound or rolled? Any other reading matter?

Answer: These are women's questions. They are good questions, but I can't answer most of them. Maybe a WAC assigned to Air Force Intelligence can. After, of course, the first twenty questions have been answered by the WAC's superiors. After all, priority still is a magic word around the Pentagon, and I want my questions answered first.

BEHIND THE FLYING SAUCERS

Chapter 17
Some Air-Conditioned Conclusions

"You can measure a circle beginning anywhere," said Charles Fort. The same is true of the flying saucer story. In three years it had completed a circle. In a very literal sense it was back to where it had started.

On June 25, 1947, Kenneth Arnold reported nine objects flying in saucer-like fashion over Mt. Rainier, Washington. On April 30, 1950, Mrs. Albert Goelitzer reported seeing eight flat cylindrical-shaped objects flying over Centralia, Washington. Were eight of them the same ones Kenneth Arnold had seen three years before? Were they looking for the missing ninth, the one that had had "magneto trouble" and had dropped out near Aztec, New Mexico?

Between those two observations and the intervening three years, thousands had seen strange objects in the sky and from trained observers to rank amateurs they almost to a man, woman, and child, had reported that they looked like flying saucers.

But the Air Force took the position that they were all out of step but Jim. Jim of the Air Force had decided that everybody else was either a little crazy or playing jokes. I have decided that when 150,000,000 persons are rated crazy it's the psychiatrist who is cracked. If this is any consolation to Jim of the Air Force, he's welcome to it.

At the beginning of this project I took the position that if the Air Force said there was such a thing as flying saucers, don't you believe them. If they said there is no such thing as flying saucers, don't you believe them. If they said I didn't know what I was talking about, don't you believe them. In brief, don't believe them. Believe me.

I have viewed with compassion those reporters who tried to get at the truth of this story, only to get slugged for playing ball with the Pentagonians. I have told them that if the pen were really mightier than the sword they were poor hands at proving it. I'd as leave go into a combat of this sort unarmed as Marines would have gone into Guadalcanal unarmed.

BEHIND THE FLYING SAUCERS

Like others, I have thrilled many times at the picture of General Douglas A. MacArthur stepping into the shallow waters of Luzon and wading ashore. But I knew before that happened that barrages had been laid down, flame throwers had cleared out all snipers and, though the beach looked a wreck, it was comparatively safe from enemy fire. I have followed the same procedure in dealing with the Pentagonians and the flying saucer story. I have treated them as a race apart and have, I hope, warned my readers to dig in and so be prepared to laugh off a counterattack. Thus when it comes all of us can say, "See, I told you the truth would burn them up!"

The hypocritical pattern is ever the same and when broken down it remains essentially the same. Note how the chancellor of the University of Denver got all steamed up about an unidentified lecturer. He issued a faculty order that all lecturers must be screened henceforth. He and his faculty knew who the speaker was. It was all a part of the great American game of chumping the common people. The military and now the intelligentsia believe Lincoln was wrong. You can fool all the people all the time, if you change your act now and then. Did that Denver chancellor ever ask that the anonymity of Air Force spokesmen be revealed? Did he ever ask them to stop snooping around, trying to get information on a project that was publicly announced as closed? Did he ever ask the newspapers not to print press handouts unless Air Force spokesmen were identified?

When I reflect on all the money that was spent on Project Saucer and how little these master minds had to show for it I wonder if the object of a military training is not only to use language to conceal thought but to make thinking appear ridiculous.

Read again the Digest of the Air Materiel Command and see if it shows an inkling of even a theoretical knowledge of magnetic propulsion. It reads like the learned essays of the pre-Copernican era-full of things which when weighed mean nothing. There was never better proof that a dull mind hides behind many a smart uniform.

It reminds me of Lee Bowman and his ship, which he designed during the war. Because high octane gas was at a premium, he designed his ship to fly on carbon dioxide. Carbon dioxide was cheap. It couldn't explode or burn. Roscoe Turner tested an X model and pronounced it well worth developing. The Navy decided it wanted it. They horsed around for eighteen months while Bowman awaited essential material. He finally said, "Listen, get this stuff or forget it." They told him to hold his horses and wait his turn. He told them to get moving and to leave the horses to the bookies. They said there were two ways to do it: their way and their way. He said, "Not with my brains." They said, "We have ways of making men do it our way." He said, "Not now you haven't, because I just pulled out of the whole deal a minute ago."

The ship was never made and Bowman is rich and the brass that tried to push him around is unwept, unhonored, and unsung. If he had been a poor scientist, forced to take that $7,500 a year and all the guff that went with it, or in a worse position where he had to rely on their caprices for essential materials, he'd have had to take their orders, or else.

Bad as that is in wartime it is absolutely intolerable between wars. The Council of the Federation of American Scientists have decided to fight back. In deploring an order against the discussion of scientific information the council stated:

"It is hard for any American to take an order from some one in Washington to 'keep his trap shut' even where there is a belated 'please' attached to it."

Gerard Piel, publisher of the Scientific American, who was ordered to burn 3,000 copies, because the issue contained material known to every scientist short of Haile Selassie's physician, said: "For the pall of secrecy which so dangerously frustrates its legitimate activities, the press must blame itself as much as anybody. Our newspapers and magazines have sold themselves a gold brick."

David Lawrence, who found himself at the receiving end of a flying saucer, asked editors to stop being confused by worn-out arguments concerning national security since "too often it can cloak a desire for a hush-hush policy that can hide incompetence behind the scenes."

Well, that's a charitable view. But suppose it hid willful duplicity. Suppose it hid the truth about something that couldn't possibly prove we were worse off than anybody else on this planet? Suppose at worst it merely proved that we are 500 years behind some other part of the universe in the matter of propelling objects through space? Is that such a disgraceful thing to confess?

Almost everybody else in the world agrees that where there is much smoke there must be some fire. But not the Air Force. To them we all have soot on our sun glasses and the moving disks we think we see are really drops of sweat. Very simple fellows in the Air Force. Too simple. If only you could put a magnet on one side of their minds and draw brains into it we might be officered by Einsteins.

There is still hope that they may decide that we the people are worth taking into their confidence. Or are we like the deceived wife, the last one to know?

By April 9, 1950, even *The New York Times* had begun to weaken. It published a feature by Joseph Nolan, entitled: ***"THOSE FLYING SAUCERS: ARE OR AREN'T THEY?"***

Everybody, including the President, the story said, "was puzzled and many guesses were made."

The only guess that came near the mark, in my opinion, was by Soviet Deputy Foreign Minister Andrei A. Gromyko, who walked into, instead of out of, this one for a change. He suggested they might be caused by a Russian discus thrower who didn't know his own strength.

Could be, for when George Washington threw that silver dollar across the Potomac he might have got on a magnetic line of force that flustered the law of gravity for a moment.

It's an old story, you see. It goes back to the lodestone and that goes back thousands of years. Official ridicule to the contrary, the world will have to go back to Thales, to Gilbert, and to Faraday, and work up from these sources to an understanding of modern magnetic research before any one can answer the question of how real or unreal are flying saucers.

With that I leave the door open for a last minute confession from the Air Force that the saucers were (a) ours, (b) Russia's, (c) from another planet, or (d) from all three. After that they may come home and all will be forgiven.

BEHIND THE FLYING SAUCERS

Appendix
The Post-Fortean File
1947-1950
1947
June 26, 1947: Los Angeles Times
9 "SAUCERS" FLYING 1200 MPH SIGHTED-BUT WHAT ARE THEY?
Pendleton, Ore. June 25 (AP) Kenneth Arnold reported seeing nine shiny objects flying at 1,200 miles an hour over the Cascade range of Western Washington. The objects were bright and saucer-like, flying at 10,000 feet altitude. When first sighted they were approximately 25-30 miles away, and flying north.

June 29, 1947: Los Angeles Daily News
MANY REPORT SEEING FLYING SAUCERS
White Sands Proving Ground, N. M. June 28 (UP) The Kenneth Arnold report of seeing nine objects which flew like flying saucers and supported by other residents in the Northwest area as having seen flying objects, was discounted by Air Force officers in New Mexico. Lt. Col. Harold R. Turner, commanding officer of the Army's rocket proving ground, said the disks must have been jet airplanes.

July 4, 1947: Los Angeles Examiner
AIR FORCE PROBES "FLYING DISKS" MYSTERY; HITS MISSILE THEORY
Wright Field, Ohio, July 3 (INS) Officers of the air research and development section of the AAF's Air Materiel Command were asked by General Carl Spaatz, the Army's air commander, to try to ascertain what the disks are. Lt. William C. Anderson, public relations officer at the field, said: "So far we haven't found anything to confirm that the disks exist. We don't think they are guided missiles." He said as things were they now appear to be either a phenomenon or figment of somebody's imagination.

BEHIND THE FLYING SAUCERS

July 4, 1947: Los Angeles Examiner
AIRLINE PILOT SIGHTS FLYING DISK CLUSTER Boise, Idaho, July 4 (AP) Captain Smith, United Airlines pilot, with co-pilot, First Officer Stevens, reported "three to five" disks at an altitude of 7,500 feet, 15 miles southwest of Ontario, Oregon. The first photograph taken of the mystery saucers was claimed by Yeoman Frank Ryman. Ryman's estimate was that the saucer was 9,000 to 10,000 feet in the air and traveling 500 m.p.h.

July 5, 1947: Los Angeles Examiner
MARS - SAYS "SAUCERS" MAY BE SIGNALS FROM PLANET
Detroit, July 5 (INS) A Detroit meteorologist, unidentified, says the disks may be signals from Mars.

July 5, 1947: Los Angeles Examiner ASTRONOMER FAILS TO LOCATE SAUCERS Flagstaff, Ariz. July 5 (UP) Dr. V. M. Slipher, director of the famed Lowell Observatory, said he hadn't noted any saucers from Arizona but that you can find anything you want to find in the heavens if you look long enough.

July 5, 1947: Los Angeles Examiner REPORTS POUR IN ON SAUCER PUZZLE UP release: Numerous reports received from all over the nation are causing scientists to wonder if many Americans just don't have a bad case of jitters; seeing spots before their eyes, aren't suffering from hallucinations or delusions. Reports noted from Pennsylvania, New Jersey, Georgia, Idaho, and other states in the far west.

July 5, 1947 : Los Angeles Examiner
STRANGE FIND-OBJECT LIKE "SAUCER" DROPS ON FARM
Circleville, Ohio, July 4 (AP) Sherman Campbell reported having found a strange object on his farm in the form of a six-pointed star, 50 inches high, 48 inches wide, covered with tinfoil, and weighing about two pounds. Port Columbus, Air field Weather Station, said object tallied with object used by the Army Air Forces to measure wind velocity.

July 5, 1947: Los Angeles Examiner
INVENTOR'S TEST OF "FLYING SAUCERS" HERE IN 1928 BARED
Leo Bentz, one time builder of automobiles, said that he and a friend saw a confidential demonstration of saucer-like flying model in Griffith Park in 1928. The inventor was George de Bay interested in a new principle for airplanes. De Bay produced drawings showing designs of contrivance that would skip through the air like a flat stone-an upside down saucer that worked on a vacuum principle requiring ten times less power for propulsion. Inventor de Bay, it is believed, may

have gone to Russia.

July 5, 1947: Los Angeles Examiner
FLIERS GET CLOSE UP-ONE SAYS OVALS "SCARED HIM SILLY"
Dan J. Whelan and Duncan Underhill of Hollywood reported that near Santa Monica at 5 P.M. on July 4, 1947, they saw a disk above them at 2,000 feet. The fliers were about 7,000 feet altitude. It was a disk-shaped object, not spinning, but resembling a rifle practice disk target, forty to fifty feet in diameter and traveling at about 400 to 500 miles an hour.

July 5, 1947: Los Angeles Examiner
FLYING DISKS V.F.W. CHIEF EXPECTS U. S. TO EXPLAIN
Columbus, Ohio, July 5 (AP) Louis E. Starr, national commander in chief of the Veterans of Foreign Wars told the V.F.W. Ohio encampment that he was expecting information from Washington regarding the "fleet of flying saucers." Commander did not indicate his source of information.

July 5,1947: Los Angeles Examiner LINK "SAUCERS" TO ATOM TESTS In headlines one and three-eighths inches high story makes a stab at tie up between atomic disturbances and saucerian curiosity. Photo with title "What is it?" shows flying disk at 10,000 feet. This is a print of the photograph taken by Yeoman Ryman.

July 9, 1947: Los Angeles Examiner
Photo 6 X 9 3/4 inches. Title: "Now What?" Captain roads, "Residents in almost every section of Kentucky reported seeing these luminous 'disks' streaking across the sky last night. A newspaper photographer was on hand to snap this picture of two of the flying objects."

1948
January 7, 1948: The Louisville Courier
F-51 AND CAPT. MANTELL DESTROYED CHASING FLYING SAUCER
Ft. Knox, Jan. 8 (UP) Capt. Thomas F. Mantel], of the Kentucky Air National Guard, a veteran of the Normandy invasion, chased either a flying saucer or the planet Venus to his death today over Godman Air Force base, near Fort Knox. Two others in the formation pulled out at 18,000 feet but Capt. Mantell went up to 20,000 feet before meeting his death.

February 18, 1948: The Omaha Herald
FLYING SAUCER SETS OFF EXPLOSION?
Stockton, Kansas, Feb. 18 (UP) A terrific explosion in northern Kansas rocked buildings, broke windows, and terrified natives. Its origin is unknown. A farmer

BEHIND THE FLYING SAUCERS

near Stockton said he saw a flying saucer before the explosion.

April 5, 1948: Manila, P. I.
SAUCER ELUDES ARMY PILOT BY 90-DEGREE TURN Manila, Apr. 8 Lt. Robert W. Meyers of the 67th Fighter Wing, 18th Fighter Group, Philippine Islands, leading a group of four F-47s, saw an aerial object three miles away, turned around to check on it and watched it make a 90-degree turn and disappear within five seconds. It was silver-colored and left no exhaust trails.

April 8, 1948:
TWO TOWNS REPORT SILVER PLATTER IN SKY Ashley, O., Apr. 8 (UP) Several witnesses reported an oblong silver streak over two Ohio towns. Perkins Observatory said there were weather balloons in the area at the time of the sighting.

July 28, 1948: Los Angeles Herald and Express GEORGIANS SEE WEIRD SKY SHOW Montgomery, Ala., July 28 (INS) At least 15 persons in Georgia report seeing a ball of fire, with a short flaming tail, which was variously described as being red, green, blue, and reddish white. Two flyers in Alabama reported seeing flying objects which were silvery moving westward very slowly. All agreed the objects were moving from west to east.

October 1, 1948:
GORMAN HAS 27-MINUTE DOG FIGHT WITH DISK LIGHT
Lt. George F. Gorman had a dog fight with a flying saucer over the Fargo, North Dakota, Air National Guard field for 27 minutes. He chased the light up and down, dodged head-on collisions and finally was lost at 14,000 feet, left behind by his assailant. Two control tower officers and civilians in another plane witnessed the fight.

1949
April 8, 1949: Los Angeles Times
SKY-GOING DISK SIGHTED BY PARK JOB WORKERS Two workmen in Griffith Park reported seeing a silver disk flying at a high rate of speed. Left a trail of white vapor, and zig-zagged northward. Estimated the altitude about one mile, and the disks to be about five feet in diameter. Griffith Observatory reported seeing or hearing nothing that day.

April 27, 1949: Los Angeles Times
FLYING SAUCERS NO JOKE, AIR FORCE SAID TO HAVE FOUND AFTER INQUIRY
Dayton, Ohio, April 26 (UP) The Air Force has not ruled out the possibility that the flying saucers are foreign aircraft. They have assigned a crew of technical intelligence agents of the Air Materiel Command to track down reports of the

BEHIND THE FLYING SAUCERS

mysterious object. A total of 240 domestic and 30 foreign incidents of saucers reported have been investigated. Thirty per cent of these found to be due to conventional objects such as weather, meteors, and cosmic ray research balloons. Commonplace answers are expected to be found for thirty per cent and the remaining forty per cent are still a mystery, the journal Herald said. "It is believed very unlikely that any other nation of the earth could have knowledge so far above the level of ours."

April 30, 1949: The Saturday Evening Post
WHAT YOU CAN BELIEVE ABOUT FLYING SAUCERS by Sidney Shalett
In a long article he says the Air Force has given him wholehearted co-operation and that the service has not been able to locate a flying saucer. He follows the "mistaken objects" party line but gives no opinion of his own that can be pinned down and quoted.

May 7, 1949: The Saturday Evening Post
WHAT YOU CAN BELIEVE ABOUT FLYING SAUCERS by Sidney Shalett
The author quotes various members of the high command—Vandenberg, Norstad, McCoy, LeMay, and Spaatz—all tending to belittle what you can believe about flying saucers. This is followed by case histories all tending to support the old "hallucinations" party line.

July 25, 1949: Los Angeles Times
WINGLESS FLAMING SKY MONSTER SEEN
Atlanta, July 24 (UP) Airline pilots reported tremendous aircraft spewing forty-foot stream of fire from rear. The space ship had a luminous glow, like a giant fluorescent light which ran along the belly of the thing. It was going between 500 and 700 miles an hour.

August 21, 1949: The Los Angeles Times
JUST OLD CONTRAPTIONS "FLYING SAUCERS" FIND PROVES FALSE ALARM
Washington, D. C. August 20 (AP) Air Force said that the two old machines found in a Maryland tobacco shed had nothing to do with the reported flying saucers. (Illustrated by a 1940 photo of rotor planes developed by Jonathan Caldwell. Remains of his works were found in Maryland.)

August 31, 1949: Los Angeles Times
U. S. OFFICERS REPORT SEEING FLYING DISKS, Feature by Marvin Miles
White Sands Proving Grounds, N. M. August 29. Flying saucers or at least some mysterious objects seen by the service personnel at this center were reported today. One officer believes the objects were space ships. Weather balloon, famil-

BEHIND THE FLYING SAUCERS

iar to observer, was therefore disqualified. Observation made through a photo theodolite, showed ship to be egg-shaped, fantastic in size, traveling at possibly three to four miles a second.

August 31, 1949: Los Angeles Daily News
WEIRD SKY MONSTER TRAILS MILE OF FLAME Report of sky giant trailing a blue flame exhaust nearly a mile long, cruising 50,000 feet above the Air Force's base at Muroc. Airport towers and CAA monitors at Lockheed Air Terminal, Palmdale and Long Beach received the startling report from a private pilot and two passengers. Bob Hanley, pilot, reported object at 12:15 A.M. over Mint Canyon. Hanley was described as a steady and reliable pilot.

September 16, 1949: Los Angeles Times
OUR FLYING DISK EXPERT READS SOME OF HIS MAIL, Feature by Marvin Miles
Written in the humorous trend, author quotes portions of letters received by writer from people, stating the various and sundry things they have seen, such as: "a huge blunt-nosed bullet," "bright golden object with bluish green light," "looked like enormous shuttlecocks." Marvin Miles would like to have a photograph, he states.

October 6, 1949: Los Angeles Daily Mirror
NEW THEORY HINTED-"FLYING SAUCERS" ARE REALLY REAL
Flying saucers are real objects not figments of imagination, reports Daily Mirror. They may even be from some other planet. Basis for the conclusion apparently was that enough evidence has been gathered from varied and far flung sources to blast the notion that "there's nothing to the flying saucers."

October 12, 1949: Variety (New York)
ONE FLYING SAUCER LANDS IN NEW MEXICO Two-column feature by Frank Scully giving full details from scientists who researched a saucer. "It was 100 feet across, with a cabin in the center that measures 18 feet in diameter and 72 inches high." It further stated that "sixteen men, intact but charred black, were found in the cabin. The space ship contains two metals never found so far on this earth."

October 31, 1949: Los Angeles Daily Mirror
WEIRD SKY MONSTER TRAILS MILE OF FLAME Aircraft inventor, William B. Stout, stated that the flying disk and weird space ships cannot be laughed off. The same story of the "mile of flame" that appeared in the August 31, 1949 issue of the Los Angeles Daily News is run here.

BEHIND THE FLYING SAUCERS

November 23, 1949: Variety (New York)
FLYING SAUCERS DISMANTLED, SECRETS MAY BE LOST
Two-column feature by Frank Scully giving added details of flying saucers revealed by him on October 12, 1949. New details indicate they traveled on magnetic lines of force and could therefore have come from a planet like Venus and have got back there in an hour. Ships, he says, were dismantled by the Air Force over the protests of magnetic research scientists.

December 27, 1949: Los Angeles Times
FLYING DISKS CALLED SPIES FROM PLANET
New York, December 26 (AP) Article refers to Donald Keyhoe's story in True Magazine, January issue. Many quotes direct from the article. A.P. story seems to accept the True article as q. correct.

December 28, 1949: Los Angeles Daily News
"FLYING SAUCER" MYTH BLOWN SKY HIGH BY AIR FORCE STUDY
Washington, December 28 (UP) The Air Force has closed project saucer, because the 375 reports that the Air Force has made of the flying saucers show no verification whatever of the reports, and attributes the reports to "misinterpretation of conventional objects, a mild form of mass hysteria or hoaxes."

December 28, 1949: Los Angeles Times
NO EVIDENCE-FLYING DISKS BRANDED "JOKE" BY AIR FORCE
Washington, December 27 (AP) Air Force said today that two years of investigation have convinced them that flying saucers are just a joke. It ordered ended a special "flying saucer" project which was set up in January, 1948. The announcement of its final report served as a denial of a story published by True Magazine, which said saucers were real and were from another planet. Analyses indicate flying objects are: (1) Misinterpretation of various conventional objects (2) a mild form of mass hysteria (3) or hoaxes.

December 28, 1949: Hollywood Citizen News
FLYING SAUCER IDEAS BLASTED BY AIR FORCE Washington, December 27 (AP) It took two years, a special team from the Air Force's science staff and help from university consultants to track down the rumors of disks. "Under Air Force definition, `various conventional objects' include such things as meteors, balloons, birds in flight, or just ordinary optical illusions."

December 29, 1949: Los Angeles Times
STRANGE BLIMP-SHAPED AIRCRAFT SEEN IN EAST Hamlet, N. C. December 28 (AP) Several residents including two pilots report seeing craft which was about

BEHIND THE FLYING SAUCERS

twenty to thirty feet in diameter. One pilot chased it and reported seeing something dropped from the craft-it resembled a man. The theory of a weather balloon was disqualified as the object was much larger than a weather balloon, and the pilot was familiar with the standard weather balloon.

December 29, 1949: Los Angeles Evening Herald and Express
WEIRD SIGNALS IN SKIES AS 1950 DAWNS
Ghostly "Trails" over Los Angeles. Also seen in the East a mystery vapor in strange designs. Four pilots chased an object over Carolina for several minutes. It resembled a streak of smoke about fifteen or twenty feet long coming from an unseen plane. Observers at the U. S. Weather Bureau spotted the trails spreading across the sky at an estimated 20,000 or 25,000 feet.

December 29, 1949: Hollywood Citizen News
FLYING "THING" ELUDES NORTH CAROLINA PILOTS Many residents reported having seen an object looking like a balloon or blimp, and it appeared to be twenty to thirty feet in diameter, over the North Carolina communities of Fayetteville, and Greenwood. It flew into the setting sun; four pilots in light planes attempted to follow it. The Weather Bureau at Charlotte said that apparently it was not a weather balloon, but the officials at Pop Field Airbase said that the object could very probably have been a balloon.

December 30, 1949: Los Angeles Times
VAPOR TRAILS TRACED IN SKY BY MILITARY PLANES
Picture showing mile long vapor trails coming from wing tips of military planes maneuvering between 25,000 and 35,000 feet. The turbulence created by the planes' passage caused a premature formation of "clouds," which appeared as streamers behind the aircraft.

December 31, 1949: Los Angeles Daily News
Editorial: Evidences skepticism as to possibility of flying disks. "It would not be too difficult to believe there are beings in the universe more intelligent than man. But it is still a bit outside the bounds of reason to believe space ships from another planet have come here." It further states: "Americans want their flying saucers and their men from Mars. They want their bugaboos and boogie men. They want their scandal and ordeals by fire. If the facts interfere with the achievement of these, to heck with the facts."

1950
January 1950: True Magazine, Volume 26, No. 152
THE FLYING SAUCERS ARE REAL by Donald E. Keyhoe Author reports that he

BEHIND THE FLYING SAUCERS

spent eight months of intensive investigation. He is convinced flying saucers are real. Article rewrites Fort and Air Force reports mainly.

January 11, 1950: Los Angeles Times
QUEER OBJECTS SIGHTED IN SKY BY WEATHERMEN Tucumcari, N. M. January 10 (AP) The report of three weathermen comparing notes regarding two strange objects. One object soared through the sky, changing from white to red to green and back to white. It disappeared twenty-two minutes after it first was sighted. The second object was much smaller; it also changed color and disappeared in about an hour.

January 11, 1950: Variety (New York)
AIR FORCE ASKED TWENTY QUESTIONS by Frank Scully
Queries indicate that flying saucers were dismantled in New Mexico and Arizona and shipped back to Wright Field, Dayton, Ohio and never heard of since. Air Force did not even bother to say "No comment," but newspapers like the L. A. Daily Mirror, The Buffalo Evening News, The Christian Science Monitor, Fortnight, The Canyon Crier and radio commentators around the country picked the questions up for further dissemination. As of April, 1950 only one of the questions has been answered, and that not by the Air Force.

January 11, 1950: Daily Variety (Review)
THE FLYING SAUCER (reviewer not given) Films Classics of Columbia Productions. "Action unfolds at the famed Taku glacier near Juneau. Much of the footage is spectacularly effective. Narrative shows race between U. S. and Russia to find saucer, and in its unfoldment there is fast action. Scenes purporting to show the lightning-like saucer are thrillingly presented." The producer, director, writer, and star is Mikel Conrad.

January 9-13, 1950: The New York Times.
EINSTEIN ANNOUNCES PROFOUND DISCOVERY Einstein used a quadratic type of equation method to describe the fact that energy and matter are not different. "Now Dr. Einstein has gone one step further. He has a series of equations which, he says, expresses all the relationships of the physical universe. Particularly, they tell the relationship between gravitation and the electromagnetic force that is all about us."
January 16, 1950: Los Angeles Daily Mirror
HERE ARE SOME NEW PUZZLERS ON FLYING SAUCERS RIDDLE
by Dick Williams
Dick Williams picks up the twenty questions asked by Frank Scully, and is interested in what the answers are to these questions.

185

BEHIND THE FLYING SAUCERS

January 20, 1950: The Kansas City Times
THE LITTLE MEN IN SPACE SHIPS SAIL BACK TO FICTION'S LIMBO
The Denver residents who told Rudy Fick about visitors from Venus and showed him "evidence" now disclaim authenticity of their conversational Frankenstein. Motorcar dealer passes story on that was told to him by an engineer from Denver named George Coulter. The story became distorted as it circulated, ending up with R. Fick actually having seen the disks instead of passing on a story which had been related to him. A prank was played on the motorcar dealer.

January 23, 1950: Los Angeles Daily Mirror
DID 15-YEAR-OLD BOY HAPPEN ON SECRET OF FLYING DISKS by Dick Williams. This is the story of a fifteen-year-old boy interested in shortwave radio construction, who accidently hit on the wave length of magnetic frequency and every time he dialed this frequency he shorted every motor-driven vehicle using the ignition system for a radius of three miles. This incident occurred back in 1941 in Appleton, Wisconsin. In check, Dick Williams found that motors of planes flying over his house were also shorted. The local airfield had made record of the phenomena several times This story is related in that the explanation of magnetic frequency as being tied in somewhere.

February 2, 1950: Los Angeles Daily Mirror
FLAMES ACROSS THE SKY-TUCSON PILOT CHASES "DISK"
Tucson, Ariz., February 2 (AP) An Air Force base pilot, Davis Monthan chased an unidentified object in his B-29. He was unable to catch the object, which left a "long black plume of smoke" as it disappeared very rapidly behind a range of mountains. White Sands Proving Ground in New Mexico said that the object was not a rocket, because there had been no firing that day.

February 9, 1950: Los Angeles Herald Express
"FLYING CONE"-CHECK REPORT OF ODD CRAFT OVER SAN FRANCISCO
San Francisco, Feb. 9. Observations made by five residents of San Leandro, California, and Lt. Commander J. L. Kraker of an object which appeared like a thirty-foot ice cream cone. It flew over the Alameda Naval Station at about 5,000 feet and disappeared southeast at from seventy-five to ninety-five miles an hour. Vapor trails were left.

February 19, 1950: Los Angeles Herald Express
FLYING SAUCER DISINTEGRATES INTO SPARKS Copenhagen, Denmark, Feb. 18. Christian Sandersen, farmer, and his wife said they saw two flying saucers. One saucer passed over the roof of the farmhouse, and the other landed in the yard and in less than a minute disintegrated into thousands of flowing sparks. The

saucer had a light shining through its apparently transparent bottom and flew a red ribbon.

February 23, 1950: Los Angeles Daily News
"SPACE SHIPS FROM ANOTHER PLANET"
New York, Feb. 23 (UP) Navy man tells about 'em (at usual rates). Commander Robert B. McLaughlin relates theory that flying saucers are really "space ships from another planet." Commander McLaughlin headed a guided missiles research unit. McLaughlin states he saw one of the disks in May of 1949. Much of the information is that contained in his article in True Magazine.

February 22, 1950: Buffalo Evening News
CRITIC OF AIR FORCE INSISTS BODIES WERE FOUND IN FLYING SAUCERS
Announcement by the Air Force that its Operation Saucer had been closed failed in its purpose. The announcement followed by twenty-four hours the appearance in True Magazine of an article by Donald E. Keyhoe. Frank Scully scoffs at Air Force announcement of closing. The article lists Scully's twenty questions.

February 23, 1950: Los Angeles Times
OTHER PLANET SEND SAUCERS, NAVY MAN SAYS New York, Feb. 22 (UP) Navy commander convinced that flying saucers are real space ships, piloted by strangers from other planets. Commander Robert B. McLaughlin, guided missile expert, is the U.P.'s authority.

March 7, 1950: Denver Post
SKY LIGHT AT GERING HURTS EYES
Gering, Neb., March 7. A blazing white light flashed across the countryside in the early morning. The object was very bright, and could not be watched continually without hurting the eyes. Appeared to be 100 feet in the air and traveled fast. It seemingly changed shape-first appearing flat and wide, then hourglass shaped, and then round. Estimated twenty to twenty-five feet in radius.

March 9, 1950: Denver Post
D. U. STUDENTS HEAR WEIRD TALE OF MIDGET DISK PILOTS LANDING
Story by Denver Post staff writer-Charles Little-gives account of a 45-minute secret discourse on flying saucers by an unidentified guest lecturer to several hundred students.

March 9, 1950: Denver Post
DISK EXPERT'S IDENTITY STILL A DARK MYSTERY Alfred C. Nelson, vice-chancellor, expressed surprise at the publicity given the lecturer, since the students of the class were urged to "exercise logic" on whatever the lecturer told them in his

address. Francis F. Broman, the class instructor, said he permitted the lecturer to speak to test the class' ability to weigh evidence of a scientific nature.

March 9, 1950: Denver Post
YANK CLAIMS HE SAW WRECKED FLYING DISK Los Angeles, March 9 (INS) Ray L. Dimmick, sales manager for the Apache Powder Co., states he saw a disk land near Mexico City, killing its pilot, who was 25 inches tall, with a big head and small body. The object was 46 feet in diameter and powered by two motors. The disk appeared to be constructed of aluminum.

March 9, 1950: Los Angeles Examiner
SHOWERS FROM THE NORTHWEST-One Word Led to Another by Arthur "Bugs" Baer. "If you have been perturbed by rumors of flying saucers don't worry until you see the rest of the dishes." In this vein he says that scientists dispute the theory that Mars is throwing the dishes-that they call it natural phenomenon unexplainable by marginal notations in a cookbook.

March 10, 1950: Los Angeles Examiner
23-IN. PILOT REPORTED KILLED IN "SAUCER" CRASH Ray L. Dimmick, business executive and well-known amateur golfer, reported that he saw a wreckage at a secret military installation near Mexico City, of a saucer which was powered by two motors. The saucer was approximately 46 feet in diameter, built of metal resembling aluminum, and contained the body of a pilot 23 inches tall, who was killed when the object supposedly crashed. The Mexican authorities roped off the area, and removed the wreckage to military installation. "Top brass" from Washington, D. C., and Air Force headquarters professed to know nothing of it, and said, "If American officers had seen the object they would have made a report."

March 10, 1950: Denver Post
IS YOUR SAUCER VIEW DIM OR DIMMICK'S?
Los Angeles, March 10 (AP) Ray L. Dimmick, a dynamite salesman, backtracked today. He said the flying saucer story was related to him by two business associates. All Dimmick actually saw, according to revised version, was a strip of metal about six feet long, eight inches wide, and three-quarters of an inch thick. Dr. Vallarta, Mexico's leading nuclear scientist, stated that the saucer-seers were viewing balloons released by the U. S. Weather stations along the border.

March 10, 1950: Denver Post
"ZOOM, SWISH, PFFT!" SAYS SAUCER SEER
Lewis Hayden, Denver aviation executive, reported that he thought he sighted

BEHIND THE FLYING SAUCERS

a saucer. "All I know-it was very high, shiny like aluminum, and shot out of sight at a rate of speed unknown to modern aviation."

March 10, 1950: Chicago Daily Times
"DISK" REPORTS START JITTERS A two-column report of the fallen saucer seen by Ray L. Dimmick, which crashed in Mexico, killing its 23-inch pilot, coupled with the Colorado version, as related by the Denver Post, of the lecturer who told several hundred students in a basic science class of the University of Denver that he knew of three saucers landing.

March 10, 1950: Los Angeles Times
COMPOSER SURE HE SAW FLYING SAUCER IN SKY Eddie Coffman, composer, and amateur astronomer, told police he had seen a genuine flying saucer about 400 feet over the San Fernando Valley. Saucer was about fifty feet in diameter, and was observed through 20-power telescope.

March 10, 1950: Denver Post
D. U. STUDENTS IMPRESSED BY TALK OF FLYING DISKS AND LITTLE MEN
Reaction of the University of Denver basic science students to the lecture they heard by an unidentified individual who claimed knowledge of disks and the men inside, was one of great interest. The class had requested to hear from an "authority" on existence of the objects.

March 1950: True Magazine, Volume 26, No. 154
HOW SCIENTISTS TRACED A FLYING SAUCER by Commander R. B. McLaughlin
Author was assigned to guided missiles at White Sands Proving
Ground, New Mexico. His article is mainly a detailed account of one saucer which he thought he saw at an altitude of twenty-five miles moving at 360 miles per hour. He said he was convinced they were space ships from another planet.

March 10, 1950: Los Angeles Times
SCIENTIST SAYS SAUCERS CARRY MARS VISITORS Mexico City, March 9 (UP) Government newspaper El Nacional quoted a Mexican scientist as saying his claim that flying saucers carry visitors from Mars, would be confirmed in the near future. The scientist said that it was obvious from the manner of light and proportions of these disks that they carry beings from another world, undoubtedly Mars.

March 12, 1950: Los Angeles Times
LITTLE MEN HERE AGAIN, THIS TIME OVER SALINAS Salinas, March 11 (UP)
Reports of saucers driving on an automobile, looping the loop and/or speeding across the horizon at low altitude, was made by a score of persons in the Salinas,

189

BEHIND THE FLYING SAUCERS

California area.

March 12, 1950: Los Angeles Times
CHILEAN NAVY REPORTS 7-INCH FLYING SAUCER Santiago, March 11 (UP)
Chilean Navy's meteorologist observatory at Punta Arenas reported spheroid
celestial body, about seven inches in diameter, and naked to the eye, which
crossed the sky in an east-to-west direction.

March 12, 1950: Los Angeles Times
AMATEUR PHOTOGRAPHER SNAPS WEIRD DISK IN SKY
Amateur photographer, Miss Bette Malles of Los Angeles, has both seen and
snapped a photograph of something resembling a flying saucer. The disk was a
circular blob, and what appears to be a cone of faint light, connects the blob to the
disk. A second cone of light, projecting backwards from the disk narrows to meet
another round blob of light which seems to serve as the disk's rear guard. The
disk and its rear guard are enclosed within a large and perfectly circular halo.

March 12, 1950: Denver Post
SAUCER-TALK MIDDLEMAN QUIZ TARGET
George T. Koehler is the middleman in bringing the mystery scientist to speak
to the basic science students of Denver University. Koehler gave his opinion: "Let's
open our minds to the possibility of the saucer, at least. Why hide our heads in the
sand? If the age is here, it is here whether there are denials that interplanetary
travel has come of age or not."

March 12, 1950: Los Angeles Times
MEXICO SEES FLYING SAUCERS OR SOMETHING Mexico City, March 11 (UP)
Ever since the True Magazine story, and the fact that the newspaper Excelsior
printed a series of articles citizens have "saucer craze." A picture taken of a strange
object appeared very much like a picture of a klieg light.

March 12, 1950: Denver Post
SAUCY SAUCER SAUSE-SHADES OF H. G. WELLS AND JULES VERNE
Feature by Thor Severson, Denver Post staff writer. Factual report of the lecture
given to the basic science students of the University of Denver by the unidentified
lecturer who reported on disks and the little men inside them.

March 12, 1950: Los Angeles Times
CALEXICO HAS NEW FLYING SAUCER TALE
Residents reported a strange round object in the sky. There seems to be a dis-
pute as to whether the object was a weather balloon, or the work of some prank-

BEHIND THE FLYING SAUCERS

ster who attempted to augment recent flying saucer reports in the Riverside area.

March 12, 1950: Los Angeles Times
FLYING SAUCERS? YOU CAN'T BE SURE by Marvin Miles Kites, balloons, reflections? Almost anything, says the Air Force. Three hundred and forty-one reports have been explained to the Air Force's satisfaction out of 375 selected reports of unidentified flying objects. States ratio is probably lower by now, and that it does not mean that the unexplained reports are necessarily space ships or high altitude cruisers from another nation.

March 14, 1950: Los Angeles News
EXPERTS SIGHT FOUR 'SAUCERS' OVER MEXICO CITY
Mexico City, March 14 (UP) Hundreds of persons said they saw four flying saucers over the city and one at Monterrey, 350 miles north. Meteorologist calculated the altitude between 35,000 and 40,000 feet. Included also was the story of the two Colorado businessmen who were chased by a strange flying object while returning from a trip to New Mexico.

March 14, 1950: Los Angeles Times
PROFESSOR'S IDEA-SAUCER PILOTS COULD BE SMART BUGS OR PLANTS
Dr. Gerard P. Kuiper, professor of astronomy at the University of Chicago, speculated that any little Martian who steps out of a flying saucer space ship will be either an intellectual insect or an even more incredible vegetable creature. Dr. Kuiper states further that Mars is composed of carbon dioxide and there is absolutely no oxygen in the atmosphere; hence no form of life such as we know it. There may be forms of insect life however.

March 15, 1950: Los Angeles Daily News
EXPERTS SIGHT FOUR "SAUCERS" OVER MEXICO CITY
Mexico City, March 14 (UP) Trained aircraft observers and meteorologists confirmed reports today of hundreds of persons who saw four "flying saucers" yesterday over the city and one at Monterrey, 350 miles north.

March 16, 1950: Denver Post ATOMIC CLOUDS?
John Leuthold, in the Open Forum Theory, submitted a letter that explained that the saucers are atomic clouds or cloudlets of released atomic ingredients arrested by, and magnetically collected on sheets or shells of the earth's magnetic field. Some of these "shells" have been detected by the scientists and named "ionospheres."

BEHIND THE FLYING SAUCERS

March 16, 1950:
TECHNICIAN GETS CLOSEUP OF FLYING SAUCER St. Mary's, Pa., March 16 (UP) Dr. Craig Hunter, 47, of Berkley Springs, W. Va., a technical director for a Washington medical instrument supply firm, reported he saw flying objects that were moving slowly from east to west. Their altitude was first noted to be about 250 to 500 feet. The objects appeared to be 50 to 150 feet in diameter and about 25 to 30 feet thick at the center.

March 16, 1950: Denver Post
DISK TALK MOVES D. U. TO SCREEN LECTURERS Chancellor Albert C. Jacobs cautioned University of Denver faculty members to screen guest lecturers carefully. This action came as a result of the mystery lecturer that spoke at the university on March 8, 1950.

March 16, 1950: Denver Post
D. U. PROFESSOR PLACES NO VALUE ON SAUCER LECTURE BY MISTER X by Thor Severson, Denver Post staff writer
Francis F. Broman, of the University of Denver, basic science instructor who permitted the controversial "mystery man" to lecture to his class on flying saucers, said, "I told this man I must present him and his remarks as an analytical study."

March 16, 1950: Denver Post
DISK PILOTS GETTING BOLDER, ONE TAKES 5-MINUTE BREAK
Denver Post Special. A Swiss engineer reported that he had seen a flying saucer that had remained suspended in the air for five minutes.

March 17, 1950: Denver Post
THE UNIVERSITY GETS A DESERVED SPANKING Denver Post Editorial. "The skirts of academic freedom are wide and are often used to cover many subjects and sins. The case of the flying saucer lecture cannot be so covered, as Chancellor Jacobs (of University of Denver) has said. It is gratifying to see the chancellor take such a strong stand on this case."

March 17, 1950: Los Angeles Daily News
(Excerpt from Matt Weinstock's column) "Granted that most reports of flying saucers are unreliable or due to wishful imagination, plenty of people have a suspicion there's more to them than meets the eye."

BEHIND THE FLYING SAUCERS

March 17, 1950: Denver Post
STUDENTS IDENTIFY SAUCER SPEAKER by Thor Severson, Denver Post staff
writer
"Mr. X" who lectured at University of Denver on flying saucers last March 8 has
been finally identified. A picture of the mystery lecturer found in the Denver Post
files has been identified as Silas M. Newton, president of the Newton Oil Company and Colorado amateur golf champion in 1942. One of the students who identified the picture as that of the lecturer was Bill Berry, who said that he "used to
caddy for Newton at the Lakewood golf course."

March 17, 1950: Los Angeles Times
FLYING SAUCER WHIRLS ABOVE BALDWIN HILLS (Los Angeles Times special)
Roy Wolford, a former jet test pilot, has designed a flying saucer that has two wings
that rotate with the disk. Mr. Wolford originally designed the string-controlled
disk as a high-speed tow target for aerial gunnery practice.

March 18, 1950: Denver Post
NEW MEXICO TOWN SURE SAUCER MASS FLIGHT SEEN
Farmington, N. M., March 18 (UP) Most of the 5,000 residents of this northwestern New Mexico oil town said today that they were "absolutely convinced" that
flying saucers exist. More than 50 witnesses-including businessmen and private
pilots-said that they saw a mass flight of disk-shaped objects yesterday which
came across the town in group waves and numbered "into the hundreds." Clayton
Boddy, advertising manager of the Farmington Daily Times, said the day was clear
with only a light scattering of cirrus clouds at an altitude estimated at 20,000 feet,
and with no strong winds capable of picking up paper or similar material.

March 18, 1950: Denver Post
AIR FORCE HOLDS FLYING DISKS "BUNK"
Washington, March 18 (UP) The Air Force still believes there is no such thing as
a flying saucer despite recent reports to the contrary. A spokesman for the Air
Force said today that the "unidentified objects result from misinterpretation of
various conventional objects, a mild form of mass hysteria, or hoaxes."

March 18,1950: Las Vegas Daily Optic
"SPACE SHIPS" CAUSE SENSATION by Walt Rogal, New Mexico Newspaper
staff writer
For the third consecutive day flying saucers have been reported over
Farmington. And on each of the three days their arrival was reported between 11
A.M. and noon. Fully half of this town's population is certain today that it saw space
ships or some strange aircraft-hundreds of them-zooming through the skies yes-

193

terday. Whatever they were, they caused a major sensation in this community, which lies only 110 air miles northwest of the huge Los Alamos atomic installation. One witness who took a triangulation sighting on one of the objects estimated its speed at about 1,000 miles an hour, and estimated its size as approximately twice that of a B-29.

March 18, 1950: Las Vegas Daily Optic Editorial titled: GIVE US THE FACTS Yesterday hundreds of reliable, sober people in Farmington saw "something" in the skies. At least half believe what they saw was an armada of space ships. Others saw something they never saw before, but won't venture a guess as to what it was. And still others say that what was seen was cotton, or jet planes or some other familiar object. The American population is not composed chiefly of children or idiots. Most of us are adults who are willing to embrace new concepts of time and space without panic. Attempts to keep the public in the dark invariably have hurt the general welfare, not helped it. We can say, however, that it is high time the government of the U. S. cast aside the cloak of evasion and secrecy surrounding these manifestations, and present to the public the findings it has reached on such matters.

March 18, 1950: Los Angeles Times
SCORES REPORT SEEING SAUCERS' FLIGHT IN FORMATION OVER NEW MEXICO
Farmington, N. M., March 17 (UP) 50 persons reported a mass flight of flying saucers over Farmington, N. Mexico. Groups commencing at 10:30 A.M. and lasted for one hour. Among the saucers was one low-flying red-hued, saucer-shaped object. All the saucers except for this one were silvery color, and all appeared to be very high except for the red-hued one.

March 21, 1950: Los Angeles Daily News
SEE SAUCER WITH WINDOWS ON BOTTOM
Memphis, Tenn., March 21 (UP) Two airline pilots report that a flying saucer with windows on the bottom and a blinking light on top flew over Arkansas last night at a tremendous rate.

March 21, 1950:
AIR FORCE FEARS MAYBE IT TALKED A LITTLE TOO MUCH
Washington, March 21 (UP) The Air Force was reported red-faced today over some of its too candid disclosures to the House Armed Services Committee. The disclosures were made in a mimeographed 71-page document justifying Air Force requests for authority to build, repair, or expand its bases in this country, Alaska, Labrador, the Azores, and Libya.

BEHIND THE FLYING SAUCERS

March 22, 1950: Los Angeles Daily News
2 VETERAN PILOTS SWEAR TO FLYING DISK
Memphis, March 22 (UP) Captain Jack Adams and First Officer G. W. Anderson reported an aircraft in controlled flight over Arkansas moving with terrific speed and possessed of a strange, strong blue-white light, which blinked rapidly on top of the object. It was not a jet. Of that they are sure.

March 22, 1950: Los Angeles Herald Express
HUNDREDS WATCH DISK 4 HOURS OVER SAN JACINTO MOUNTAINS
Idyllwild, Calif. March 22. Hundreds of people watched a saucer-like object over Idyllwild, California, while watching exhaust trails from a jet aircraft. The disk was estimated to be flying at 30,000 feet and moving northward.

March 23, 1950. Los Angeles Daily News
Matt Weinstock column. Weinstock relates the story of a Los Angeles business-man who inadvertently landed, due to carburetor trouble with his plane, in an area where a disk presumably had landed. He met with eight hours of question-ing by Air Force and was grounded.

March 23, 1950: Variety
Harry Hincle of Tucson, Arizona, tries to talk an ex-Air Corps pilot out of some 16 m footage of flying saucer for George Pal's "When Worlds Collide."

March 23, 1950: Los Angeles Daily News
"SAUCERS" POP UP IN L. A. AREA-8 SEEN OFF COAST Picture and story of Bill Elder and Bob O'Hara, from the Air Force reserve training center in Long Beach, California. They swear they saw something in the sky near Idyllwild, California, that they had never seen before. They did not say it was a space ship from another planet or "anything else." They saw eight things of an elliptical shape about 100 feet in diameter at 2,000 feet.

March 24, 1950: Denver Post
Ken White On The Air column. Ralph Edwards on the "Truth or Consequence" program will offer $1,000 to the first person to show up on his program with one of those little men from an interplanetary space ship.

March 25, 1950: The Mirror
FLYING "DISK" DAZZLES L. A. WRITER
Daniel Swinton, writer from North Hollywood, California, observed object sighted near his home as being elliptical in shape, brilliant, and undimming.

BEHIND THE FLYING SAUCERS

March 26, 1950: Denver Post
SAUCERS OR BALLOONS? PICCARD NOT CERTAIN by William L. Hathaway
Minneapolis, March 25. An exclusive interview by the press with Dr. Auguste Piccard, famed scientist and balloonist. Dr. Piccard states that "most saucers may be experimental balloons which travel hundreds of miles." Air Force investigation has given no bases for belief that there are high-speed disks in the skies, says the editor of Denver Post. Piccard says there will always be unexplained phenomena-however fewer today than a few hundred years ago . . . most saucers can be explained by competent, scientifically-trained observers.

March 27, 1950: Los Angeles Daily News REPORT DISK SEEN NEAR U. S. CAPITAL Washington, March 27 (UP) Bertram A. Totten, clerk at the Congressional Library, saw an aluminum-colored disk about forty feet in diameter and ten feet thick, while flying over Fairfax county on the outskirts of Washington.

March 27, 1950: Los Angeles Times
PLANET OR SAUCER? MYSTERY SKY VISITOR SIGHTED BY AIR FORCE
Las Vegas, March 26. Officers and men at the Air Force's Indian Springs gunnery range today were taking turns looking into an antiaircraft scope to glimpse "something bright in the sky." No one said it was a saucer-just wild guesses.

March 27, 1950: Los Angeles Daily News
CAN DISKS BE NEW FLYING TARGET DRONE?
Austin, Texas, March 28 (UP) Target drones of apparently fantastic speed are being created by University of Texas scientists for sky scrimmages with new guided missiles. The Air Force has repeatedly denied the existence of flying saucers. Radio announcer, Henry J. Taylor, broadcast that "These disks that are flying saucers are real but that this nation need not be alarmed."

March 27, 1950:
Tulsa, Okla., March 27 (AP) Seven Tulsans relate how they saw flying saucers riding high in the dust storm that silted the city.

March 28, 1950: Los Angeles Times
SAUCERS SEEN AS SECRET OF OUR AIR FORCE
Dallas, March 28 (AP) Henry J. Taylor, radio commentator, said in his opinion flying saucers are real and that when the U. S. Air Force confirms the news it will be wonderful.

March 30, 1950: Los Angeles Mirror
NAVY "PANCAKE" MAY ANSWER FLYING DISKS by Dick Williams

BEHIND THE FLYING SAUCERS

Picture of disk-like plane that had windows underneath and rows of ports across the front. The plane is the aircraft jet models of the original XF5U. This radically-different type of Navy plane can hang stationary in mid-air or zoom through the skies at speeds up to 550 miles per hour.

March 30, 1950: The New York Times
MORE "FLYING SAUCERS" IN MEDITERRANEAN, ORIENT
London, March 29. Reports of objects in skies above the Mediterranean as looking like strange bodies emitting smoke trails, moons with wakes of fire, like full moons. In Hong Kong three flying fireballs were reported.

March 31, 1950: Los Angeles Times NAVY PLANE
Washington, March 31 (UP) The Navy today discounted a California report that perhaps its twin-engine Chance-Vought XF5U fighter plane had been mistaken for a flying saucer. This type of aircraft was not found to be successful. One was purchased by the Navy two years ago.

April 3, 1950: New York World-Telegram
THEY USE BIG WORDS TO CONFUSE PUBLIC from Washington Notebook by Peter Edson
Washington, April 3. The biggest off-the-record story in Washington is the flying saucer. Air Force say "there ain't no such animal. They have never seen one and have no photographs or visible proof." Peter Edson says, however, that "privately most officials believe there's something to it."

April 3, 1950: Los Angeles Times
AIR SAUCERS CALLED TOP SECRET OF U. S.
New York, April 3 (UP) Flying saucers actually are two types of top-secret U. S. military inventions, radio commentator Henry J. Taylor said. The real facts are good news for the nation. One type a disk that whizzes through space, halts suspended in the air, soars to 30,000 feet and more, drops to 1,000 feet and then usually disintegrates in the air. Saucers are harmless, pilotless disks-20 inches to 250 feet in diameter. The other objects are Flying Phantoms, XF5U, jet propelled.

"The Navy is not experimenting with or doing research on any type of plane or guided missile that resembles in any way a flying saucer." (quote by Navy spokesman) The XF5U-1 was unsuccessful and never flown.

It was June 25, 1947, commentator H. J. Taylor said, that saucer experiments began, and they have been expanded constantly ever since. (The Air Force denied Taylor's story.) These words, Taylor says are stenciled on the back of every real saucer: "Anyone damaging or revealing description or whereabouts of this missile is subject to prosecution by the U. S. Government. Call collect at once."

BEHIND THE FLYING SAUCERS

April 3, 1950: Los Angeles Evening Herald & Express
BARE FLYING SAUCERS AS REAL AIRCRAFT BEING DEVELOPED BY U. S.
Washington, April 3. Reference to the U. S. News and World Report article which stated that there is competent evidence that flying saucers are real aircraft of revolutionary design, developed in the United States. "Flying saucers, seen by hundreds of competent observers over most parts of the United States, are accepted as real. Evidence is that they are aircraft of a revolutionary type, a combination of heliocopter and fast jet plane." It states that early models were built by engineers of the National Advisory Committee for Aeronautics.

April 3, 1950: (Drew Pearson) CONGRESSIONAL FLYING SAUCERS
Congressman Mel Price, East St. Louis, Illinois, recently acted as a committee of one from House Armed Services in badgering the Air Force into an investigation of flying saucers. Price's official Air Force reply was "There is absolutely nothing to them," he said. "They are caused by retina retention, mistaken identity, a mild form of mass hysteria, and just plain hoaxes."

April 3, 1950: Hollywood Citizen News
"FLYING SAUCERS" REAL THING? NAVY TESTING SECRET PLANES, SAYS MAGAZINE.
Washington, April 3 (AP) The weekly news magazine, U. S. News and World Report concludes that the Navy is doing the development relative to flying saucers being real aircraft. It is noted that an Air Force inquiry into saucer reports was called off last December and says this indicates clearly that top Air Force officials know where the saucers originate and are not concerned about them.

April 3, 1950: New York World-Telegram
DISHING OUT THE DIRT ON FLYING SAUCERS Washington, April 3. Cartoon by B. Pause with caption, "The Flying Saucers seen around the country were arpad's latest dish washing service to conserve water. . . ." There are quotations from the U. S. News and World Report article of the validity of flying saucers being real aircraft, developed in the United States.

April 4, 1950: Los Angeles Times
AIR SAUCERS CALLED TOP U. S. SECRET
New York, April 3 (UP) Quotations from commentator Henry J. Taylor that flying saucers are two types of top-secret U. S. military inventions.

April 4, 1950: New York Herald Tribune
FLYING SAUCERS CALLED SECRET U. S. WARCRAFT OF TERRIFIC SPEED
Washington, April 3. Picture given, which was also included in the U. S. News

BEHIND THE FLYING SAUCERS

and World Report article, of the one-third scale model built in 1942. The model is said to be the prototype of flying saucers which the U. S. News and World Report article said are real aircraft.

April 4, 1950:
TRUMAN, JOHNSON TRY TO DOWN THE DISKS Washington, April 4 (UP) Mr. Truman announced through his press secretary at Key West, Florida that he knows nothing of any flying saucers being developed by this or any other country. "We are not denying this because of any developments of secret weapons, but purely because we know of nothing to support these rumors," said Press Secretary Charles G. Ross.

April 4, 1950: The New York Times "SAUCERS" CALLED REAL NAVY PLANES Washington, April 3 (AP) Recap of the magazine article from U. S. News and World Report, which declares evidence indicating revolutionary craft are of U. S. development. Included a picture of scale model built in 1942 mounted for wind tunnel tests at Langley, Va.

April 4, 1950: Denver Post
U. S. DENIES SAUCERS TEST WEAPONS
Washington, April 4 (UP) Air Force and Navy say they are not experimenting with any plane or weapon that could account for widespread reports about the flying disks. A spokesman for the Air Force after investigation of hundreds of saucer stories said the armed services are standing on conclusions reached last December that flying saucers just don't exist.

April 5, 1950: The New York Times
TRUMAN, JOHNSON RIDICULE "SAUCERS"
Key West, Fla. April 4 (Special) President Truman said today he knew nothing about the flying saucer, while other White House comment relegated the reputed wanderer to the realm of myths. The Miami Daily News has been publishing copyrighted photographs of a glowing concave object which it identifies as the saucer that flies.... Charles G. Ross, White House secretary, quoted Brig. General Robert B. Landry and Rear Admiral Robert L. Dennison as saying they knew nothing of the flying saucers. Mr. Ross said he wasn't denying them for security reasons, that he thought it extremely unlikely they could be part of a secret weapon project concealed even from the President and as far he knew no other country had them. Secretary of Defense Johnson said he wouldn't mind having a few squadrons if they increased security.

BEHIND THE FLYING SAUCERS

April 5, 1950. Los Angeles Times
WHITE HOUSE POOH-POOHS "SECRET WEAPON" SAUCERS
Key West, Fla., April 4 (AP) Dr. Clark B. Millikan, chairman of the Armed Forces Guided Missile Committee, gave a flat denial to chain-reaction rumors of government disk developments. He confirmed the reports that work is being done on space rockets capable of streaking out of the earth's atmosphere.

April 5, 1950: New York Journal American
DO SAUCERS FLY? LEADERS SAY YES AND NO Washington, April 1 (UP) One House member who should know said flatly there is no such thing as a flying saucer. But another member equally qualified said he has seen one himself. "I am confident of this," said Rep. Engel (R.-Mich.) "If there are any such things as saucers they are ours, not somebody else's."

April 5,1950: New York journal American
NOT ENEMY ACTIVITY SAYS DEFENSE DEPT. Washington, April 5 (UP) Here is text of Defense Department statement on flying saucers: "There is no intention of reopening Project Saucer, an Air Force Special project officially closed three months ago. However the Air Force has and will continue to receive and evaluate through normal field intelligence channels any substantial reports of any unusual aerial phenomena."

April 6, 1950: Hollywood Advertiser
GRIFFITH PARK DIRECTOR SCOFFS AT FLYING DISKS
Just their imagination, says Dr. Dinsmore Alter, Director of the Griffith Park Observatory. "Flying saucers are all kinds of imagination-flavored things-but they certainly aren't space ships from Mars." He goes further to state that "The saucers just are `ordinary phenomena,' twisted by untrained observers, whose reading and discussions about the possibility of space travel lead them to interpret some of what they see on high as saucers."

April 6, 1950: Rocky Mountain News
FLYING ORANGE SPOTTED IN SKIES: Disk, Too, Seen Performing Aerial Antics
A woman called the Rocky Mountain News reporting that she saw an object completely round except that it was silver and gray in color instead of orange. It was spinning in a conventional flying disk manner. This object was sighted by four other persons. Another object sighted in the same area was disk-like in shape, but not round as the orange one reported.

April 6, 1950: Los Angeles Times
REACTIONARY HOLD OUT AGAINST SAUCERS THAT FLY by Max Hamilton.

BEHIND THE FLYING SAUCERS

Hamilton states that if there were flying saucers they would have to originate either on the earth or elsewhere in the universe. The latter, he feels, is preposterous. "Not even atomic fission, the most sensational discovery in history, burst full blown upon the world. The possibilities of it were discussed generations before. But no reputable aeronautical engineer has ever suggested that a saucer-shaped vehicle would be a wonderful new way of conquering the air," further states Hamilton.

April 7, 1950: Denver Post ANOTHER DISK GUESS
"It isn't hard at all to explain the flying `saucer,'" writes Cornelius Donovan, of New York City. "It is a `secret' project of an earth government, namely the United States of America. . . - Quite understandably, government officials deny having anything to do with the `flying saucer' method of taking the American taxpayer for a ride through the stratosphere! Could they be just a bit ashamed, by any chance?"

April 7, 1950: Los Angeles Daily News "FLYING CANDLES" ARE THE LATEST El Centro, April 7 (UP) Several residents reported seeing hundreds of lights hovering over the city. Some moved fast-others more slowly-before disappearing.

April 7, 1950: Los Angeles Daily News
EXPERT SAYS FLYING SAUCERS U. S. MILITARY SECRET
Montvale, N. J. April 7 (UP) Willy Ley, one of the world's outstanding authorities on rockets and flight above the stratosphere, said he firmly believed that the flying saucers have been winging across the U. S. He said they are not rocket-propelled. The U. S. might very probably have learned how to send disks soaring over the nation in controlled flight. He gives three possibilities: (1) They are a U. S. military secret, (2) They are the secret of some foreign power, or (3) The flying saucers are from another planet. Ley's personal opinion is that the flying saucers are a U. S. military secret.

April 7, 1950: Hollywood Citizen News
FLYING DISKS NOT HOAXES. Syndicated feature by David Lawrence.
Washington, D. C. Quotes from the U. S. News and World Report, also Ken Purdy, editor of True, which published the two articles written by Donald Keyhoe and Commander McLaughlin. "You are quite correct in saying that the flying saucers exist," Lawrence quoted Purdy as saying. "Of course they do, and I think no one can properly write this story without reference to the fact that we first made the statement in December 1949." Lawrence added, that "clearly something is lacking to explain what the competent Air Force flyers wrote in reporting their observations of the flying saucers-which reports are reposing in official files and have never been made

BEHIND THE FLYING SAUCERS

April 9, 1950: Denver Post
VIEWER BREAKS SILENCE TO TELL OF L. A. SAUCER Denver, April 9, Denver Post Special. One Denver flying-saucer-viewer broke a ten month silence Saturday to describe what he says must surely have been a flying saucer he viewed one afternoon last July in Los Angeles. Mr. J. S. Stankavage, a retired painter, said he kept quiet because "my wife and I were afraid if I said anything about it people would accuse me of 'seeing' things." Stankavage said the heart-shaped object he saw appeared to have two portholes along the side. It did not spin, but moved with the point of the heart headed forward.

April 9, 1950: The New York Times
THOSE FLYING SAUCERS: ARE OR AREN'T THEY? by Joseph Nolan.
In a by-lined story spreading over four columns the Times recapitulated stories of the flying saucers. Everybody had been left puzzled, including the President and many guesses were made.

April 10, 1950: Los Angeles Times
SCORCHED BOY INSISTS HE TOUCHED SAUCER Amarillo, Tex., April 9 (UP) David Lightfood, 12, sighted what was at first thought to be a balloon, but turned out to be an object about the same circumference as an automobile tire, and about 18 inches thick. It was rounded on the bottom with a top resembling a flat plate. He barely touched it when he claimed it was slick like a snake and hot. It was blue-gray in color and had no opening other than the divided section. There was some release of gas or spray when the object took off, which turned his arms and face bright red, causing welts. A younger boy of 9 confirmed this story.

April 10, 1950: The Salinas Sun SALINAN SPOTS FLYING SAUCER Lindsborg, April 10. P. E. Patchin of Lindsborg, said he saw a gray-white, clam-shaped object streaking across the sky near Lindsborg at 11:30 A.M. Wednesday. The object was visible to him for about five and one-third miles. It made no noise, and according to Patchin's mathematical calculations, it was heading southwest at about 650 miles per hour and at an altitude of two miles.

April 10, 1950: Los Angeles Daily News
LINKS FLYING DISKS WITH MYSTERY SUB
Boise, Idaho, April 10 (UP) Kenneth Arnold is again in the news. Arnold believes there is a link between the flying saucers and the mysterious submarines reported off the U. S. coastline. He agrees with those who think that the strange aircraft might be space ships from another planet.

BEHIND THE FLYING SAUCERS

April 11, 1950: Los Angeles Times
CHROMELIKE "SAUCER" SEEN OVER MONTEREY Monterey, April 10 (AP) A chromelike flying saucer was spotted here today by seven persons. It was cruising at a high rate of speed over Monterey. The object was 30 feet in diameter and was at an altitude of approximately 4,000 feet.

April 14, 1950: Los Angeles Daily News FLYING DISK DESIGNED 23 YEARS AGO Monterey, Calif., April 14 (UP) Alexander G. Weygers, a mechanical engineer and architect, designed a "discopter" 23 years ago. The patented designs for this gas or jet powered craft were rejected by Consolidated Vultee Aircraft Corp. in April, 1945 as being "too advanced."

April 19, 1950: Los Angeles Daily News
TEXANS REPORT SEEING FLYING BANANA-SYMINGTON POOH-POOHS IT
Dallas, Tex., April 19 (UP) Bewildered Texans today sought an explanation for flying saucers, flying bananas, and even a dinner plate which they thought they saw in the sky. Hundreds saw them, in Fort Worth, Austin, and Clarendon as well as Dallas.
Ira Maxey, a Fort Worth veteran of 3,600 hours of Air Force flying, produced pictures of curved banana-like objects which he photographed. He said they left vapor trails. Air Force Secretary Symington, who wasn't in Texas, but in San Francisco at the time, said "there is nothing at all to such reports."

April 20, 1950: Denver Post
AIR FORCE ORDERS "SAUCER" WATCH IN TEXAS SKIES
Fort Worth, Tex., April 20, 1950 (AP) The 8th Air Force still doesn't believe in flying saucers but its pilots will keep an eye out for "any unusual aerial phenomena" said a recent memorandum issued by 8th Air Force Headquarters.

April 20, 1950: Los Angeles Times
RANCHER CAPTURES FLYING DISK: SAYS IT'S NAVY PROPERTY
Douglas, Wyo., April 20 (UP) Everett Fletcher, a rancher, sighted a flying ball in the skies 32 miles north of here and followed it to the ground. Stamped on a nameplate was, "this scientific apparatus is the joint property of the U. S. Navy and the University of Minnesota. Made in Lexington, Kentucky." A telephone call to Minneapolis said it was a Navy instrument used for measuring cosmic rays. "Don't open it," a Naval officer warned. "Ship it here immediately, but don't touch it."

April 22, 1950: Los Angeles Daily News
MAN CHASED BY FLYING SAUCER SHOWERING SPARKS
Lufkin, Tex., April 22 (UP) Jack Robertson, 28, a pharmacist graduated from the

BEHIND THE FLYING SAUCERS

University of Texas, was motoring along Highway 94 west of town. He felt something following him. He stopped and got out of his car. An object approached, hovered 200 feet over him, turned a 50-degree angle and speeded off, dropping sparks as it climbed. It whirled like a flying saucer. Five minutes later his face started burning. His experience changed his views about the nonexistence of flying saucers, Air Force or no Air Force.

April 26, 1950: The New York Times
CIVILIAN TRAINING IN ATOM DETECTION
"I believe," said Paul J. Larson, director of the Office of Civilian Mobilization of the National Security Resources Board, "it is essential that, insofar as it is possible, all of us tell the same story."

April 28, 1950: The Rangely Driller
OIL BASIN FOLKS WONDER, DID THEY SEE FLYING SAUCERS?
Rangely, Colo., April 27 Seven persons including the Continental Oil Co. Superintendent A. W. Jay and his wife and daughter, said that they simultaneously saw a glowing object flash across the sky Thursday night in this northwestern Colorado oil town. Mr. and Mrs. Glen Holden saw one 50 to 75 feet away. It was circular and appeared to be covered with a "phosphorescent metallic paint." Also Ronnie Grisdale and Carley Cook, oil field workers, reported a "strange glow which seemed to hang in the sky." By their reports, one flew fast, one flew low, one stood still.

April 29, 1950: The Chicago Times
AIRLINER FLIRTS WITH A "DISK"; 'TWAS RED, ROUND AND GLOWING
South Bend, April 29 (Chicago Times, Special) Capt. Robert Adickes, a veteran TWA pilot, and several passengers said they saw a mysterious "round, glowing mass" in the air as they flew over South Bend Thursday night. "I used to laugh at all those flying saucer reports, but it's no laughing matter now," Adickes said. "I saw one." Adickes' story was confirmed by First Officer Robert Manning and several of the 19 passengers aboard the Washington to Chicago flight. "It appeared to be controlled by repulse radar," Adickes said. "As I'd turn toward it, it would veer away, keeping the same distance."

April 29, 1950: Los Angeles Examiner
SAUCER GLOWS AS IT GOES
Kansas City, April 28 (AP) Captain Robert Adickes, veteran Trans World Airline pilot, 29, described a flying saucer he saw as twenty to fifty feet in diameter and about five feet thick. His first officer, his hostess, and nineteen passengers in flight from Washington to Chicago backed him up. They saw it too.

BEHIND THE FLYING SAUCERS

April 29, 1950: Canyon Crier (Los Angeles)
HILLSIDER SWEARS HE'S SEEN, FILMED, AND INSPECTED FLYING SAUCERS
Mikel Conrad, who lives at 1401 N. Sierra Bonita, in Los Angeles, swears he photographed eight flying saucers, landing and taking off, 40 miles north of Juneau, Alaska. The government confiscated 900 feet of his film and released it with certain restrictions a year later. "I give information I'm permitted to the press," he said, "and they try to verify it in Washington and get no answers. Questions are completely ignored. But if you want to, go ahead and print it. It's all true."

April 29, 1950: Los Angeles Times
VENUS TAKES A BOW
San Bruno, Calif., April 29 (UP) Police in these bay area peninsula towns were a little shamefaced when an officer reported a flying saucer. Police radios hummed with talk about the flaming saucer, but stations went silent when a dispatcher, an amateur astronomer, announced that the saucer "was nothing but the planet Venus taking a bow."

April 30, 1950: Los Angeles Times
FLYING SAUCERS NOW GO IN FORMATION—8 OF THEM
Centralia, Wash., April 29 (UP) Mrs Albert Goelitzer said, "I happened to look out the window, and saw two saucers, but they were immediately joined by six others." She reported that they were all of the same flat cylindrical shape generally described by others who have reported seeing the objects, but one was tinged a dark red.

May 1, 1950: Quick Magazine
New York Quick predicts: "The high command will have to make its demands stronger to stop flying saucer rumors. The Pentagon is full of officers who don't know what to believe."

May 22, 1950:
MOST THINK DISKS ARE SECRET WEAPONS
Princeton, N. J. May 21 George Gallup reported that the American Institute of Public Opinion's latest poll indicated that the largest number of people believe that flying saucers are new experimental weapons or flying contraptions being tested by the Army or Navy. This represents quite a change from 1947 when the largest number labeled tham as nothing more than an illusion or a hoax. Five percent thought they were something from another planet and six percent thought they were some kind of new airplane. Only three percent thought they were something from Russia.

BEHIND THE FLYING SAUCERS

May 1950: The Way of St. Francis

MYTH OR FACT

If proof is forthcoming that the flying saucers carry visitors from another planet, then the Biblical story of creation and Christianity are disproved, according to the reader. The fact is that, first, that "if" is a big one. Besides that, the Bible and Christianity are God's provision for dealing with the children of Adam of this earth. Moreover, the truth of all that is contained in the Bible and Christianity in no way excluded the possibility that God has created other groups of intelligent beings, who may or may not inhabit other planets. In fact the Bible tells us many times of a group of intelligent beings, called angels. It even records the visitations of a few of these beings to our earth. God has told us about the angels; there could be other beings He has created about which He has told us nothing. After all, there are some men who find it difficult to accept what He *has* told them.

If they aren't out there, why do we continue to see them?"

www.ingramcontent.com/pod-product-compliance
Lightning Source LLC
Chambersburg PA
CBHW080502110426
42742CB00017B/2972